CODE OF FEDERAL
REGULATIONS

Title 1
General Provisions

Revised as of January 1, 2019

Containing a codification of documents
of general applicability and future effect

As of January 1, 2019

Published by the Office of the Federal Register
National Archives and Records Administration
as a Special Edition of the Federal Register

Table of Contents

Cite this Code: **CFR**

To cite the regulations in this volume use title, part and section number. Thus, 1 CFR 1.1 refers to title 1, part 1, section 1.

Explanation

The Code of Federal Regulations is a codification of the general and permanent rules published in the Federal Register by the Executive departments and agencies of the Federal Government. The Code is divided into 50 titles which represent broad areas subject to Federal regulation. Each title is divided into chapters which usually bear the name of the issuing agency. Each chapter is further subdivided into parts covering specific regulatory areas.

Each volume of the Code is revised at least once each calendar year and issued on a quarterly basis approximately as follows:

Title 1 through Title 16...as of January 1
Title 17 through Title 27 ....as of April 1
Title 28 through Title 41 ....as of July 1
Title 42 through Title 50..as of October 1

The appropriate revision date is printed on the cover of each volume.

LEGAL STATUS

The contents of the Federal Register are required to be judicially noticed (44 U.S.C. 1507). The Code of Federal Regulations is prima facie evidence of the text of the original documents (44 U.S.C. 1510).

HOW TO USE THE CODE OF FEDERAL REGULATIONS

The Code of Federal Regulations is kept up to date by the individual issues of the Federal Register. These two publications must be used together to determine the latest version of any given rule.

To determine whether a Code volume has been amended since its revision date (in this case, January 1, 2019), consult the "List of CFR Sections Affected (LSA)," which is issued monthly, and the "Cumulative List of Parts Affected," which appears in the Reader Aids section of the daily Federal Register. These two lists will identify the Federal Register page number of the latest amendment of any given rule.

EFFECTIVE AND EXPIRATION DATES

Each volume of the Code contains amendments published in the Federal Register since the last revision of that volume of the Code. Source citations for the regulations are referred to by volume number and page number of the Federal Register and date of publication. Publication dates and effective dates are usually not the same and care must be exercised by the user in determining the actual effective date. In instances where the effective date is beyond the cutoff date for the Code a note has been inserted to reflect the future effective date. In those instances where a regulation published in the Federal Register states a date certain for expiration, an appropriate note will be inserted following the text.

OMB CONTROL NUMBERS

The Paperwork Reduction Act of 1980 (Pub. L. 96–511) requires Federal agencies to display an OMB control number with their information collection request.

Many agencies have begun publishing numerous OMB control numbers as amendments to existing regulations in the CFR. These OMB numbers are placed as close as possible to the applicable recordkeeping or reporting requirements.

PAST PROVISIONS OF THE CODE

Provisions of the Code that are no longer in force and effect as of the revision date stated on the cover of each volume are not carried. Code users may find the text of provisions in effect on any given date in the past by using the appropriate List of CFR Sections Affected (LSA). For the convenience of the reader, a "List of CFR Sections Affected" is published at the end of each CFR volume. For changes to the Code prior to the LSA listings at the end of the volume, consult previous annual editions of the LSA. For changes to the Code prior to 2001, consult the List of CFR Sections Affected compilations, published for 1949-1963, 1964-1972, 1973-1985, and 1986-2000.

"[RESERVED]" TERMINOLOGY

The term "[Reserved]" is used as a place holder within the Code of Federal Regulations. An agency may add regulatory information at a "[Reserved]" location at any time. Occasionally "[Reserved]" is used editorially to indicate that a portion of the CFR was left vacant and not accidentally dropped due to a printing or computer error.

INCORPORATION BY REFERENCE

What is incorporation by reference? Incorporation by reference was established by statute and allows Federal agencies to meet the requirement to publish regulations in the Federal Register by referring to materials already published elsewhere. For an incorporation to be valid, the Director of the Federal Register must approve it. The legal effect of incorporation by reference is that the material is treated as if it were published in full in the Federal Register (5 U.S.C. 552(a)). This material, like any other properly issued regulation, has the force of law.

What is a proper incorporation by reference? The Director of the Federal Register will approve an incorporation by reference only when the requirements of 1 CFR part 51 are met. Some of the elements on which approval is based are:

(a) The incorporation will substantially reduce the volume of material published in the Federal Register.

(b) The matter incorporated is in fact available to the extent necessary to afford fairness and uniformity in the administrative process.

(c) The incorporating document is drafted and submitted for publication in accordance with 1 CFR part 51.

What if the material incorporated by reference cannot be found? If you have any problem locating or obtaining a copy of material listed as an approved incorporation by reference, please contact the agency that issued the regulation containing that incorporation. If, after contacting the agency, you find the material is not available, please notify the Director of the Federal Register, National Archives and Records Administration, 8601 Adelphi Road, College Park, MD 20740-6001, or call 202-741-6010.

CFR INDEXES AND TABULAR GUIDES

A subject index to the Code of Federal Regulations is contained in a separate volume, revised annually as of January 1, entitled CFR INDEX AND FINDING AIDS. This volume contains the Parallel Table of Authorities and Rules. A list of CFR titles, chapters, subchapters, and parts and an alphabetical list of agencies publishing in the CFR are also included in this volume.

An index to the text of "Title 3—The President" is carried within that volume.

The Federal Register Index is issued monthly in cumulative form. This index is based on a consolidation of the "Contents" entries in the daily Federal Register.

A List of CFR Sections Affected (LSA) is published monthly, keyed to the revision dates of the 50 CFR titles.

REPUBLICATION OF MATERIAL

There are no restrictions on the republication of material appearing in the Code of Federal Regulations.

INQUIRIES

For a legal interpretation or explanation of any regulation in this volume, contact the issuing agency. The issuing agency's name appears at the top of odd-numbered pages.

For inquiries concerning CFR reference assistance, call 202–741–6000 or write to the Director, Office of the Federal Register, National Archives and Records Administration, 8601 Adelphi Road, College Park, MD 20740-6001 or e-mail *fedreg.info@nara.gov*.

SALES

The Government Publishing Office (GPO) processes all sales and distribution of the CFR. For payment by credit card, call toll-free, 866-512-1800, or DC area, 202-512-1800, M-F 8 a.m. to 4 p.m. e.s.t. or fax your order to 202-512-2104, 24 hours a day. For payment by check, write to: US Government Publishing Office – New Orders, P.O. Box 979050, St. Louis, MO 63197-9000.

ELECTRONIC SERVICES

The full text of the Code of Federal Regulations, the LSA (List of CFR Sections Affected), The United States Government Manual, the Federal Register, Public Laws, Public Papers of the Presidents of the United States, Compilation of Presidential Documents and the Privacy Act Compilation are available in electronic format via *www.ofr.gov*. For more information, contact the GPO Customer Contact Center, U.S. Government Publishing Office. Phone 202-512-1800, or 866-512-1800 (toll-free). E-mail, *ContactCenter@gpo.gov*.

The Office of the Federal Register also offers a free service on the National Archives and Records Administration's (NARA) World Wide Web site for public law numbers, Federal Register finding aids, and related information. Connect to NARA's web site at *www.archives.gov/federal-register*.

The e-CFR is a regularly updated, unofficial editorial compilation of CFR material and Federal Register amendments, produced by the Office of the Federal Register and the Government Publishing Office. It is available at *www.ecfr.gov*.

OLIVER A. POTTS,
Director,
Office of the Federal Register.
January 1, 2019.

THIS TITLE

Title 1—GENERAL PROVISIONS is composed of one volume. This volume is comprised of Chapter I—Administrative Committee of the Federal Register, Chapter II—Office of the Federal Register, Chapter III—Administrative Conference of the United States, Chapter IV—Miscellaneous Agencies, and Chapter VI— National Capital Planning Commission. The contents of this volume represents all current regulations codified under this title of the CFR as of January 1, 2019.

Chapter IV contains the current Privacy Act, Freedom of Information Act, and Rehabilitation Act regulations issued by miscellaneous agencies.

For this volume, Ann Worley was Chief Editor. The Code of Federal Regulations publication program is under the direction of John Hyrum Martinez, assisted by Stephen J. Frattini.

Title 1—General Provisions

CHAPTER I—ADMINISTRATIVE COMMITTEE OF THE FEDERAL REGISTER

3

SUBCHAPTER A—GENERAL

PART 1—DEFINITIONS

AUTHORITY: 44 U.S.C. 1506; sec. 6, E.O. 10530, 19 FR 2709; 3 CFR, 1954–1958 Comp., p.189.

§ 1.1 Definitions.

As used in this chapter, unless the context requires otherwise—

Administrative Committee means the Administrative Committee of the Federal Register established under section 1506 of title 44, United States Code;

Agency means each authority, whether or not within or subject to review by another agency, of the United States, other than the Congress, the courts, the District of Columbia, the Commonwealth of Puerto Rico, and the territories and possessions of the United States;

Document includes any Presidential proclamation or Executive order, and any rule, regulation, order, certificate, code of fair competition, license, notice, or similar instrument issued, prescribed, or promulgated by an agency;

Document having general applicability and legal effect means any document issued under proper authority prescribing a penalty or course of conduct, conferring a right, privilege, authority, or immunity, or imposing an obligation, and relevant or applicable to the general public, members of a class, or persons in a locality, as distinguished from named individuals or organizations; and

Filing means making a document available for public inspection at the Office of the Federal Register during official business hours. A document is filed only after it has been received, processed and assigned a publication date according to the schedule in part 17 of this chapter.

Regulation and *rule* have the same meaning.

[37 FR 23603, Nov. 4, 1972, as amended at 50 FR 12466, Mar. 28, 1985]

PART 2—GENERAL INFORMATION

AUTHORITY: 44 U.S.C. 1506; sec. 6, E.O. 10530, 19 FR 2709; 3 CFR, 1954–1958 Comp., p. 189; 1 U.S.C. 112; 1 U.S.C. 113.

SOURCE: 37 FR 23603, Nov. 4, 1972, unless otherwise noted.

§ 2.1 Scope and purpose.

(a) This chapter sets forth the policies, procedures, and delegations under which the Administrative Committee of the Federal Register carries out its general responsibilities under chapter 15 of title 44, United States Code.

(b) A primary purpose of this chapter is to inform the public of the nature and uses of Federal Register publications.

§ 2.2 Administrative Committee of the Federal Register.

(a) The Administrative Committee of the Federal Register is established by section 1506 of title 44, United States Code.

(b) The Committee consists of—

(1) The Archivist, or Acting Archivist, of the United States, who is the Chairman;

(2) An officer of the Department of Justice designated by the Attorney General; and

(3) The Public Printer or Acting Public Printer.

(c) The Director of the Federal Register is the Secretary of the Committee.

(d) Any material required by law to be filed with the Committee, and any correspondence, inquiries, or other material intended for the Committee or which relate to Federal Register publications shall be sent to the Director of the Federal Register.

§ 2.3 Office of the Federal Register; location; office hours.

(a) The Office of the Federal Register is a component of the National Archives and Records Administration.

(b) The Office is located at 800 North Capitol, NW., suite 700, Washington, DC.

(c) The mailing address is: Office of the Federal Register, National Archives and Records Administration, Washington, DC 20408.

(d) Office hours are 8:45 a.m. to 5:15 p.m., Monday through Friday, except for official Federal holidays.

[37 FR 23603, Nov. 4, 1972, as amended at 54 FR 9676, Mar. 7, 1989; 57 FR 40024, Sept. 1, 1992]

§ 2.4 General authority of Director.

(a) The Director of the Federal Register is delegated authority to administer generally this chapter, the related provisions of chapter 15 of title 44, United States Code, and the pertinent provisions of statutes and regulations contemplated by section 1505 of title 44, United States Code.

(b) The Director may return to the issuing agency any document submitted for publication in the FEDERAL REGISTER, or a special edition thereof, if in the Director's judgment the document does not meet the minimum requirements of this chapter.

[37 FR 23603, Nov. 4, 1972, as amended at 54 FR 9676, Mar. 7, 1989]

§ 2.5 Publication of statutes, regulations, and related documents.

(a) The Director of the Federal Register is responsible for the central filing of the original acts enacted by Congress and the original documents containing Executive orders and proclamations of the President, other Presidential documents, regulations, and notices of proposed rulemaking and other notices, submitted to the Director by officials of the executive branch of the Federal Government.

(b) Based on the acts and documents filed under paragraph (a) of this section, the Office of the Federal Register publishes the "slip laws," the "United States Statutes at Large," the daily FEDERAL REGISTER and the "Code of Federal Regulations."

(c) Based on source materials that are officially related to the acts and documents filed under paragraph (a) of this section, the Office also publishes "The United States Government Manual," the "Public Papers of the Presidents of the United States," the "Daily Compilation of Presidential Documents," the "FEDERAL REGISTER Index," and the "LSA (List of CFR Sections Affected)."

[37 FR 23603, Nov. 4, 1972, as amended at 54 FR 9676, Mar. 7, 1989; 74 FR 3952, Jan. 21, 2009]

§ 2.6 Unrestricted use.

Any person may reproduce or republish, without restriction, any material appearing in any regular or special edition of the FEDERAL REGISTER.

PART 3—SERVICES TO THE PUBLIC

Sec.
3.1 Information services.
3.2 Public inspection of documents.
3.3 Reproduction and certification of copies of acts and documents.

AUTHORITY: 44 U.S.C. 1506; sec. 6, E.O. 10530, 19 FR 2709; 3 CFR, 1954–1958 Comp., p. 189.

SOURCE: 37 FR 23604, Nov. 4, 1972, unless otherwise noted.

§ 3.1 Information services.

Except in cases where the time required would be excessive, information concerning the publications described in § 2.5 of this chapter and the original acts and documents filed with the Office of the Federal Register is provided by the staff of that Office. However, the staff may not summarize or interpret substantive text of any act or document.

§ 3.2 Public inspection of documents.

(a) Documents filed with the Office of the Federal Register pursuant to law are available for public inspection at 800 North Capitol Street, NW., suite 700, Washington, DC, during the Office of the Federal Register office hours. There are no formal inspection procedures or requirements.

(b) The Director of the Federal Register shall cause each document received by the office to be filed for public inspection not later than the working day preceding the publication day for that document.

(c) The Director shall cause to be placed on the original and certified copies of each document a notation of the day and hour when it was filed and made available for public inspection.

(d) Photocopies of documents or excerpts may be made at the inspection desk.

[37 FR 23604, Nov. 4, 1972, as amended at 54 FR 9676, Mar. 7, 1989; 57 FR 40025, Sept. 1, 1992]

§3.3 Reproduction and certification of copies of acts and documents.

The regulations for the public use of records in the National Archives (36 CFR parts 1252–1258) govern the furnishing of reproductions of acts and documents and certificates of authentication for them. Section 1258.14 of those regulations provides for the advance payment of appropriate fees for reproduction services and for certifying reproductions.

[51 FR 27017, July 29, 1986, as amended at 54 FR 9676, Mar. 7, 1989]

SUBCHAPTER B—THE FEDERAL REGISTER

PART 5—GENERAL

AUTHORITY: 44 U.S.C. 1506; sec. 6, E.O. 10530, 19 FR 2709; 3 CFR, 1954–1958 Comp., p. 189.

SOURCE: 37 FR 23604, Nov. 4, 1972, unless otherwise noted.

§5.1 Publication policy.

(a) Pursuant to chapter 15 of title 44, United States Code, and this chapter, the Director of the Federal Register shall publish a serial publication called the FEDERAL REGISTER to contain the following:

(1) Executive orders, proclamations, and other Presidential documents.

(2) Documents required to be published therein by law.

(3) Documents accepted for publication under §5.3.

(b) Each document required or authorized to be filed for publication shall be published in the FEDERAL REGISTER as promptly as possible, within limitations imposed by considerations of accuracy, usability, and reasonable costs.

(c) In prescribing regulations governing headings, preambles, effective dates, authority citations, and similar matters of form, the Administrative Committee does not intend to affect the validity of any document that is filed and published under law.

§5.2 Documents required to be filed for public inspection and published.

The following documents are required to be filed for public inspection with the Office of the Federal Register and published in the FEDERAL REGISTER:

(a) Presidential proclamations and Executive orders in the numbered series, and each other document that the President submits for publication or orders to be published.

(b) Each document or class of documents required to be published by act of Congress.

(c) Each document having general applicability and legal effect.

[37 FR 23604, Nov. 4, 1972, as amended at 54 FR 9676, Mar. 7, 1989]

§5.3 Publication of other documents.

Whenever the Director of the Federal Register considers that publication of a document not covered by §5.2 would be in the public interest, the Director may allow that document to be filed for public inspection with the Office of the Federal Register and published in the FEDERAL REGISTER.

[54 FR 9676, Mar. 7, 1989]

§5.4 Publication not authorized.

(a) Chapter 15 of title 44, United States Code, does not apply to treaties, conventions, protocols, or other international agreements, or proclamations thereof by the President.

(b) Chapter 15 of title 44, United States Code, prohibits the publication in the FEDERAL REGISTER of comments or news items.

(c) The Director of the Federal Register may not accept any document for filing and publication unless it is the official action of the agency concerned. Chapter 15 of title 44, United States Code, does not authorize or require the filing and publication of other papers from an agency.

§5.5 Supplement to the Code of Federal Regulations.

The FEDERAL REGISTER serves as a daily supplement to the Code of Federal Regulations. Each document that is subject to codification and published in a daily issue shall be keyed to the Code of Federal Regulations.

§5.6 Daily publication.

There shall be an edition of the FEDERAL REGISTER published for each official Federal working day.

[54 FR 9676, Mar. 7, 1989]

§5.7 Delivery and mailing.

The Government Printing Office shall distribute the FEDERAL REGISTER by delivery or by deposit at a post office at or before 9 a.m. on the publication day, except that each FEDERAL REGISTER dated for a Monday shall be deposited at a post office at or before 9 a.m. on the preceding Saturday.

§5.8 Form of citation.

Without prejudice to any other form of citation, FEDERAL REGISTER material may be cited by volume and page number, and the short form "FR" may be used for "FEDERAL REGISTER". For example, "37 FR 6803" refers to material beginning on page 6803 of volume 37 of the daily issues.

§5.9 Categories of documents.

Each document published in the FEDERAL REGISTER shall be placed under one of the following categories, as indicated:

(a) *The President.* This category contains each Executive order or Presidential proclamation and each other Presidential document that the President submits for publication or orders to be published.

(b) *Rules and regulations.* This category contains each document having general applicability and legal effect, except those covered by paragraph (a) of this section. This category includes documents subject to codification, general policy statements concerning regulations, interpretations of agency regulations, statements of organization and function, and documents that affect other documents previously published in the rules and regulations section.

(c) *Proposed rules.* This category contains each notice of proposed rulemaking submitted pursuant to section 553 of title 5, United States Code, or any other law, which if promulgated as a rule, would have general applicability and legal effect. This category includes documents that suggest changes to regulations in the Code of Federal Regulations, begin a rulemaking proceeding, and affect or relate to other documents previously published in the proposed rules section.

(d) *Notices.* This category contains miscellaneous documents applicable to the public and not covered by paragraphs (a), (b), and (c) of this section. This category includes announcements of meetings and other information of public interest.

[37 FR 23604, Nov. 4, 1972, as amended at 54 FR 9676, Mar. 7, 1989]

§5.10 Forms of publication.

Pursuant to section 1506 of title 44, United States Code, the Administrative Committee publishes the FEDERAL REGISTER in the following formats: paper; microfiche; and online on GPO Access (44 U.S.C. 4101).

[61 FR 68118, Dec. 27, 1996]

PART 6—INDEXES AND ANCILLARIES

Sec.
6.1 Index to daily issues.
6.2 Analytical subject indexes.
6.3 Daily lists of parts affected.
6.4 Monthly list of sections affected.
6.5 Indexes, digests, and guides.

AUTHORITY: 44 U.S.C. 1506; sec. 6, E.O. 10530, 19 FR 2709; 3 CFR, 1954–1958 Comp., p. 189.

SOURCE: 37 FR 23605, Nov. 4, 1972, unless otherwise noted.

§6.1 Index to daily issues.

Each daily issue of the FEDERAL REGISTER shall be appropriately indexed.

§6.2 Analytical subject indexes.

Analytical subject indexes covering the contents of the FEDERAL REGISTER shall be published as currently as practicable and shall be cumulated and separately published at least once each calendar year.

§6.3 Daily lists of parts affected.

(a) Each daily issue of the FEDERAL REGISTER shall carry a numerical list of the parts of the Code of Federal Regulations specifically affected by documents published in that issue.

(b) Beginning with the second issue of each month, each daily issue shall also carry a cumulated list of the parts affected by documents published during that month.

§ 6.4 Monthly list of sections affected.

A monthly list of sections of the Code of Federal Regulations affected shall be separately published on a cumulative basis during each calendar year. The list shall identify the sections of the Code specifically affected by documents published in the FEDERAL REGISTER during the period it covers.

§ 6.5 Indexes, digests, and guides.

(a) The Director of the Federal Register may order the preparation and publication of indexes, digests, and similar guides, based on laws, Presidential documents, regulatory documents, and notice materials published by the Office, which will serve users of the FEDERAL REGISTER. Indexes, digests, and similar guides will be published yearly or at other intervals as necessary to keep them current and useful.

(b) Each index, digest, and guide is considered to be a special edition of the FEDERAL REGISTER whenever the public need requires special printing or special binding in substantial numbers.

[54 FR 9676, Mar. 7, 1989]

SUBCHAPTER C—SPECIAL EDITIONS OF THE FEDERAL REGISTER

PART 8—CODE OF FEDERAL REGULATIONS

AUTHORITY: 44 U.S.C. 1506, 1510; sec. 6, E.O. 10530, 19 FR 2709, 3 CFR, 1954–1958 Comp., p. 189.

SOURCE: 37 FR 23605, Nov. 4, 1972, unless otherwise noted.

§ 8.1 Policy.

(a) Pursuant to chapter 15 of title 44, United States Code, the Director of the Federal Register shall publish periodically a special edition of the FEDERAL REGISTER to present a compact and practical code called the "Code of Federal Regulations", to contain each Federal regulation of general applicability and legal effect.

(b) The Administrative Committee intends that every practical means be used to keep the Code as current and readily usable as possible, within limitations imposed by dependability and reasonable costs.

[37 FR 23605, Nov. 4, 1972, as amended at 54 FR 9677, Mar. 7, 1989]

§ 8.2 Orderly development.

To assure orderly development of the Code of Federal Regulations along practical lines, the Director of the Federal Register may establish new titles in the Code and rearrange existing titles and subordinate assignments. However, before taking an action under this section, the Director shall consult with each agency directly affected by the proposed change.

§ 8.3 Periodic updating.

(a) *Criteria.* Each book of the Code shall be updated at least once each calendar year. If no change in its contents has occurred during the year, a simple notation to that effect may serve as the supplement for that year. More frequent updating of any unit of the Code may be made whenever the Director of the Federal Register determines that the content of the unit has been substantially superseded or otherwise determines that such action would be consistent with the intent and purpose of the Administrative Committee as stated in § 8.1.

(b) *Staggered publication.* The Code will be produced over a 12-month period under a staggered publication system to be determined by the Director of the Federal Register.

(c) *Cutoff dates.* Each updated title of the Code will reflect each amendment to that title published as a codified regulation in the FEDERAL REGISTER on or before the "As of" date. Thus, each title updated as of July 1 each year will reflect all amendatory documents appearing in the daily FEDERAL REGISTER on or before July 1.

[37 FR 23605, Nov. 4, 1972, as amended at 54 FR 9677, Mar. 7, 1989]

§ 8.4 Indexes.

A subject index to the entire Code shall be annually revised and separately published. An agency-prepared index for any individual book may be published with the approval of the Director of the Federal Register.

§ 8.5 Ancillaries.

The Code shall provide, among others, the following-described finding aids:

(a) *Parallel tables of statutory authorities and rules.* In the Code of Federal Regulations Index or at such other place as the Director of the Federal Register considers appropriate, numerical lists of all sections of the current edition of the United States Code (except section 301 of title 5) which are cited by issuing agencies as rulemaking authority for currently effective regulations in the Code of Federal Regulations. The lists shall be arranged in the order of the titles and sections of the United States Code with parallel citations to the pertinent titles and parts of the Code of Federal Regulations.

(b) *Parallel tables of Presidential documents and agency rules.* In the Code of Federal Regulations Index, or at such other place as the Director of the Federal Register considers appropriate, tables of proclamations, Executive orders, and similar Presidential documents which are cited as rulemaking authority in currently effective regulations in the Code of Federal Regulations.

(c) *List of CFR sections affected.* Following the text of each Code of Federal Regulations volume, a numerical list of sections which are affected by documents published in the FEDERAL REGISTER. (Separate volumes, "List of Sections Affected, 1949–1963" and "List of CFR Sections Affected, 1964–1972", list all sections of the Code which have been affected by documents published during the period January 1, 1949, to December 31, 1963, and January 1, 1964, to December 31, 1972, respectively.)[1] Listings shall refer to FEDERAL REGISTER pages and shall be designed to enable the user of the Code to find the precise text that was in effect on a given date in the period covered.

[37 FR 23605, Nov. 4, 1972, as amended at 54 FR 9677, Mar. 7, 1989]

§ 8.6 Forms of publication.

(a) Under section 1506 of title 44, United States Code, the Administrative Committee authorizes publication of the Code of Federal Regulations in the following formats:

(1) Paper;

(2) Microfiche; and

(3) Online on GPO Access (44 US.C. 4101).

(b) The Director of the Federal Register is authorized to regulate the format of the Code of Federal Regulations according to the needs of users and compatibility with the facilities of the Government Printing Office. The Director may provide for the Code of Federal Regulations to be printed in as many separately bound books as nec-

---

[1] A three volume set, "List of CFR Sections Affected, 1973–1985", lists all sections of the Code which have been affected during the period January 1, 1973 to December 31, 1985.

essary, set requirements for microfiche images, and oversee the organization and means of access to material in the online edition.

[65 FR 8843, Feb. 23, 2000]

§ 8.7 Agency cooperation.

Each agency shall cooperate in keeping publication of the Code current by complying promptly with deadlines set by the Director of the Federal Register and the Public Printer.

§ 8.9 Form of citation.

The Code of Federal Regulations may be cited by title and section, and the short form "CFR" may be used for "Code of Federal Regulations." For example, "1 CFR 10.2" refers to title 1, Code of Federal Regulations, part 10, section 2.

PART 9—THE UNITED STATES GOVERNMENT MANUAL

Sec.
9.1 Publication required.
9.2 Scope.

AUTHORITY: 5 U.S.C. 552; 44 U.S.C. 1506; sec. 6, E.O. 10530, 19 FR 2709; 3 CFR, 1954–1958 Comp., p. 189.

SOURCE: 76 FR 6312, Feb. 4, 2011, unless otherwise noted.

§ 9.1 Publication required.

(a) The Director publishes a special edition of the FEDERAL REGISTER called "The United States Government Manual" as authorized by the Administrative Committee.

(b) The Director may update the *Manual* when such supplementation is considered to be in the public interest.

§ 9.2 Scope.

(a) The *Manual* will contain appropriate information about the Executive, Legislative, and Judicial branches of the Federal Government, which for the major Executive agencies will include—

(1) Descriptions of the agency's legal authorities, public purposes, programs, and functions;

(2) Established places and methods whereby the public may obtain information and make submittals or requests; and

(3) Lists of officials heading major operating units.

(b) The *Manual* will also contain brief information about quasi-official agencies and supplemental information that, in the opinion of the Director, is of enough public interest to warrant.

PART 10—PRESIDENTIAL PAPERS

Subpart A—Regular Publication

AUTHORITY: 44 U.S.C. 1506; sec. 6, E.O. 10530, 19 FR 2709, 3 CFR, 1954–1958 Comp., p. 189.

SOURCE: 50 FR 12467, Mar. 28, 1985, unless otherwise noted.

Subpart A—Regular Publication

§ 10.1   Publication required.

The Director publishes a special edition of the FEDERAL REGISTER compiling recent presidential documents, called "The Daily Compilation of Presidential Documents."

[74 FR 3952, Jan. 21, 2009]

§ 10.2   Scope and sources.

(a) The text of the publication consists of oral statements by the President or of writing subscribed by the President, and selected from transcripts or text issued by the Office of the White House Press Secretary, including—

(1) Communications to Congress;
(2) Public addresses and remarks;
(3) News conferences and interviews;
(4) Public messages and letters;
(5) Statements released on miscellaneous subjects; and
(6) Formal executive documents promulgated in accordance with law.

(b) In addition, each publication includes selections, either in full text or ancillary form, from the following groups of documents, when issued by the Press Office.

(1) Announcements of Presidential appointments and nominations;
(2) White House statements and announcements on miscellaneous subjects;
(3) Statements by the Press Secretary or Deputy Press Secretary;
(4) Statements and news conferences by senior administration officials; and
(5) Fact sheets.

[50 FR 12467, Mar. 28, 1985, as amended at 74 FR 3952, Jan. 21, 2009]

§ 10.3   Format.

The Daily Compilation of Presidential Documents is published online on the Government Printing Office access system.

[74 FR 3952, Jan. 21, 2009]

Subpart B—Annual Publication

§ 10.10   Publication required.

The Director of the Federal Register shall publish annually a special edition of the FEDERAL REGISTER called the "Public Papers of the Presidents of the United States".

§ 10.11   Scope and sources.

The basic text of the Public Papers consists of the documents compiled under subpart A of this part.

[74 FR 3952, Jan. 21, 2009]

§ 10.12   Format, indexes, and ancillaries.

(a) Each publication covers one calendar year, unless procedures require otherwise, and is divided into books according to the amount of material to be included. The publication is published in the binding and style that the Administrative Committee of the Federal Register considers suitable to the dignity of the Office of the President of the United States.

(b) Each publication is appropriately indexed and contains additional ancillary information and illustrative material respecting significant Presidential documents and activities.

§ 10.13   Coverage of prior years.

The Administrative Committee may authorize the publication of volumes of papers of the Presidents covering specified years before 1945 after consulting with the National Historical Publications and Records Commission.

SUBCHAPTER D—AVAILABILITY OF OFFICE OF THE FEDERAL REGISTER PUBLICATIONS

PART 11—SUBSCRIPTIONS

AUTHORITY: 44 U.S.C. 1506; sec. 6, E.O. 10530, 19 FR 2709, 3 CFR, 1954–1958 Comp., p. 189.

SOURCE: 54 FR 9677, Mar. 7, 1989, unless otherwise noted.

§ 11.1 Subscription by the public.

The Government Printing Office produces the paper and microfiche editions of the publications described in § 2.5 of this chapter, and the Superintendent of Documents, Government Printing Office, Washington, DC 20402, makes them available for sale to the public. All fees are payable in advance to the Superintendent of Documents, Government Printing Office. They are not available for free distribution to the public.

[54 FR 9677, Mar. 7, 1989, as amended at 61 FR 68118, Dec. 27, 1996]

§ 11.2 Federal Register.

(a) The subscription price for the paper edition of the daily FEDERAL REGISTER is $749 per year. A combined subscription to the daily FEDERAL REGISTER, the monthly FEDERAL REGISTER Index, and the monthly LSA (List of CFR Sections Affected) is $808 per year for the paper edition, or $165 per year for the microfiche edition. Six-month subscriptions for the paper and microfiche editions are also available at one-half the annual rate. Those prices exclude postage. The prevailing postal rates will be applied to orders according to the delivery method requested. The price of a single copy of the daily FEDERAL REGISTER, including postage, is based on the number of pages: $11 for an issue containing less than 200 pages; $22 for an issue containing 200 to 400 pages; and $33 for an issue containing more than 400 pages. Single issues of the microfiche edition may be purchased for $3 per copy, including postage.

(b) The online edition of the FEDERAL REGISTER, issued under the authority of the Administrative Committee, is available on GPO Access, a service of the Government Printing Office (44 U.S.C. 4101).

[61 FR 68119, Dec. 27, 1996, as amended at 65 FR 8843, Feb. 23, 2000; 66 FR 44524, Aug. 24, 2001; 69 FR 12783, Mar. 18, 2004]

§ 11.3 Code of Federal Regulations.

(a) The subscription price for a complete set of the Code of Federal Regulations is $1,019 per year for the bound, paper edition, or $247 per year for the microfiche edition. Those prices exclude postage. The prevailing postal rates will be applied to orders according to the delivery method requested. The Government Printing Office sells individual volumes of the paper edition of the Code of Federal Regulations at prices determined by the Superintendent of Documents under the general direction of the Administrative Committee. The price of a single volume of the microfiche edition is $4 per copy, including postage.

(b) The online edition of the Code of Federal Regulations, issued under the authority of the Administrative Committee, is available on GPO Access, a service of the Government Printing Office (44 U.S.C. 4101).

[65 FR 8843, Feb. 23, 2000, as amended at 66 FR 44524, Aug. 24, 2001; 69 FR 12783, Mar. 18, 2004]

§ 11.4 The United States Government Manual.

(a) The online edition of the *Manual*, issued under the authority of the Administrative Committee, is available through the Government Printing Office's Web site.

(b) Copies of a bound, paper edition of the *Manual* may be sold at a price determined by the Superintendent of

Documents under the general direction of the Administrative Committee.

[76 FR 6313, Feb. 4, 2011]

§ 11.5 Public Papers of the Presidents of the United States.

Copies of annual clothbound volumes are sold at a price determined by the Superintendent of Documents under the general direction of the Administrative Committee.

§ 11.6 [Reserved]

§ 11.7 Federal Register Index.

The annual subscription price for the monthly FEDERAL REGISTER Index, purchased separately, in paper form, is $29. The price excludes postage. The prevailing postal rates will be applied to orders according to the delivery method requested.

[69 FR 12783, Mar. 18, 2004]

§ 11.8 LSA (List of CFR Sections Affected).

The annual subscription price for the monthly LSA (List of CFR Sections Affected), purchased separately, in paper form, is $30. The price excludes postage. The prevailing postal rates will be applied to orders according to the delivery method requested.

[69 FR 12783, Mar. 18, 2004]

PART 12—OFFICIAL DISTRIBUTION WITHIN FEDERAL GOVERNMENT

Sec.
12.1 Federal Register.
12.2 Code of Federal Regulations.
12.4 Weekly Compilation of Presidential Documents.
12.5 Public Papers of the Presidents of the United States.

AUTHORITY: 44 U.S.C. 1506; sec. 6, E.O. 10530, 19 FR 2709; 3 CFR, 1954–1958 Comp., p. 189.

SOURCE: 54 FR 9678, Mar. 7, 1989, unless otherwise noted.

§ 12.1 Federal Register.

(a) Copies of the daily FEDERAL REGISTER in paper or microfiche form shall be made available to the following without charge:

(1) *Members of Congress.* Each Senator and each Member of the House of Representatives will be provided with not more than five copies of each daily issue based on a written request to the Director of the Federal Register.

(2) *Congressional committees.* Each committee of the Senate and the House of Representatives will be provided with the number of copies needed for official use based on a written request from the chairperson, or authorized delegate, to the Director of the Federal Register.

(3) *Supreme Court.* The Supreme Court will be provided with the number of copies needed for official use based on a written request to the Director of the Federal Register.

(4) *Other courts.* Other constitutional or legislative courts of the United States will be provided with the number of copies needed for official use based on a written request from the Director of the Administrative Office of the U.S. Courts, or authorized delegate, to the Director of the Federal Register.

(5) *Executive agencies.* Each Federal executive agency will be provided with the number of copies needed for official use based on a written request from the agency Federal Register authorizing officer, or the alternate, designated under § 16.1 of this chapter, to the Director of the Federal Register.

(b) Requisitions for quantity overruns of specific issues to be paid for by the agency are available as follows:

(1) To meet its needs for special distribution of the FEDERAL REGISTER in substantial quantity, any agency may request an overrun of a specific issue.

(2) An advance printing and binding requisition on Standard Form 1 must be submitted by the agency directly to the Government Printing Office, to be received not later than 12 noon on the working day before publication.

(c) Requisitions for quantity overruns of separate part issues to be paid for by the agency are available as follows:

(1) Whenever it is determined by the Director of the Federal Register to be in the public interest, one or more documents may be published as a separate part (e.g., part II, part III) of the FEDERAL REGISTER.

(2) Advance arrangements for this service must be made with the Office of the Federal Register.

(3) Any agency may request an overrun of such a separate part by submitting an advance printing and binding requisition on Standard Form 1 directly to the Government Printing Office, to be received not later than 12 noon on the working day before the publication date.

(d) An agency may order limited quantities of extra copies of a specific issue of the FEDERAL REGISTER for official use, from the Superintendent of Documents, to be paid for by that agency.

(e) Copies of the Federal Register Index and LSA (List of CFR Sections Affected) are included with each FEDERAL REGISTER official distribution.

§12.2 Code of Federal Regulations.

(a) Copies of the Code of Federal Regulations in paper or microfiche form shall be made available to the following without charge:

(1) *Congressional committees.* Each committee of the Senate and House of Representatives will be provided with the number of copies needed for official use based on a written request from the chairperson, or authorized delegate, to the Director of the Federal Register.

(2) *Supreme Court.* The Supreme Court will be provided with the number of copies needed for official use based on a written request to the Director of the Federal Register.

(3) *Other courts.* Other constitutional and legislative courts of the United States will be provided with the number of copies needed for official use based on a written request from the Director of the Administrative Office of the U.S. Courts, or authorized delegate, to the Director of the Federal Register.

(4) *Executive agencies.* Each Federal executive agency will be provided with the number of copies needed for official use, not to exceed 300 copies of individual titles per agency, based on a written request from the agency Federal Register authorizing officer, or the alternate, designated under §16.1 of this chapter, to the Director of the Federal Register.

(b) Legislative, judicial, and executive agencies of the Federal Government may obtain additional copies of selected units of the Code, at cost, for official use, by submission, before the press run, of a printing and binding requisition to the Government Printing Office on Standard Form 1.

(c) After the press run, each request for extra copies of selected units of the Code must be addressed to the Superintendent of Documents, to be paid for by the agency making the request.

§12.4 Weekly Compilation of Presidential Documents.

(a) Copies of the Weekly Compilation of Presidential Documents shall be made available to the following without charge:

(1) *Members of Congress.* Each Senator and each Member of the House of Representatives will be provided with the number of copies needed for official use based on a written request to the Director of the Federal Register.

(2) *Congressional committees.* Each committee of the Senate and the House of Representatives will be provided with the number of copies needed for official use based on a written request from the chairperson, or authorized delegate, to the Director of the Federal Register.

(3) *Supreme Court.* The Supreme Court will be provided with the number of copies needed for official use based on a written request to the Director of the Federal Register.

(4) *Other courts.* Other constitutional and legislative courts of the United States will be provided with the number of copies needed for official use based on a written request from the Director of the Administrative Office of the U.S. Courts, or authorized delegate, to the Director of the Federal Register.

(5) *Executive agencies.* Each Federal executive agency will be provided with the number of copies needed for official use based on a written request from the agency Federal Register authorizing officer, or the alternate designated under §16.1 of this chapter, to the Director of the Federal Register.

(b) Legislative, judicial, and executive agencies of the Federal Government may obtain additional copies of selected issues of the Weekly Compilation of Presidential Documents, at cost, for official use, by submission, before the press run, of a printing and binding requisition to the Government Printing Office on a Standard Form 1.

(c) After the press run, each request for extra copies of selected issues must be addressed to the Superintendent of Documents, to be paid for by the agency making the request.

§ 12.5 Public Papers of the Presidents of the United States.

(a) Copies of the Public Papers of the Presidents of the United States shall be made available to the following without charge:

(1) *Members of Congress.* Each Senator and each Member of the House of Representatives will be provided with one copy of each annual publication published during the Member's term in office based on a written request to the Director of the Federal Register.

(2) *Supreme Court.* The Supreme Court will be provided with not more than 12 copies of each publication based on a written request to the Director of the Federal Register.

(3) *Executive agencies.* Each head of a Federal executive agency will be provided with one copy of each annual publication based on a written request from the agency Federal Register authorizing officer, or the alternate, designated under § 16.1 of this chapter, to the Director of the Federal Register.

(b) Legislative, judicial, and executive agencies of the Federal Government may obtain additional copies, at cost, for official use, by submission before the press run, of a printing and binding requisition to the Government Printing Office on Standard Form 1.

(c) After the press run, each request for extra copies must be addressed to the Superintendent of Documents, to be paid for by the agency making the request.

SUBCHAPTER E—PREPARATION, TRANSMITTAL, AND PROCESSING OF DOCUMENTS

PART 15—SERVICES TO FEDERAL AGENCIES

Subpart A—General

Subpart B—Special Assistance

AUTHORITY: 44 U.S.C. 1506; sec. 6, E.O. 10530, 19 FR 2709; 3 CFR, 1954–1958 Comp., p. 189.

SOURCE: 37 FR 23607, Nov. 4, 1972, unless otherwise noted.

Subpart A—General

§ 15.1 Cooperation.

The Director of the Federal Register shall assist each agency in complying with the pertinent publication laws to assure efficient public service in promulgating administrative documents having the effect of legal notice or of law.

§ 15.2 Information services.

The Director of the Federal Register shall provide for the answering of each appropriate inquiry presented in person, by telephone, or in writing. Each written communication and each matter involving the Administrative Committee shall be sent to the Director, Office of the Federal Register, National Archives and Records Administration, Washington, DC 20408.

[50 FR 12468, Mar. 28, 1985]

§ 15.3 Staff assistance.

The staff of the Office of the Federal Register shall provide informal assistance and advice to officials of the various agencies with respect to general or specific programs of regulatory drafting, procedures, and promulgation practices.

§ 15.4 Reproduction and certification of copies of acts and documents.

The Director of the Federal Register shall furnish to requesting agencies, at cost, reproductions or certified copies of original acts and documents filed with that Office that are needed for official use unless funds are appropriated for that purpose.

[50 FR 12468, Mar. 28, 1985, as amended at 54 FR 9679, Mar. 7, 1989]

Subpart B—Special Assistance

§ 15.10 Information on drafting and publication.

The Director of the Federal Register may prepare, and distribute to agencies, information and instructions designed to promote effective compliance with the purposes of chapter 15 of title 44, United States Code, sections 552–553 of title 5, United States Code, related statutes, and this chapter. The Director may also develop and conduct programs of technical instruction.

PART 16—AGENCY REPRESENTATIVES

AUTHORITY: 44 U.S.C. 1506; sec. 6, E.O. 10530, 19 FR 2709; 3 CFR, 1954–1958 Comp., p. 189.

SOURCE: 37 FR 23608, Nov. 4, 1972, unless otherwise noted.

§ 16.1 Designation.

(a) Each agency shall designate, from its officers or employees, persons to serve in the following capacities with relation to the Office of the Federal Register:

(1) A liaison officer and an alternate.

(2) A certifying officer and an alternate.

(3) An authorizing officer and an alternate.

The same person may be designated to serve in one or more of these positions.

(b) In choosing its liaison officer, each agency should consider that this officer will be the main contact between that agency and the Office of the Federal Register and that the liaison officer will be charged with the duties set forth in § 16.2. Therefore, the agency should choose a person who is directly involved in the agency's regulatory program.

(c) Each agency shall notify the Director of the name, title, address, and telephone number of each person it designates under this section and shall promptly notify the Director of any changes.

§ 16.2 Liaison duties.

Each agency liaison officer shall—

(a) Represent the agency in all matters relating to the submission of documents to the Office of the Federal Register, and respecting general compliance with this chapter;

(b) Be responsible for the effective distribution and use within the agency of Federal Register information on document drafting and publication assistance authorized by § 15.10 of this chapter;

(c) Promote the agency's participation in the technical instruction authorized by § 15.10 of this chapter; and

(d) Be available to discuss documents submitted for publication with the editors of the FEDERAL REGISTER.

[54 FR 9679, Mar. 7, 1989]

§ 16.3 Certifying duties.

The agency certifying officer is responsible for attaching the required number of true copies of each original document submitted by the agency to the Office of the Federal Register and for making the certification required by §§ 18.5 and 18.6 of this chapter.

[54 FR 9679, Mar. 7, 1989]

§ 16.4 Authorizing duties.

The agency authorizing officer is responsible for furnishing, to the Director of the Federal Register, a current mailing list of officers or employees of the agency who are authorized to receive the FEDERAL REGISTER, the Code of Federal Regulations, and the Weekly Compilation of Presidential Documents for official use.

[54 FR 9679, Mar. 7, 1989]

PART 17—FILING FOR PUBLIC INSPECTION AND PUBLICATION SCHEDULES

Sec.

Subpart A—Receipt and Processing

17.1 Receipt and processing.

Subpart B—Regular Schedule

17.2 Procedure and timing for regular schedule.

Subpart C—Emergency Schedule

17.3 Criteria for emergency publication.
17.4 Procedure and timing for emergency publication.
17.5 Criteria for emergency filing for public inspection.
17.6 Procedure and timing for emergency filing for public inspection.

Subpart D—Deferred Schedule

17.7 Criteria for deferred schedule.

AUTHORITY: 44 U.S.C. 1506; sec. 6, E.O. 10530, 19 FR 2709; 3 CFR, 1954–1958 Comp., p. 189.

SOURCE: 37 FR 23608, Nov. 4, 1972, unless otherwise noted.

Subpart A—Receipt and Processing

§ 17.1 Receipt and processing.

Unless special arrangements are made with the Director of the Federal Register, the Office of the Federal Register receives documents only during official working hours. Upon receipt, each document shall be held for confidential processing until it is filed for public inspection.

Subpart B—Regular Schedule

§ 17.2 Procedure and timing for regular schedule.

(a) Each document received shall be filed for public inspection only after it has been received, processed and assigned a publication date.

(b) Except as provided in paragraph (d) of this section, each document received by 2:00 p.m. which meets the requirements of this chapter shall be assigned to the regular schedule. Unless the issuing agency makes special arrangements otherwise, or the Office determines that the document requires a deferred schedule (see 1 CFR 17.7), receipt of a document by 2:00 p.m. is considered to be a request for filing for public inspection and publication on the regular schedule. Documents received after 2:00 p.m. which meet the requirements of this chapter shall be assigned to the next working day's regular schedule.

(c) The regular schedule for filing for public inspection and publication is as follows:

Received before 2:00 p.m.	Filed for public inspection	Published
Monday	Wednesday	Thursday
Tuesday	Thursday	Friday
Wednesday	Friday	Monday
Thursday	Monday	Tuesday
Friday	Tuesday	Wednesday

Where a legal Federal holiday intervenes, one additional work day is added.

(d) Each notice of meeting issued under the "Government in the Sunshine Act" (5 U.S.C. 552b(e)(3)) is placed on immediate public inspection after it has been received, processed, and assigned a publication date.

(1) Each notice received before 4:00 p.m. is scheduled to be published 2 working days later.

(2) Each notice received after 4:00 p.m. is scheduled to be published 3 working days later.

[54 FR 9680, Mar. 7, 1989]

Subpart C—Emergency Schedule

§ 17.3 Criteria for emergency publication.

The emergency schedule is designed to provide the fastest possible publication of a document involving the prevention, alleviation, control, or relief of an emergency situation.

[37 FR 23608, Nov. 4, 1972, as amended at 54 FR 9680, Mar. 7, 1989]

§ 17.4 Procedure and timing for emergency publication.

(a) Each agency requesting publication on the emergency schedule shall briefly describe the emergency and the benefits to be attributed to immediate publication in the FEDERAL REGISTER. The request must be made by letter.

(b) The Director of the Federal Register shall assign a document to the emergency schedule whenever the Director concurs with a request for that action and it is feasible.

(c) Each document assigned to the emergency schedule shall be published as soon as possible.

(d) Each document assigned to the emergency schedule for publication will be filed for public inspection on the working day before publication unless emergency filing for public inspection is also requested.

[37 FR 23608, Nov. 4, 1972, as amended at 54 FR 9680, Mar. 7, 1989]

§ 17.5 Criteria for emergency filing for public inspection.

An agency may request emergency filing for public inspection for documents to be published under the regular, emergency or deferred publication schedules. Emergency filing for public inspection provides for the fastest possible public access to a document after it has been received, processed and assigned a publication date. Emergency filing for public inspection is considered a special arrangement under § 17.2 of this part that results in deviation from the regular schedule for filing for public inspection. A document receiving emergency filing for public inspection remains on public inspection until it is published according to the schedule for publication.

[54 FR 9680, Mar. 7, 1989]

§ 17.6 Procedure and timing for emergency filing for public inspection.

(a) Each agency requesting emergency filing for public inspection shall briefly describe the emergency and the benefits to be attributed to immediate public access. The request must be made by letter.

(b) The Director of the Federal Register shall approve an emergency filing for public inspection request whenever the Director concurs with a request for that action and it is feasible.

(c) Each document approved for emergency filing for public inspection shall be filed as soon as possible following processing and scheduling.

[54 FR 9680, Mar. 7, 1989]

Subpart D—Deferred Schedule

§ 17.7 Criteria for deferred schedule.

(a) A document may be assigned to the deferred schedule under the following conditions:

(1) There are technical problems, unusual or lengthy tables, or illustrations, or the document is of such size as to require extraordinary processing time.

(2) The agency concerned requests a deferred publication date.

(b) The Office of the Federal Register staff will notify the agency if its documents must be assigned to a deferred schedule.

[37 FR 23608, Nov. 4, 1972, as amended at 54 FR 9680, Mar. 7, 1989; 54 FR 23343, May 31, 1989]

PART 18—PREPARATION AND TRANSMITTAL OF DOCUMENTS GENERALLY

AUTHORITY: 44 U.S.C. 1506; sec. 6, E.O. 10530, 19 FR 2709; 3 CFR, 1954–1958 Comp., p. 189.

SOURCE: 37 FR 23609, Nov. 4, 1972, unless otherwise noted.

§ 18.1 Original and copies required.

Except as provided in § 19.2 of this subchapter for Executive orders and proclamations, each agency submitting a document to be filed and published in the FEDERAL REGISTER shall send an original and two duplicate originals or certified copies.[1] However, if the document is printed or processed on both sides, one of the copies sent by the agency must be a collated, single-sided copy.

[54 FR 9680, Mar. 7, 1989]

§ 18.2 Prohibition on combined category documents.

(a) The Director of the Federal Register will not accept a document for filing and publication if it combines material that must appear under more than one category in the FEDERAL REGISTER. For example, a document may not contain both rulemaking and notice of proposed rulemaking material.

(b) Where two related documents are to be published in the same FEDERAL REGISTER issue, the agency may insert a cross-reference in each document.

[54 FR 9680, Mar. 7, 1989]

§ 18.3 Submission of documents and letters of transmittal.

(a) Each document authorized or required by law to be filed for public inspection with the Office of the Federal Register and published in the FEDERAL REGISTER shall be sent to the Director of the Federal Register.

(b) Except for cases involving special handling or treatment, there is no need for a letter of transmittal for a document submitted for filing and FEDERAL REGISTER publication.

(c) Receipt dates are determined at the time a signed original and clear and legible copies are received.

[37 FR 23609, Nov. 4, 1972, as amended at 54 FR 9680, Mar. 7, 1989]

§ 18.4 Form of document.

(a) A printed or processed document may be accepted for filing for public inspection and publication if it is on

---

[1] Agencies with computer processed data are urged to consult with the Office of the Federal Register staff about possible use of the data in the publication process.

bond or similar quality paper, legible, and free of adhesive or correction tape.[2]

(b) A document in the form of a letter or press release may not be accepted for filing for public inspection or publication in the rules and regulations, proposed rules, or notices categories of the FEDERAL REGISTER.

(c) Original documents submitted by telecommunication and authenticated by digital signatures consistent with applicable Federal standards and Office of the Federal Register technical specifications may be accepted for publication.[3]

[54 FR 9681, Mar. 7, 1989, as amended at 61 FR 68119, Dec. 27, 1996]

§18.5 Certified copies.

The certified copies or duplicate originals of each document must be submitted with the original. Each copy or duplicate must be entirely clear and legible.

[54 FR 9681, Mar. 7, 1989]

§18.6 Form of certification.

Each copy of each document submitted for filing and publication, except a Presidential document or a duplicate original, must be certified as follows:

(Certified to be a true copy of the original)

The certification must be signed by a certifying officer designated under §16.1 of this chapter.

[54 FR 9681, Mar. 7, 1989]

§18.7 Signature.

The original and each duplicate original document must be signed in ink, with the name and title of the official signing the document typed or stamped beneath the signature. Initialed or impressed signatures will not be accepted. Documents submitted under §18.4(c) may be authenticated as

original documents by digital signatures.

[37 FR 23609, Nov. 4, 1972, as amended at 54 FR 9681, Mar. 7, 1989; 61 FR 68119, Dec. 27, 1996]

§18.8 Seal.

Use of a seal on an original document or certified copy is optional with the issuing agency.

§18.9 Style.

Each document submitted by an agency for filing and publication shall conform to the current edition of the U.S. Government Printing Office Style Manual in punctuation, capitalization, spelling, and other matters of style.

[54 FR 9681, Mar. 7, 1989]

§18.10 Illustrations, tabular material, and forms.

(a) If it is necessary to publish a form or illustration, a clear and legible original form or illustration, or a clear and completely legible reproduction approximately 8 ½ by 11 inches, shall be included in the original document and each certified copy.

(b) A document that includes tabular material may be assigned to the deferred publication schedule. See §17.7.

[54 FR 9681, Mar. 7, 1989]

§18.12 Preamble requirements.

(a) Each agency submitting a proposed or final rule document for publication shall prepare a preamble which will inform the reader, who is not an expert in the subject area, of the basis and purpose for the rule or proposal.

(b) The preamble shall be in the following format and contain the following information:

AGENCY: _____
      (Name of issuing agency)

ACTION: _____
(Notice of Intent), (Advance Notice of Proposed Rulemaking), (Proposed Rule), (Final Rule), (Other).

SUMMARY: _____
(Brief statements, in simple language, of: (i) the action being taken; (ii) the circumstances which created the need for the action; and (iii) the intended effect of the action.)

DATES: _____

---

[2] Agencies with computer processed data are urged to consult with the Office of the Federal Register staff about possible use of the data in the publication process.

[3] At present, submission of documents by telecommunication is limited to selected pilot projects.

(Comments must be received on or before: _____.) (Proposed effective date: _____.) (Effective date: _____.) (Hearing: _____.) (Other: _____.)

ADDRESSES: _____

(Any relevant addresses.)

FOR FURTHER INFORMATION CONTACT: _____

(For Executive departments and agencies, the name and telephone number of a person in the agency to contact for additional information about the document [Presidential Memorandum, 41 FR 42764, September 28, 1976].)

SUPPLEMENTARY INFORMATION: _____

(See paragraph (c) of this section.)

(c) The agency may include the following information in the preamble, as applicable:

(1) A discussion of the background and major issues involved;

(2) In the case of a final rule, any significant differences between it and the proposed rule;

(3) A response to substantive public comments received; and

(4) Any other information the agency considers appropriate.

[41 FR 56624, Dec. 29, 1976, as amended at 54 FR 9681, Mar. 7, 1989]

§ 18.13 Withdrawal or correction of filed documents.

(a) A document that has been filed for public inspection with the Office of the Federal Register but not yet published, may be withdrawn from publication or corrected by the submitting agency. Withdrawals or minor corrections may be made with a timely letter, signed by a duly authorized representative of the agency. Extensive corrections may require agency withdrawal of the document from publication.

(b) Both the originally filed document and the withdrawing or correcting letter shall remain on file. The original document and the withdrawing or correcting letter will be retained by the Office of the Federal Register after the public inspection period expires.

[54 FR 9681, Mar. 7, 1989]

§ 18.15 Correction of errors in printing.

(a) Typographical or clerical errors made in the printing of the FEDERAL REGISTER shall be corrected by insertion of an appropriate notation or a reprinting in the FEDERAL REGISTER published without further agency documentation, if the Director of the Federal Register determines that—

(1) The error would tend to confuse or mislead the reader; or

(2) The error would affect text subject to codification.

(b) The issuing agency shall review published documents and notify the Office of the Federal Register of printing errors found in published documents.

(c) If the error was in the document as submitted by the agency, the issuing agency must prepare and submit for publication a correction document.

[50 FR 12468, Mar. 28, 1985]

§ 18.16 Reinstatement of expired regulations.

Agencies may reinstate regulations removed from the Code of Federal Regulations data base which have expired by their own terms only by republishing the regulations in full text in the FEDERAL REGISTER.

[54 FR 9681, Mar. 7, 1989]

§ 18.17 Effective dates and time periods.

(a) Each document submitted for publication in the FEDERAL REGISTER that includes an effective date or time period should either set forth a date certain or a time period measured by a certain number of days after publication in the FEDERAL REGISTER. When a document sets forth a time period measured by a certain number of days after publication, Office of the Federal Register staff will compute the date to be inserted in the document as set forth in paragraph (b) of this section.

(b) Dates certain will be computed by counting the day after the publication day as one, and by counting each succeeding day, including Saturdays, Sundays, and holidays. However, where the final count would fall on a Saturday, Sunday, or holiday, the date certain will be the next succeeding Federal business day.

(c) In the event an effective date is dependent upon Congressional action, or an act of Congress or a dispositive Federal court decision establishes or changes the effective date of an agency's regulation, the issuing agency shall promptly publish a document in the FEDERAL REGISTER announcing the effective date.

[37 FR 23609, Nov. 4, 1972, as amended at 54 FR 9681, Mar. 7, 1989]

§18.20 Identification of subjects in agency regulations.

(a) *Federal Register documents.* Each agency that submits a document that is published in the Rules and Regulations section or the Proposed Rules section of the FEDERAL REGISTER shall—

(1) Include a list of index terms for each Code of Federal Regulations part affected by the document; and

(2) Place the list of index terms as the last item in the Supplementary Information portion of the preamble for the document.

(b) *Federal Register Thesaurus.* To prepare its list of index terms, each agency shall use terms contained in the Federal Register Thesaurus of Indexing Terms. Agencies may include additional terms not contained in the Thesaurus as long as the appropriate Thesaurus terms are also used. Copies of the Federal Register Thesaurus of Indexing Terms are available from the Office of the Federal Register, National Archives and Records Administration, Washington, D.C. 20408.

[46 FR 7163, Jan. 22, 1981, as amended at 54 FR 9681, Mar. 7, 1989]

PART 19—EXECUTIVE ORDERS AND PRESIDENTIAL PROCLAMATIONS

Sec.
19.1 Form.
19.2 Routing and approval of drafts.
19.3 Routing and certification of originals and copies.
19.4 Proclamations calling for the observance of special days or events.
19.5 Proclamations of treaties excluded.
19.6 Definition.

AUTHORITY: Secs. 1 to 6 of E.O. 11030, 27 FR 5847, 3 CFR, 1959–1963 Comp., p. 610; E.O. 11354, 32 FR 7695, 3 CFR, 1966–1970 Comp., p. 652; and E.O. 12080, 43 FR 42235, 3 CFR, 1978 Comp., p. 224.

SOURCE: 37 FR 23610, Nov. 4, 1972, unless otherwise noted.

§19.1 Form.

Proposed Executive orders and proclamations shall be prepared in accordance with the following requirements:

(a) The order or proclamation shall be given a suitable title.

(b) The order or proclamation shall contain a citation of the authority under which it is issued.

(c) Punctuation, capitalization, spelling, and other matters of style shall, in general, conform to the most recent edition of the U.S. Government Printing Office Style Manual.

(d) The spelling of geographic names shall conform to the decisions of the Board on Geographic Names, established by section 2 of the Act of July 25, 1947, 61 Stat. 456 (43 U.S.C. 364a).

(e) Descriptions of tracts of land shall conform, so far as practicable, to the most recent edition of the "Specifications for Descriptions of Tracts of Land for Use in Executive Orders and Proclamations,"[1] prepared by the Bureau of Land Management, Department of the Interior.

(f) Proposed Executive orders and proclamations shall be typewritten on paper approximately 8 × 13 inches, shall have a left-hand margin of approximately 1½ inches and a right-hand margin of approximately 1 inch, and shall be double-spaced except that quotations, tabulations, and descriptions of land may be single-spaced.

(g) Proclamations issued by the President shall conclude with the following-described recitation:

IN WITNESS WHEREOF, I have hereunto set my hand this ____ day of _____, in the year of our Lord _____, and of the Independence of the United States of America the _____.

[37 FR 23610, Nov. 4, 1972, as amended at 54 FR 9681, Mar. 7, 1989]

§19.2 Routing and approval of drafts.

(a) A proposed Executive order or proclamation shall first be submitted, with seven copies thereof, to the Director of the Office of Management and Budget, together with a letter, signed

---

[1] Agencies with computer processed data are urged to consult with the Office of the Federal Register staff about possible use of the data in the publication process.

by the head or other properly authorized officer of the originating Federal agency, explaining the nature, purpose, background, and effect of the proposed Executive order or proclamation and its relationship, if any, to pertinent laws and other Executive orders or proclamations.

(b) If the Director of the Office of Management and Budget approves the proposed Executive order or proclamation, he shall transmit it to the Attorney General for his consideration as to both form and legality.

(c) If the Attorney General approves the proposed Executive order or proclamation, he shall transmit it to the Director of the Office of the Federal Register, National Archives and Records Administration: *Provided,* That in cases involving sufficient urgency the Attorney General may transmit it directly to the President: *And provided further,* That the authority vested in the Attorney General by this section may be delegated by him, in whole or in part, to the Deputy Attorney General, Solicitor General, or to such Assistant Attorney General as he may designate.

(d) After determining that the proposed Executive order or proclamation conforms to the requirements of § 19.1 and is free from typographical or clerical error, the Director of the Office of the Federal Register shall transmit it and three copies thereof to the President.

(e) If the proposed Executive order or proclamation is disapproved by the Director of the Office of Management and Budget or by the Attorney General, it shall not thereafter be presented to the President unless it is accompanied by a statement of the reasons for such disapproval.

§ 19.3 Routing and certification of originals and copies.

(a) If the order or proclamation is signed by the President, the original and two copies shall be forwarded to the Director of the Federal Register for publication in the FEDERAL REGISTER.

(b) The Office of the Federal Register shall cause to be placed upon the copies of all Executive orders and proclamations forwarded as provided in paragraph (a) of this section the following notation, to be signed by the Director

or by some person authorized by him to sign such notation: "Certified to be a true copy of the original."

§ 19.4 Proclamations calling for the observance of special days or events.

Except as may be otherwise provided by law, responsibility for the preparation and presentation of proposed proclamations calling for the observance of special days, or other periods of time, or events, shall be assigned by the Director of the Office of Management and Budget to such agencies as he may consider appropriate. Such proposed proclamations shall be submitted to the Director at least 60 days before the date of the specified observance. Notwithstanding the provisions of § 19.2, the Director shall transmit any approved commemorative proclamations to the President.

[37 FR 23610, Nov. 4, 1972, as amended at 54 FR 9681, Mar. 7, 1989]

§ 19.5 Proclamations of treaties excluded.

Consonant with the provisions of chapter 15 of title 44 of the United States Code (44 U.S.C. 1511), nothing in these regulations shall be construed to apply to treaties, conventions, protocols, or other international agreements, or proclamations thereof by the President.

§ 19.6 Definition.

The term "Presidential proclamations and Executive orders," as used in chapter 15 of title 44 of the United States Code (44 U.S.C. 1505(a)), shall, except as the President or his representative may hereafter otherwise direct, be deemed to include such attachments thereto as are referred to in the respective proclamations or orders.

PART 20—HANDLING OF THE UNITED STATES GOVERNMENT MANUAL STATEMENTS

Sec.
20.1 Liaison officers.
20.2 Preparation of agency statements.
20.3 Organization.
20.4 Description of program activities.
20.5 Sources of information.
20.6 Form, style, arrangement and apportionment of space.

20.7 Deadline dates.

AUTHORITY: 44 U.S.C. 1506; sec. 6, E.O. 10530, 19 FR 2709; 3 CFR, 1954–1958 Comp., p. 189.

SOURCE: 37 FR 23611, Nov. 4, 1972, unless otherwise noted.

§20.1 Liaison officers.

(a) Each of the following shall appoint an officer to maintain liaison with the Office on matters relating to The United States Government Manual:

(1) Agencies of the legislative and judicial branches.

(2) Executive agencies that do not have a liaison officer designated under §16.1 of this chapter or who wish to appoint a liaison officer for Manual matters other than the one designated under such §16.1.

(3) Quasi-official agencies represented in the Manual.

(4) Any other agency that the Director believes should be included in the Manual.

(b) Each liaison officer will insure agency compliance with part 9 of this chapter and this part 20.

[37 FR 23611, Nov. 4, 1972, as amended at 50 FR 12468, Mar. 28, 1985; 54 FR 9682, Mar. 7, 1989]

§20.2 Preparation of agency statements.

In accordance with schedules established under §20.7 each agency shall submit for publication in the Manual an official draft of the information required by §9.2 of this chapter and this part 20.

§20.3 Organization.

(a) Information about lines of authority and organization may be reflected in a chart if the chart clearly delineates the agency's organizational structure. Charts must be prepared so as to be perfectly legible when reduced to the size of a Manual page. Charts that do not meet this requirement will not be included in the Manual.

(b) Listings of heads of operating units should be arranged whenever possible to reflect relationships between units.

(c) Narrative descriptions of organizational structure or hierarchy that duplicate information conveyed by charts or by lists of officials will not be published in the Manual.

[37 FR 23611, Nov. 4, 1972, as amended at 54 FR 9682, Mar. 7, 1989]

§20.4 Description of program activities.

(a) Descriptions should clearly state the public purposes that the agency serves, and the programs that carry out those purposes.

(b) Descriptions of the responsibilities of individuals or of administrative units common to most agencies will not be accepted for publication in the Manual.

[54 FR 9682, Mar. 7, 1989]

§20.5 Sources of information.

Pertinent sources of information useful to the public, in areas of public interest such as employment, consumer activities, contracts, services to small business, and other topics of public interest should be provided with each agency statement. These sources of information shall plainly identify the places at which the public may obtain information or make submittals or requests.

§20.6 Form, style, arrangement and apportionment of space.

The form, style, and arrangement of agency statements and other materials included in the Manual and the apportionment of space therein shall be determined by the Director of the Federal Register. The U.S. Government Printing Office Style Manual is the applicable reference work in determining style.

§20.7 Deadline dates.

The Manual is published on a schedule designed to provide the public with information about their Government on a timely basis. Therefore, agencies must comply with the deadline dates established by the Director of the Federal Register for transmittal of statements and charts and for the verification of proofs. Failure to do so may result in publication of an outdated statement or the omission of important material, thus depriving members of the public of information they have a right to expect in a particular edition of the Manual.

PART 21—PREPARATION OF DOCUMENTS SUBJECT TO CODIFICATION

AUTHORITY: 44 U.S.C. 1506; sec. 6, E.O. 10530, 19 FR 2709; 3 CFR, 1954–1958 Comp., p. 189.

SOURCE: 37 FR 23611, Nov. 4, 1972, unless otherwise noted.

Subpart A—General

§ 21.1   Drafting.

(a) Each agency that prepares a document that is subject to codification shall draft it as an amendment to the Code of Federal Regulations, in accordance with this subchapter, before submitting it to the Office of the Federal Register.

(b) Each agency that prepares a document that is subject to codification shall include words of issuance and amendatory language that precisely describes the relationship of the new provisions to the Code.

[37 FR 23611, Nov. 4, 1972, as amended at 54 FR 9682, Mar. 7, 1989]

§ 21.6   Notice of expiration of codified material.

Whenever a codified regulation expires after a specified period by its own terms or by law, the issuing agency shall submit a notification by document for publication in the FEDERAL REGISTER.

[54 FR 9682, Mar. 7, 1989]

CODE STRUCTURE

§ 21.7   Titles and subtitles.

(a) The major divisions of the Code are titles, each of which brings together broadly related Government functions.

(b) Subtitles may be used to distinguish between materials emanating from an overall agency and the material issued by its various components. Subtitles may also be used to group chapters within a title.

§ 21.8   Chapters and subchapters.

(a) The normal divisions of a title are chapters, assigned to the various agencies within a title descriptive of the subject matter covered by the agencies' regulations.

(b) Subchapters may be used to group related parts within a chapter.

(c) Chapter and subchapter assignments are made by the Office of the

Federal Register after agency consultation.

[37 FR 23611, Nov. 4, 1972, as amended at 54 FR 9682, Mar. 7, 1989]

§21.9 Parts, subparts, and undesignated center heads.

(a) The normal divisions of a chapter are parts, consisting of a unified body of regulations applying to a specific function of an issuing agency or devoted to specific subject matter under the control of that agency.

(b) Subparts or undesignated center heads may be used to group related sections within a part. Undesignated center heads may also be used to group sections within a subpart.

§21.10 Sections.

(a) The normal divisions of a part are sections. Sections are the basic units of the Code.

(b) When internal division is necessary, a section may be divided into paragraphs, and paragraphs may be further subdivided using the lettering indicated in §21.11.

NUMBERING

§21.11 Standard organization of the Code of Federal Regulations.

The standard organization consists of the following structural units:

(a) Titles, which are numbered consecutively in Arabic throughout the Code;

(b) Subtitles, which are lettered consecutively in capitals throughout the title;

(c) Chapters, which are numbered consecutively in Roman capitals throughout each title;

(d) Subchapters, which are lettered consecutively in capitals throughout the chapter;

(e) Parts, which are numbered in Arabic throughout each title;

(f) Subparts, which are lettered in capitals;

(g) Sections, which are numbered in Arabic throughout each part. A section number includes the number of the part followed by a period and the number of the section. For example, the section number for section 15 of part 21 is "§21.15"; and

(h) Paragraphs, which are designated as follows:

level 1 (a), (b), (c), etc.
level 2 (1), (2), (3), etc.
level 3 (i), (ii), (iii), etc.
level 4 (A), (B), (C), etc.
level 5 (*1*), (*2*), (*3*), etc.
level 6 (*i*), (*ii*), (*iii*), etc.

[54 FR 9682, Mar. 7, 1989; 54 FR 23343, May 31, 1989]

§21.12 Reservation of numbers.

In a case where related parts or related sections are grouped under a heading, numbers may be reserved at the end of each group to allow for expansion.

[37 FR 23611, Nov. 4, 1972, as amended at 54 FR 9682, Mar. 7, 1989]

§21.14 Deviations from standard organization of the Code of Federal Regulations.

(a) Any deviation from standard Code of Federal Regulations designations must be approved in advance by the Office of the Federal Register. Requests for approval must be submitted in writing at least five working days before the agency intends to submit the final rule document for publication and include a copy of the final rule document.

(b) The Director of the Federal Register may allow the keying of section numbers to correspond to a particular numbering system used by an agency only when the keying will benefit both that agency and the public.

[54 FR 9682, Mar. 7, 1989]

HEADINGS

§21.16 Required document headings.

(a) Each rule and proposed rule document submitted to the Office of the Federal Register shall contain the following headings, when appropriate, on separate lines in the following order:

(1) Agency name;

(2) Subagency name;

(3) Numerical references to the CFR title and parts affected;

(4) Agency numbers of identifying symbol in brackets, if used;

(5) Brief subject heading describing the document.

(b) Each CFR section in the regulatory text of the document shall have a brief descriptive heading, preceding the text, on a separate line.

[50 FR 12468, Mar. 28, 1985]

§ 21.18 Tables of contents.

A table of contents shall be used at the beginning of the part whenever a new part is introduced, an existing part is completely revised, or a group of sections is revised or added and set forth as a subpart or otherwise separately grouped under a center head. The table shall follow the part heading and precede the text of the regulations in that part. It shall also list the headings for the subparts, undesignated center headings, sections in the part, and appendix headings to the part or subpart.

[37 FR 23611, Nov. 4, 1972, as amended at 54 FR 9682, Mar. 7, 1989]

§ 21.19 Composition of part headings.

Each part heading shall indicate briefly the general subject matter of the part. Phrases such as "Regulations under the Act of July 28, 1955" or other expressions that are not descriptive of the subject matter may not be used. Introductory expressions such as "Regulations governing" and "Rules applicable to" may not be used.

AMENDMENTS

§ 21.20 General requirements.

(a) Each amendatory document shall identify in specific terms the unit amended, and the extent of the changes made.

(b) The number and heading of each section amended shall be set forth in full on a separate line.

REFERENCES

§ 21.21 General requirements: References.

(a) Each reference to the Code of Federal Regulations shall be in terms of the specific titles, chapters, parts, sections, and paragraphs involved. Ambiguous references such as "herein", "above", "below", and similar expressions may not be used.

(b) Each document that contains a reference to material published in the Code shall include the Code citation as a part of the reference.

(c) Each agency shall publish its own regulations in full text. Cross-references to the regulations of another agency may not be used as a substitute for publication in full text, unless the Office of the Federal Register finds that the regulation meets any of the following exceptions:

(1) The reference is required by court order, statute, Executive order or reorganization plan.

(2) The reference is to regulations promulgated by an agency with the exclusive legal authority to regulate in a subject matter area, but the referencing agency needs to apply those regulations in its own programs.

(3) The reference is informational or improves clarity rather than being regulatory.

(4) The reference is to test methods or consensus standards produced by a Federal agency that have replaced or preempted private or voluntary test methods or consensus standards in a subject matter area.

(5) The reference is to the Department level from a subagency.

[37 FR 23611, Nov. 4, 1972, as amended at 50 FR 12468, Mar. 28, 1985]

§ 21.23 Parallel citations of Code and Federal Register.

For parallel reference, the Code of Federal Regulations and the FEDERAL REGISTER may be cited in the following forms, as appropriate:

_____ CFR _____ (_____ FR _____). § _____ of this chapter (_____ FR _____).

§ 21.24 References to 1938 edition of Code.

When reference is made to material codified in the 1938 edition of the Code of Federal Regulations, or a supplement thereto, the following forms may be used, as appropriate:

_____ CFR, 1938 Ed., _____.
_____ CFR, 1943, Cum. Supp., _____.
_____ CFR, 1946 Supp., _____.

EFFECTIVE DATE STATEMENT

§ 21.30 General.

Each document subject to codification shall include a clear statement as to the date or dates upon which its contents become effective.

§ 21.35 OMB control numbers.

To display OMB control numbers in agency regulations, those numbers shall be placed parenthetically at the end of the section or displayed in a table or codified section.

[50 FR 12468, Mar. 28, 1985]

Subpart B—Citations of Authority

§ 21.40 General requirements: Authority citations.

Each section in a document subject to codification must include, or be covered by, a complete citation of the authority under which the section is issued, including—

(a) General or specific authority delegated by statute; and

(b) Executive delegations, if any, necessary to link the statutory authority to the issuing agency.

[50 FR 12468, Mar. 28, 1985]

§ 21.41 Agency responsibility.

(a) Each issuing agency is responsible for the accuracy and integrity of the citations of authority in the documents it issues.

(b) Each issuing agency shall formally amend the citations of authority in its codified material to reflect any changes therein.

§ 21.42 Exceptions.

The Director of the Federal Register may make exceptions to the requirements of this subpart relating to placement and form of citations of authority whenever the Director determines that strict application would impair the practical use of the citations.

[37 FR 23611, Nov. 4, 1972, as amended at 54 FR 9682, Mar. 7, 1989]

§ 21.43 Placing and amending authority citations.

(a) The requirements for placing authority citations vary with the type of amendment the agency is making in a document. The agency shall set out the full text of the authority citation for each part affected by the document.

(1) If a document sets out an entire CFR part, the agency shall place the complete authority citation directly after the table of contents and before the regulatory text.

(2) If a document amends only certain sections within a CFR part, the agency shall present the complete authority citation to this part as the first item in the list of amendments.

(i) If the authority for issuing an amendment is the same as the authority listed for the whole CFR part, the agency shall simply restate the authority.

(ii) If the authority for issuing an amendment changes the authority citation for the whole CFR part, the agency shall revise the authority citation in its entirety. The agency may specify the particular authority under which certain sections are amended in the revised authority citation.

(b) The agency shall present a centralized authority citation. The authority citation shall appear at the end of the table of contents for a part or after each subpart heading within the text of a part. Citations of authority for particular sections may be specified within the centralized authority citation.

[50 FR 12469, Mar. 28, 1985, as amended at 54 FR 9682, Mar. 7, 1989]

§ 21.45 Nonstatutory authority.

Citation to a nonstatutory document as authority shall be placed after the statutory citations. For example:

AUTHORITY: Sec. 9, Pub. L. 89–670, 80 Stat. 944 (49 U.S.C. 1657). E.O. 11222, 30 FR 6469, 3 CFR, 1965 Comp., p. 10.

[37 FR 23611, Nov. 4, 1972, as amended at 54 FR 9682, Mar. 7, 1989]

§ 21.51 General.

(a) Formal citations of authority shall be in the shortest form compatible with positive identification and ready reference.

(b) The Office of the Federal Register shall assist agencies in developing model citations.

§ 21.52 Statutory material.

(a) *United States Code.* All citations to statutory authority shall include a

United States Code citation, where available. Citations to titles of the United States Code, whether or not enacted into positive law, may be cited without Public Law or U.S. Statutes at Large citation. For example:

AUTHORITY: 10 U.S.C. 501.

(b) *Public Laws and U.S. Statutes at Large.* Citations to Public Laws and U.S. Statutes at Large are optional when the United States Code is cited. Citations to current public laws and to the U.S. Statutes at Large shall refer to the section of the public law and the volume and page of the U.S. Statutes at Large to which they have been assigned. The page number shall refer to the page on which the section cited begins. For example:

AUTHORITY: Sec. 5, Pub. L. 89–670, 80 Stat. 935 (49 U.S.C. 1654); sec. 313, Pub. L. 85–726, 72 Stat. 752 (49 U.S.C. 1354).

[54 FR 9682, Mar. 7, 1989]

§ 21.53　Nonstatutory materials.

Nonstatutory documents shall be cited by document designation and by FEDERAL REGISTER volume and page, followed, if possible, by the parallel citation to the Code of Federal Regulations. For example:

AUTHORITY: Special Civil Air Reg. SR–422A, 28 FR 6703, 14 CFR part 4b. E.O. 11130, 28 FR 12789; 3 CFR 1959–1963 Comp.

[37 FR 23611, Nov. 4, 1972, as amended at 54 FR 9683, Mar. 7, 1989]

PART 22—PREPARATION OF NOTICES AND PROPOSED RULES

Subpart A—Notices

AUTHORITY: 44 U.S.C. 1506; sec. 6, E.O. 10530, 19 FR 2709; 3 CFR, 1954–1958 Comp., p. 189.

SOURCE: 37 FR 23614, Nov. 4, 1972, unless otherwise noted.

Subpart A—Notices

§ 22.1　Name of issuing agency and subdivision.

(a) The name of the agency issuing a notice shall be placed at the beginning of the document.

(b) Whenever a specific bureau, service, or similar unit within an agency issues a notice, the name of that bureau, service, or unit shall be placed on a separate line below the name of the agency.

(c) An agency that uses file numbers, docket numbers, or similar identifying symbols shall place them in brackets immediately below the other headings required by this section.

(d) A suitable short title identifying the subject shall be provided beginning on a separate line immediately after the other required caption or captions. Whenever appropriate, an additional brief caption indicating the nature of the document shall be used.

§ 22.2　Authority citation.

The authority under which an agency issues a notice shall be cited in narrative form within text or in parentheses on a separate line following text.

Subpart B—Proposed Rules

§ 22.5　General requirements.

Each proposed rule required by section 553 of title 5, United States Code, or any other statute, and any similar document voluntarily issued by an agency shall include a statement of—

(a) The time, place, and nature of public rulemaking proceedings; and

(b) Reference to the authority under which the regulatory action is proposed.

[37 FR 23614, Nov. 4, 1972, as amended at 54 FR 9683, Mar. 7, 1989]

§ 22.6　Code designation.

The area of the Code of Federal Regulations directly affected by a proposed regulatory action shall be identified by placing the appropriate CFR citation immediately below the name of the issuing agency. For example:

1 CFR part 22

[37 FR 23614, Nov. 4, 1972, as amended at 54 FR 9683, Mar. 7, 1989]

§22.7 Codification.

Any part of a proposed rule document that contains the full text of a pro-posed regulation shall also conform to the pertinent provisions of part 21 of this chapter.

[37 FR 23614, Nov. 4, 1972, as amended at 54 FR 9683, Mar. 7, 1989]

PARTS 23–49 [RESERVED]

CHAPTER II—OFFICE OF THE FEDERAL REGISTER

PART 50 [RESERVED]

PART 51—INCORPORATION BY REFERENCE

AUTHORITY: 5 U.S.C. 552(a).

SOURCE: 47 FR 34108, Aug. 6, 1982, unless otherwise noted.

§ 51.1 Policy.

(a) Section 552(a) of title 5, United States Code, provides, in part, that "matter reasonably available to the class of persons affected thereby is deemed published in the FEDERAL REGISTER when incorporated by reference therein with the approval of the Director of the Federal Register."

(b) The Director will interpret and apply the language of section 552(a) together with other requirements which govern publication in the FEDERAL REGISTER and the Code of Federal Regulations. Those requirements which govern publication include—

(1) The Federal Register Act (44 U.S.C. 1501 *et seq.*)

(2) The Administrative Procedure Act (5 U.S.C. 551 *et seq.*);

(3) The regulations of the Administrative Committee of the Federal Register under the Federal Register Act (1 CFR Ch. I); and

(4) The acts which require publication in the FEDERAL REGISTER (See CFR volume entitled "CFR Index and Finding Aids.")

(c) The Director will assume in carrying out the responsibilities for incorporation by reference that incorporation by reference—

(1) Is intended to benefit both the Federal Government and the members of the class affected; and

(2) Is not intended to detract from the legal or practical attributes of the system established by the Federal Register Act, the Administrative Procedure Act, the regulations of the Administrative Committee of the Federal Register, and the acts which require publication in the FEDERAL REGISTER.

(d) The Director will carry out the responsibilities by applying the standards of part 51 fairly and uniformly.

(e) Publication in the FEDERAL REGISTER of a document containing an incorporation by reference does not of itself constitute an approval of the incorporation by reference by the Director.

(f) Incorporation by reference of a publication is limited to the edition of the publication that is approved. Future amendments or revisions of the publication are not included.

§ 51.3 When will the Director approve a publication?

(a)(1) The Director will informally approve the proposed incorporation by reference of a publication when the preamble of a proposed rule meets the requirements of this part (See § 51.5(a)).

(2) If the preamble of a proposed rule does not meet the requirements of this part, the Director will return the document to the agency (See 1 CFR 2.4).

(b) The Director will formally approve the incorporation by reference of a publication in a final rule when the following requirements are met:

(1) The publication is eligible for incorporation by reference (See § 51.7).

(2) The preamble meets the requirements of this part (See § 51.5(b)(2)).

(3) The language of incorporation meets the requirements of this part (See § 51.9).

(4) The publication is on file with the Office of the Federal Register.

(5) The Director has received a written request from the agency to approve the incorporation by reference of the publication.

(c) The Director will notify the agency of the approval or disapproval of an incorporation by reference in a final rule within 20 working days after the agency has met all the requirements for requesting approvals (See § 51.5).

[79 FR 66278, Nov. 7, 2014]

§ 51.5 How does an agency request approval?

(a) For a proposed rule, the agency does not request formal approval but must:

(1) Discuss, in the preamble of the proposed rule, the ways that the materials it proposes to incorporate by reference are reasonably available to interested parties or how it worked to make those materials reasonably available to interested parties; and

(2) Summarize, in the preamble of the proposed rule, the material it proposes to incorporate by reference.

(b) For a final rule, the agency must request formal approval. The formal request package must:

(1) Send a letter that contains a written request for approval at least 20 working days before the agency intends to submit the final rule document for publication;

(2) Discuss, in the preamble of the final rule, the ways that the materials it incorporates by reference are reasonably available to interested parties and how interested parties can obtain the materials;

(3) Summarize, in the preamble of the final rule, the material it incorporates by reference;

(4) Send a copy of the final rule document that uses the proper language of incorporation with the written request (See § 51.9); and

(5) Ensure that a copy of the incorporated material is on file at the Office of the Federal Register.

(c) Agencies may consult with the Office of the Federal Register at any time with respect to the requirements of this part.

[79 FR 66278, Nov. 7, 2014]

§ 51.7　What publications are eligible?

(a) A publication is eligible for incorporation by reference under 5 U.S.C. 552(a) if it—

(1) Conforms to the policy stated in § 51.1;

(2)(i) Is published data, criteria, standards, specifications, techniques, illustrations, or similar material; and

(ii) Does not detract from the usefulness of the FEDERAL REGISTER publication system; and

(3) Is reasonably available to and usable by the class of persons affected. In determining whether a publication is usable, the Director will consider—

(i) The completeness and ease of handling of the publication; and

(ii) Whether it is bound, numbered, and organized, as applicable.

(b) The Director will assume that a publication produced by the same agency that is seeking its approval is inappropriate for incorporation by reference. A publication produced by the agency may be approved, if, in the judgment of the Director, it meets the requirements of paragraph (a) and possesses other unique or highly unusual qualities. A publication may be approved if it cannot be printed using the FEDERAL REGISTER/Code of Federal Regulations printing system.

(c) The following materials are not appropriate for incorporation by reference:

(1) Material published previously in the FEDERAL REGISTER.

(2) Material published in the *United States Code.*

[47 FR 34108, Aug. 6, 1982, as amended at 79 FR 66278, Nov. 7, 2014]

§ 51.9　What is the proper language of incorporation?

(a) The language incorporating a publication by reference must be precise, complete, and clearly state that the incorporation by reference is intended and completed by the final rule document in which it appears.

(b) The language incorporating a publication by reference is precise and complete if it—

(1) Uses the words "incorporated by reference;"

(2) States the title, date, edition, author, publisher, and identification number of the publication;

(3) Informs the user that the incorporated publication is a requirement;

(4) Makes an official showing that the publication is in fact available by stating where and how copies may be examined and readily obtained with maximum convenience to the user; and

(5) Refers to 5 U.S.C. 552(a).

(c) If the Director approves a publication for incorporation by reference in a final rule, the agency must include—

(1) The following language under the **DATES** caption of the preamble to the final rule document (See 1 CFR 18.12 Preamble requirements):

The incorporation by reference of certain publications listed in the regulations is approved by the Director of the Federal Register as of _____.

(2) The preamble requirements set out in 51.5(b).

(3) The term "incorporation by reference" in the list of index terms (See 1 CFR 18.20 Identification of subjects in agency regulations).

[47 FR 34108, Aug. 6, 1982, as amended at 79 FR 66278, Nov. 7, 2014]

§51.11 How does an agency change or remove an approved incorporation?

(a) An agency that seeks approval for a change to a publication that is approved for incorporation by reference must—

(1) Publish notice of the change in the FEDERAL REGISTER and amend the Code of Federal Regulations;

(2) Ensure that a copy of the amendment or revision is on file at the Office of the Federal Register; and

(3) Notify the Director of the Federal Register in writing that the change is being made.

(b) If a regulation containing an incorporation by reference fails to become effective or is removed from the Code of Federal Regulations, the agency must notify the Director of the Federal Register in writing of that fact within 5 working days of the occurrence.

PARTS 52–299 [RESERVED]

CHAPTER III—ADMINISTRATIVE CONFERENCE OF THE UNITED STATES

PART 300 [RESERVED]

PART 301—ORGANIZATION AND PURPOSE

Sec.

AUTHORITY: 5 U.S.C. 552, 591–96.

SOURCE: 75 FR 68941, Nov. 10, 2010, unless otherwise noted.

§ 301.1 Establishment and location.

The Administrative Conference of the United States was established as a permanent independent agency of the Federal Government by the Administrative Conference Act (5 U.S.C. 591–96), as amended. The Conference offices are located at 1120 20th Street, NW., South Lobby, Suite 706, Washington, DC 20036. The offices are open from 8:30 a.m. to 5 p.m., Monday through Friday, excluding legal holidays, unless otherwise stated. General correspondence and filings should be delivered to the foregoing address. Electronic filings should be transmitted as specified by the Conference. The public may obtain information about the Conference either by accessing its Web site at *http://www.acus.gov*, by calling the Conference offices at (202) 480–2080, or by contacting *info@acus.gov*. The Conference's recommendations may be obtained by accessing its Web site or by visiting the reading room at its offices.

§ 301.2 Purposes.

The purposes of the Administrative Conference are—

(a) To provide suitable arrangements through which Federal agencies, assisted by outside experts, may cooperatively study mutual problems, exchange information, and develop recommendations for action by proper authorities to the end that private rights may be fully protected and regulatory activities and other Federal responsibilities may be carried out expeditiously in the public interest;

(b) To promote more effective public participation and efficiency in the rulemaking process;

(c) To reduce unnecessary litigation in the regulatory process;

(d) To improve the use of science in the regulatory process; and

(e) To improve the effectiveness of laws applicable to the regulatory process.

§ 301.3 Organization.

(a) The Chairman of the Administrative Conference of the United States is appointed by the President, with the advice and consent of the Senate, for a five-year term.

(b) The Council consists of the Chairman and 10 other members who are appointed by the President for three-year terms, of whom not more than one-half may be employees of Federal regulatory agencies or Executive departments.

(c) The total membership of the Conference may not, by statute, be lower than 75 or higher than 101. It comprises, in addition to the Council, approximately 50 Government members (from Executive departments and agencies designated by the President and independent regulatory boards or commissions) and approximately 40 non-Government or public members appointed by the Chairman with the approval of the Council (lawyers in private practice, scholars in the field of administrative law or government, or others specially informed by knowledge and experience with respect to Federal administrative procedure). Public members are selected so as to provide broad representation of the views of private citizens and utilize diverse experience.

(d) Members of the Conference, except the Chairman, are not entitled to pay for service; although public members are entitled to travel reimbursement.

(e) The membership is divided into six standing committees, each assigned a broad area of interest as follows: Adjudication, Administration, Public Processes, Judicial Review, Regulation, and Rulemaking.

(f) The membership meeting in plenary session is called the Assembly of the Administrative Conference. The Council must call at least one plenary session each year. The Assembly has authority to adopt bylaws for carrying out the functions of the Conference.

§ 301.4 **Activities.**

(a) The Conference may study the efficiency, adequacy, and fairness of the administrative procedure used by administrative agencies in carrying out administrative programs. Subjects for inquiry by the Conference are developed by the Chairman, the Council, the committees, and the Assembly. The committees, with the assistance of staff and consultants, conduct thorough studies of these subjects and develop proposed recommendations and supporting reports. Reports and recommendations are considered by the Council and distributed to the membership, with the views and recommendations of the Council, to be placed on the agenda of a plenary session. The Assembly has complete authority to approve, amend, remand, or reject recommendations presented by the committees. The deliberations of the Assembly are public. Recommendations may be made to administrative agencies, collectively or individually, and to the President, Congress, or the Judicial Conference of the United States, as the Conference considers appropriate.

(b) The Conference may arrange for interchange among administrative agencies of information potentially useful in improving administrative procedure, collect information and statistics from administrative agencies and publish such reports as it considers useful for evaluating and improving administrative procedure, and enter into arrangements with any administrative agency or major organizational unit within an administrative agency pursuant to which the Conference performs any of the functions described in this section.

(c) The Conference may provide assistance in response to requests relating to the improvement of administrative procedure in foreign countries, subject to the concurrence of the Secretary of State or the Administrator of the Agency for International Development, as appropriate, except that:

(1) Such assistance shall be limited to the analysis of issues relating to administrative procedure, the provision of training of foreign officials in ad-

ministrative procedure, and the design or improvement of administrative procedure, where the expertise of members of the Conference is indicated; and

(2) Such assistance may only be undertaken on a fully reimbursable basis, including all direct and indirect administrative costs.

(d) For purposes of this section:

(1) "Administrative program" includes a Federal function which involves protection of the public interest and the determination of rights, privileges, and obligations of private persons through rulemaking, adjudication, licensing, or investigation, except that it does not include a military or foreign affairs function of the United States; and

(2) "Administrative procedure" means procedure used in carrying out an administrative program and is to be broadly construed to include any aspect of agency organization, procedure, or management which may affect the equitable consideration of public and private interests, the fairness of agency decisions, the speed of agency action, and the relationship of operating methods to later judicial review, but does not include the scope of agency responsibility as established by law or matters of substantive policy committed by law to agency discretion.

§ 301.5 **Office of the Chairman.**

The Chairman is the chief executive of the Conference. The Chairman presides at meetings of the Council and at each plenary session of the Conference. Among his powers is the authority to encourage Federal agencies to adopt the recommendations of the Conference. The Chairman is also authorized to make inquiries into matters he considers important for Conference consideration, including matters proposed by individuals inside or outside the Federal Government. The purpose of such inquiries is not to review the results in particular cases, but rather to determine whether the problems should be made the subject of Conference study in the interests of developing fair and effective procedures for such cases. Upon request of the head of an agency, the Chairman is authorized to furnish assistance and advice on matters of administrative procedure.

The Chairman may request agency heads to provide information needed by the Conference, which information shall be supplied to the extent permitted by law.

PARTS 302–303 [RESERVED]

PART 304—DISCLOSURE OF RECORDS OR INFORMATION

Subpart A—Procedures for Disclosure of Records Under the Freedom of Information Act

Subpart B—Protection of Privacy and Access to Individual Records Under the Privacy Act of 1974

SOURCE: 76 FR 18635, Apr. 5, 2011, unless otherwise noted.

Subpart A—Procedures for Disclosure of Records Under the Freedom of Information Act

AUTHORITY: 5 U.S.C. 552, 591–96.

§304.1 General provisions.

(a) This subpart contains the rules that the Administrative Conference of the United States ("ACUS" or "the agency") follows in processing requests for disclosure of records under the Freedom of Information Act ("FOIA" or "the Act"), 5 U.S.C. 552, as amended, and in meeting its responsibilities under the Act. Note that electronic records are treated as records for the purposes of the FOIA. These rules should be read together with the text of the FOIA itself and the Uniform Freedom of Information Fee Schedule and Guidelines published by the Office of Management and Budget (OMB Guidelines). They also may be read in conjunction with the agency's "Freedom of Information Act Reference Guide," which provides basic information about use of the Act in relation to the agency's records. Requests made by individuals for records about themselves under the Privacy Act of 1974, 5 U.S.C. 552a, are processed in accordance with the agency's Privacy Act regulations as well as under this subpart.

(b) The agency will withhold records or information only when it reasonably foresees that disclosure would harm an interest protected by an exemption of the FOIA or when disclosure is prohibited by law. Where full disclosure is not possible, the agency will consider whether partial disclosure is possible and, if so, will take reasonable steps to segregate and release nonexempt information. These policies do not create any right enforceable in court.

(c) The agency has designated its General Counsel as its Chief FOIA Officer, who has agency-wide responsibility for efficient and appropriate compliance with the FOIA and these implementing regulations. The Chief FOIA Officer has designated the agency's FOIA Public Liaison, who can assist individuals in locating and obtaining particular agency records. Contact information for the Chief FOIA Officer and the FOIA Public Liaison are clearly indicated on the agency's Web site at *https://www.acus.gov/foia.*

[82 FR 7632, Jan. 23, 2017]

§ 304.2 Proactive disclosures.

(a) Records that the FOIA requires ACUS to make regularly available for public inspection in an electronic format, including any records that have been requested three or more times, or were previously released and are likely to become the subject of subsequent requests or appear to be of general interest, may be accessed through the agency's Web site at *https://www.acus.gov.* A subject matter index of such records (or comparable tool) may also be accessed through the agency's Web site and will be updated on an ongoing basis.

(b) Information routinely provided to the public as part of a regular agency activity, including information posted on the agency's Web site (for example, press releases or recommendations adopted by the Conference pursuant to the Administrative Conference Act, 5 U.S.C. 591 *et seq.*), may be provided to the public without following this subpart.

(c) Any requester needing assistance in locating proactively disclosed or other agency records may contact the agency's FOIA Public Liaison at (202) 480–2080.

[82 FR 7632, Jan. 23, 2017]

§ 304.3 Requirements for making requests.

(a) *How made and addressed.* You may make a request for records by using the FOIA Request form on the ACUS Web site at *https://www.acus.gov/foia.* You may also send a written request letter to the agency either by mail addressed to FOIA Public Liaison, Administrative Conference of the United States, 1120 20th Street NW., Suite 706 South, Washington, DC 20036, or by fax delivery to (202) 386–7190. For the quickest possible handling of a mail request, you should mark both your request letter and the envelope "Freedom of Information Act Request." (You may find the agency's "Freedom of Information Act Reference Guide"—which is available in electronic format on its Web

site and in paper form—helpful in making your request.) If you are making a request for records about yourself, see § 304.21(d) for additional requirements. If you are making a request for records about another individual, then either a written authorization signed by that individual permitting disclosure of those records to you or proof that that individual is deceased (for example, a copy of a death certificate or an obituary notice) will help the processing of your request. Your request will be considered received as of the date upon which it is logged in as received by the agency's FOIA Public Liaison.

(b) *Description of records sought.* (1) You must describe the records that you seek in enough detail to enable agency personnel to locate them with a reasonable amount of effort. Whenever possible, your request should include specific information about each record sought, such as the date, title or name, author, recipient, and subject matter of the record. If known, you should include any file designations or similar descriptions for the records that you want. As a general rule, the more specific you are about the records or type of records that you want, the more likely that the agency will be able to locate those records in response to your request. Before submitting your request, you may contact the agency's FOIA Public Liaison at (202) 480–2080 for assistance in describing the records.

(2) If the agency determines that your request does not reasonably describe records, then it will tell you either what additional information is needed or why your request is otherwise insufficient. It also will give you an opportunity to discuss your request by telephone so that you may modify it to meet the requirements of this section. Additionally, if your request does not reasonably describe the records you seek, the agency's response to it may be delayed as an initial matter.

(c) *Format of records sought.* Requests may specify the preferred form or format (including electronic formats) for the records you seek. The agency will accommodate your request if the record is readily reproducible in that form or format.

(d) *Agreement to pay fees.* When you make a FOIA request, it will be considered to be an agreement by you to pay all applicable fees charged under §304.9, up to $50.00, unless you specifically request a waiver of fees. The agency ordinarily will confirm this agreement in an acknowledgment letter. When making a request, you may specify a willingness to pay a greater or lesser amount. Your agreement will not prejudice your ability to seek a waiver or reduction of any applicable fee at a later time.

[82 FR 7632, Jan. 23, 2017]

§304.4 Responsibility for responding to requests.

(a) *In general.* The agency will be responsible for responding to a request in all respects, except in the case of a referral to another agency as is described in paragraphs (b), (c), and (d) of this section. In determining which records are responsive to a request, the agency ordinarily will include only records in its possession and control as of the date upon which it begins its search for them. If any other date is used, the agency will inform the requester of that date.

(b) *Consultations and referrals.* When the agency receives a request for a record in its possession and control, it will determine whether another agency of the Federal Government is better able to determine whether the record is exempt from disclosure under the FOIA and, if so, whether it should be disclosed as a matter of administrative discretion. If the agency determines that it is best able to process the record in response to the request, then it will do so. If the agency determines that it is not best able to process the record, then it will either:

(1) Respond to the request regarding that record, after consulting with the agency that is best able to determine whether to disclose it and with any other agency that has a substantial interest in it; or

(2) Refer the responsibility for responding to the request regarding that record to another agency that originated the record (but only if that agency is subject to the FOIA). Ordinarily, the agency that originated a record will be presumed to be best able to determine whether to disclose it.

(c) *Notice of referral.* When the agency refers all or any part of the responsibility for responding to a request to another agency, it ordinarily will notify the requester of the referral and inform the requester of the name of the agency to which the request has been referred and of the part of the request that has been referred.

(d) *Timing of responses to consultations and referrals.* All consultations and referrals will be handled according to the date upon which the FOIA request initially was received by the first agency, and not any later date.

(e) *Agreements regarding consultations and referrals.* The agency may make agreements with other agencies designed to eliminate the need for consultations or referrals regarding particular types of records.

§304.5 Timing of responses to requests.

(a) *In general.* The agency ordinarily will respond to requests according to their order of receipt.

(b) *Multi-track processing.* The agency generally uses two processing tracks that distinguish between simple and complex requests. In determining the appropriate track for a request, the agency considers, among other factors, the number of records requested, the number of pages involved in processing the request and the need for consultations or referrals. When a request is placed on the complex track, the agency will provide the requester with an opportunity to narrow or modify the request so that it can be placed on the simple track. The agency will contact the requester by telephone, email or letter, whichever is most efficient, in each case.

(c) *Unusual circumstances.* (1) Where the statutory time limit of 20 days for processing a request cannot be met because of "unusual circumstances," as defined in the FOIA, and the agency extends the time limits on that basis, it will, before expiration of the 20-day period, notify the requester in writing of the unusual circumstances and of the date by which the agency estimates processing of the request can be expected to be completed. Where the extension is likely to exceed ten working days, the agency will provide the requester with an opportunity to modify the request or arrange an alternative time period for processing the original or modified request. In such instances, the agency's FOIA Public Liaison will contact the requester, and the requester will be informed of the mediation services offered by the Office of Government Information Services ("OGIS")—see *https://www.archives.gov/ogis*.

(2) Where the agency reasonably believes that multiple requests submitted by a requester, or by a group of requesters acting in concert, constitute a single request that would otherwise involve unusual circumstances, and the requests involve clearly related matters, they may be aggregated. Multiple requests involving unrelated matters will not be aggregated.

(d) *Expedited processing.* (1) Requests and appeals will be taken out of order and given expedited treatment whenever it is determined that they involve:

(i) Circumstances in which the lack of expedited treatment could reasonably be expected to pose an imminent threat to the life or physical safety of an individual;

(ii) An urgency to inform the public concerning actual or alleged federal government activity, if made by a person primarily engaged in disseminating information; or

(iii) Other circumstances as determined by the agency.

(2) A request for expedited processing may be made at the time of the initial request for records (i.e., as part of the initial request) or at any later time.

(3) A requester who seeks expedited processing must submit a statement, certified to be true and correct to the best of that person's knowledge and belief, explaining in detail the basis for requesting expedited processing. For example, a requester within the category in paragraph (d)(1)(ii) of this section, if not a full-time member of the news media, must establish that he or she is a person whose main professional activity or occupation is information dissemination, though it need not be his or her sole occupation. That requester also must establish a particular urgency to inform the public about the government activity involved in the request, beyond the public's right to know about government activity generally. The formality of certification may be waived by the agency as a matter of administrative discretion.

(4) Within ten calendar days of its receipt of a request for expedited processing, the agency will decide whether to grant it and will notify the requester of the decision. If a request for expedited treatment is granted, then the request will be given priority and will be processed as soon as practicable. If a request for expedited processing is denied, then any appeal of that decision will be acted on expeditiously.

[76 FR 18635, Apr. 5, 2011, as amended at 82 FR 7632, Jan. 23, 2017]

§ 304.6   Responses to requests.

(a) *Acknowledgments of requests.* On receipt of a request, if the agency cannot provide the requested information within two working days, then an acknowledgment letter or email message will be sent to the requester that will confirm the requester's agreement to pay fees under § 304.3(d) and will provide a request tracking number for further reference. Requesters may use this tracking number to determine the status of their request—including the date of its receipt and the estimated date on which action on it will be completed—by calling the agency's FOIA Public Liaison at (202) 480–2080. In some cases, the agency may seek further information or clarification from the requester.

(b) *Grants of requests.* Ordinarily, the agency will have 20 working days from when a request is received to determine whether to grant or deny the request. Once the agency makes such a determination, it will immediately notify the requester in writing. The agency will inform the requester in the notice of any fee charged under § 304.9 and will disclose records to the requester promptly upon payment of any applicable fee. The agency will also inform the requester of the availability of its FOIA Public Liaison to offer assistance.

(c) *Adverse determinations of requests.* Whenever the agency makes an adverse determination denying a request in any respect, it will notify the requester of that determination in writing. Adverse determinations, or denials of requests, consist of: A determination to withhold any requested record in whole or in part; a determination that a requested record does not exist or cannot be located; a determination that a record is not readily reproducible in the form or format sought by the requester; a determination that what has been requested is not a record subject to the FOIA; a determination on any disputed fee matter, including a denial of a request for a fee waiver; and a denial of a request for expedited treatment. The denial letter will include:

(1) The name and title or position of the person responsible for the denial;

(2) A brief statement of the reason(s) for the denial, including any FOIA exemption(s) applied by the agency in denying the request;

(3) An estimate of the volume of records or information withheld, in number of pages or in some other reasonable form of estimation. This estimate does not need to be provided if the volume is otherwise indicated through deletions on records disclosed in part, or if providing an estimate would harm an interest protected by an applicable exemption; and

(4) An indication on the released portion of a record of each exemption applied, at the place at which it was applied, if technically feasible.

(5) A statement that the denial may be appealed under §304.8(a) and a description of the requirements of §304.8(a).

(6) A statement notifying the requester of the assistance available from the agency's FOIA Public Liaison and the dispute resolution services offered by OGIS.

(d) *Markings on released documents.* Records disclosed in part will be marked or annotated to show the amount of information deleted, unless doing so would harm an interest protected by an applicable exemption. The location of the information deleted also will be indicated on the record, if technically feasible.

[82 FR 7633, Jan. 23, 2017]

§304.7 Business information.

(a) *In general.* Business information obtained by the agency will be disclosed under the FOIA only under this section and in accordance with Executive Order 12,600, 3 CFR part 235 (1988).

(b) *Definitions.* For purposes of this section:

(1) "Business information" means privileged or confidential commercial or financial information obtained by the agency from a submitter that may be protected from disclosure under Exemption 4 of the FOIA.

(2) "Submitter" means any person or entity from whom the agency obtains business information, either directly or indirectly. The term includes corporations; state, local, and tribal governments; and foreign governments.

(c) *Designation of business information.* A submitter of business information will use good-faith efforts to designate, by appropriate markings, either at the time of submission or at a reasonable time thereafter, any and all portion(s) of its submission that it considers to be protected from disclosure under Exemption 4. These designations will expire ten years after the date of the submission unless the submitter requests, and provides justification for, a longer designation period.

(d) *Notice to submitters.* The agency will provide a submitter with prompt written notice of a FOIA request or administrative appeal that seeks its business information wherever required under paragraph (e) of this section, except as provided in paragraph (h) of this section, in order to give the submitter an opportunity to object to disclosure of any specified portion of that information under paragraph (f) of this section. The notice will either describe the business information requested or include copies of the requested records or record portions containing the information. When notification of a voluminous number of submitters is required, notification may be made by posting or publishing the notice in a place reasonably likely to accomplish it.

(e) *Where notice is required.* Notice will be given to a submitter wherever:

(1) The information has been designated in good faith by the submitter as information considered protected from disclosure under Exemption 4; or

49

(2) The agency has reason to believe that the information may be protected from disclosure under Exemption 4.

(f) *Opportunity to object to disclosure.* The agency will allow a submitter a reasonable time to respond to the notice described in paragraph (d) of this section and will specify that time period within the notice. If a submitter has any objection to disclosure, it is required to submit a detailed written statement. The statement must specify all grounds for withholding any portion of the information under any exemption of the FOIA and, in the case of Exemption 4, it must show why the information is a trade secret or commercial or financial information that is privileged or confidential. In the event that a submitter fails to respond to the notice within the time specified in it, the submitter will be considered to have no objection to disclosure of the information. Information provided by the submitter that is not received by the agency until after its disclosure decision has been made will not be considered by the agency. Information provided by a submitter under this paragraph may itself be subject to disclosure under the FOIA.

(g) *Notice of intent to disclose.* The agency will consider a submitter's objections and specific grounds for nondisclosure in deciding whether to disclose business information. Whenever the agency decides to disclose business information over the objection of a submitter, it will give the submitter written notice, which will include:

(1) A statement of the reason(s) why each of the submitter's disclosure objections was not sustained;

(2) A description of the business information to be disclosed; and

(3) A specified disclosure date, which will be a reasonable time subsequent to the notice.

(h) *Exceptions to notice requirements.* The notice requirements of paragraphs (d) and (g) of this section will not apply if:

(1) The agency determines that the information should not be disclosed;

(2) The information lawfully has been published or has been officially made available to the public;

(3) Disclosure of the information is required by statute (other than the

FOIA) or by a regulation issued in accordance with the requirements of Executive Order 12,600; or

(4) The designation made by the submitter under paragraph (c) of this section appears obviously frivolous—except that, in such a case, the agency will, within a reasonable time prior to a specified disclosure date, give the submitter written notice of any final decision to disclose the information.

(i) *Notice of FOIA lawsuit.* Whenever a requester files a lawsuit seeking to compel the disclosure of business information, the agency will promptly notify the submitter.

(j) *Corresponding notice to requesters.* Whenever the agency provides a submitter with notice and an opportunity to object to disclosure under paragraph (d) of this section, it will also notify the requester(s). Whenever the agency notifies a submitter of its intent to disclose requested information under paragraph (g) of this section, it will also notify the requester(s). Whenever a submitter files a lawsuit seeking to prevent the disclosure of business information, the agency will notify the requester(s).

§ 304.8 Appeals.

(a) *Appeals of adverse determinations.* If you are dissatisfied with the response to your request, you may appeal an adverse determination denying your request, in any respect, to the Chairman of the agency. You must make your appeal in writing, by email or letter, and it must be received by the agency within 90 calendar days of the date of the agency's response denying your request. Your appeal should provide reasons and supporting information as to why the initial determination was incorrect. The appeal should clearly identify the particular determination (including the assigned request number, if known) that you are appealing. For the quickest possible handling of a mail request, you should mark your appeal "Freedom of Information Act Appeal." The Chairman or his or her designee will act on the appeal, except that an appeal ordinarily will not be acted on if the request becomes a matter of FOIA litigation.

(b) *Responses to appeals.* The decision on your appeal will be communicated to you by email or letter, ordinarily within 20 working days of receipt of your appeal. A decision affirming an adverse determination in whole or in part will contain a statement of the reason(s) for the affirmance, including any FOIA exemption(s) applied, and will inform you of the FOIA provisions for court review of the decision. The decision will also inform you of the mediation services offered by OGIS as a non-exclusive alternative to FOIA litigation. If the adverse determination is reversed or modified on appeal, in whole or in part, then you will be notified in a written decision and your request will be reprocessed in accordance with that appeal decision.

(c) *Engaging in dispute resolution services provided by OGIS.* Mediation is a voluntary process. If the agency agrees to participate in the mediation services provided by OGIS, it will actively engage in the process in an attempt to resolve the dispute.

(d) *When appeal is required.* As a general rule, if you wish to seek review by a court of any adverse determination, you must first appeal it in a timely fashion under this section.

[82 FR 7633, Jan. 23, 2017]

§304.9 Fees.

(a) *In general.* The agency will charge for processing requests under the FOIA in accordance with paragraph (c) of this section and with the OMB Guidelines. The agency ordinarily will collect all applicable fees before sending copies of requested records to a requester. Requesters must pay fees by check or money order made payable to the Treasury of the United States.

(b) *Definitions.* For purposes of this section:

(1) "Commercial use request" means a request from or on behalf of a person who seeks information for a use or purpose that furthers his or her commercial, trade, or profit interests, including furthering those interests through litigation. The agency will determine, whenever reasonably possible, the use to which a requester will put the requested records. When it appears that the requester will put the records to a commercial use, either because of the nature of the request itself or because the agency has reasonable cause to

doubt a requester's stated use, the agency will provide the requester a reasonable opportunity to submit further clarification.

(2) "Direct costs" means those expenses that an agency actually incurs in searching for and duplicating (and, in the case of commercial use requests, reviewing) records to respond to a FOIA request. Direct costs include, for example, the salary of the employee performing the work (the basic rate of pay for the employee, plus 16 percent of that rate to cover benefits) and the cost of operating duplication machinery. Not included in direct costs are overhead expenses such as the costs of space and heating or lighting of the facility in which the records are kept.

(3) "Duplication" means the making of a copy of a record, or of the information contained in it, necessary to respond to a FOIA request. Copies can take the form of paper, audiovisual materials, or electronic records, among others. The agency will honor a requester's specified preference of form or format of disclosure if the record is readily reproducible with reasonable efforts in the requested form or format.

(4) "Educational institution" means a preschool, a public or private elementary or secondary school, an institution of undergraduate higher education, an institution of graduate higher education, an institution of professional education, or an institution of vocational education, that operates a program of scholarly research. To qualify under this category, a requester must show that the request is authorized by and is made under the auspices of a qualifying institution and that the records are not sought for a commercial use but are sought to further scholarly research.

(5) "Noncommercial scientific institution" means an institution that is not operated on a "commercial" basis, as that term is defined in paragraph (b)(1) of this section, and that is operated solely for the purpose of conducting scientific research the results of which are not intended to promote any particular product or industry. To qualify under this category, a requester must show that the request is authorized by and is made under the auspices of a qualifying institution and

that the records are not sought for a commercial use but are sought to further scientific research.

(6) "Representative of the news media," or "news-media requester," means any person or entity that gathers information of potential interest to a segment of the public, uses its editorial skills to turn the raw materials into a distinct work, and distributes that work to an audience. For this purpose, the term "news" means information that is about current events or that would be of current interest to the public. Examples of news-media entities are television or radio stations broadcasting to the public at large and publishers of periodicals (but only if such entities qualify as disseminators of "news") who make their products available for purchase by or subscription by or free distribution to the general public. These examples are not all-inclusive. Moreover, as methods of news delivery evolve (for example, the adoption of the electronic dissemination of newspapers through telecommunications services), such alternative media shall be considered to be news-media entities. A freelance journalist shall be regarded as working for a news-media entity if the journalist can demonstrate a solid basis for expecting publication through that entity, whether or not the journalist is actually employed by the entity. A publication contract would present a solid basis for such an expectation; the agency may also consider the past publication record of the requester in making such a determination. To qualify under this category, a requester must not be seeking the requested records for a commercial use. A request for records supporting the news-dissemination function of the requester will not be considered to be for a commercial use.

(7) "Review" means the examination of a record located in response to a request in order to determine whether any portion of it is exempt from disclosure. It also includes processing any record for disclosure—for example, doing all that is necessary to redact it and prepare it for disclosure. Review costs are recoverable even if a record ultimately is not disclosed. Review time includes time spent considering any formal objection to disclosure made by a business submitter under § 304.7 but does not include time spent resolving general legal or policy issues regarding the application of exemptions.

(8) "Search" means the process of looking for and retrieving records or information responsive to a request. It includes page-by-page or line-by-line identification of information within records and also includes reasonable efforts to locate and retrieve information from records maintained in electronic form or format. The agency will conduct searches in the most efficient and least expensive manner reasonably possible. For example, it will not search on a line-by-line basis where duplicating an entire document would be quicker and less expensive.

(c) *Fees charged.* In responding to FOIA requests, the agency will charge the following fees unless a waiver or reduction of fees has been granted under paragraph (k) of this section:

(1) *Search.* (i) Search fees will be charged for all requests (other than requests made by educational institutions, noncommercial scientific institutions, or representatives of the news media) subject to the limitations of paragraph (d) of this section. The agency may charge for time spent searching even if it does not locate any responsive record or if it withholds the record(s) located as entirely exempt from disclosure.

(ii) For each quarter hour spent by clerical personnel in searching for and retrieving a requested record, the fee will be $5.00. Where a search and retrieval cannot be performed entirely by clerical personnel (for example, where the identification of records within the scope of a request requires the use of professional personnel) the fee will be $10.00 for each quarter hour of search time spent by professional personnel. Where the time of managerial personnel is required, the fee will be $15.00 for each quarter hour of time spent by those personnel.

(iii) For computer searches of records, requesters will be charged the direct costs of conducting the search, although certain requesters (as provided in paragraph (d)(1) of this section) will be charged no search fee and certain other requesters (as provided in paragraph (d)(3) of this section) will be entitled to the cost equivalent of two hours of manual search time without charge. These direct costs will include the costs of operator/programmer salary apportionable to the search.

(2) *Duplication.* Duplication fees will be charged to all requesters, subject to the limitations of paragraph (d) of this section. For a paper photocopy of a record (no more than one copy of which need be supplied), the fee will be ten cents per page. For copies produced by computer, such as tapes, disks, or printouts, the agency will charge the direct costs, including operator time, of producing the copy. For other forms of duplication, the agency will charge the direct costs of that duplication.

(3) *Review.* Review fees will be charged to requesters who make a commercial use request. Review fees will be charged only for the initial record review, when the agency determines whether an exemption applies to a particular record or record portion at the initial request level. No charge will be made for review at the administrative appeal level regarding an exemption already applied. However, records or record portions withheld under an exemption that is subsequently determined not to apply may be reviewed again to determine whether any other exemption not previously considered applies; the costs of that review are chargeable where it is made necessary by such a change of circumstances. Review fees will be charged at the same rates as those used for a search under paragraph (c)(1)(ii) of this section.

(d) *Limitations on charging fees.* (1) No search fee will be charged for requests by educational institutions, noncommercial scientific institutions, or representatives of the news media.

(2) No search fee or review fee will be charged for a quarter-hour period unless more than half of that period is required for search or review.

(3) Except for requesters seeking records for a commercial use, the agency will provide without charge:

(i) The first 100 pages of duplication (or the cost equivalent); and

(ii) The first two hours of search (or the cost equivalent).

(4) Whenever a total fee calculated under paragraph (c) of this section is

$20.00 or less for any request, no fee will be charged.

(5) The provisions of paragraphs (d)(3) and (4) of this section work together. This means that for requesters other than those seeking records for a commercial use, no fee will be charged unless the cost of search in excess of two hours plus the cost of duplication in excess of 100 pages totals more than $20.00.

(6) (i) If the agency fails to comply with the FOIA's time limits in which to respond to a request, it may not charge search fees, or, in the instances of requests from requesters described in paragraph (d)(1) of this section, may not charge duplication fees, except as described in (d)(6)(ii)–(iv).

(ii) If the agency has determined that unusual circumstances as defined by the FOIA apply and the agency provided timely written notice to the requester in accordance with the FOIA, a failure to comply with the time limit will be excused for an additional 10 working days.

(iii) If the agency has determined that unusual circumstances, as defined by the FOIA, apply and more than 5,000 pages are necessary to respond to the request, the agency may charge search fees, or, in the case of requesters described in paragraph (d)(1) of this section, may charge duplication fees, if the following steps are taken. The agency must have provided timely written notice of unusual circumstances to the requester in accordance with the FOIA and the agency must have discussed with the requester via written mail, email, or telephone (or made not less than three good-faith attempts to do so) how the requester could effectively limit the scope of the request in accordance with 5 U.S.C. 552(a)(6)(B)(ii). If this exception is satisfied, the agency may charge all applicable fees incurred in the processing of this request.

(iv) If a court has determined that exceptional circumstances exist, as defined by the FOIA, a failure to comply with the time limits will be excused for the length of time provided by the court order.

(e) *Notice of anticipated fees in excess of $50.00.* (1) When the agency determines or estimates that the fees to be charged under this section will amount to more than $50.00, it will notify the requester of the actual or estimated amount of the fees, unless the requester has indicated a willingness to pay fees as high as those anticipated. If only a portion of the fee can be estimated readily, the agency will advise the requester that the estimated fee might be only a portion of the total fee. In cases in which a requester has been notified that actual or estimated fees amount to more than $50.00, the request will not be considered received and further work will not be done on it until the requester agrees to pay the total anticipated fee. Any such agreement should be memorialized in writing. A notice under this paragraph will offer the requester an opportunity to discuss the matter with agency personnel in order to reformulate the request to meet the requester's needs at a lower cost.

(2) If the requester has indicated a willingness to pay some designated amount of fees, but the agency estimates that the total fee will exceed that amount, the agency will suspend the processing of the request when it notifies the requester of the estimated fees in excess of the amount the requester has indicated a willingness to pay. The agency will inquire whether the requester wishes to revise the amount of fees the requester is willing to pay or modify the request. Once the requester responds, the time to respond will resume from where it was at the date of the notification.

(3) The agency will make its FOIA Public Liaison available to assist any requester in reformulating a request to meet the requester's needs at a lower cost.

(f) *Charges for other services.* Apart from the other provisions of this section, when the agency chooses as a matter of administrative discretion to provide a special service—such as certifying that records are true copies or sending them by other than ordinary mail—the direct costs of providing the service ordinarily will be charged.

(g) *Charging interest.* The agency may charge interest on any unpaid bill starting on the 31st day following the date of the billing of the requester. Interest charges will be assessed at the rate provided in 31 U.S.C. 3717 and will accrue from the date of the billing until payment is received by the agency. The agency will follow the provisions of the Debt Collection Act of 1982, Public Law 97–365, 96 Stat. 1749, as amended, and regulations pursuant thereto.

(h) *Aggregating requests.* Wherever the agency reasonably believes that a requester or a group of requesters acting together is attempting to divide a request into a series of requests for the purpose of avoiding fees, it may aggregate those requests and charge accordingly. In so doing, it will presume that multiple requests of this type made within a 30-day period have been made in order to avoid fees. Where requests are separated by a longer period, the agency will aggregate them only where there exists a solid basis for determining that aggregation is warranted under all the circumstances involved. Multiple requests involving unrelated matters will not be aggregated.

(i) *Advance payments.* (1) For requests other than those described in paragraphs (i)(2) and (i)(3) of this section, the agency will not require the requester to make an advance payment—in other words, a payment made before work is begun or continued on a request. Payment owed for work already completed (i.e., a prepayment before copies are sent to a requester) is not an advance payment.

(2) Where the agency determines or estimates that a total fee to be charged under this section will be more than $250.00, it may require the requester to make an advance payment of an amount up to the amount of the entire anticipated fee before beginning to process the request, except where it receives a satisfactory assurance of full payment from a requester that has a history of prompt payment.

(3) Where a requester has previously failed to pay a properly charged FOIA fee to the agency within 30 calendar days of the date of billing, the agency may require the requester to pay the full amount due, plus any applicable interest, and to make an advance payment of the full amount of any anticipated fee, before it begins to process a new request or continues to process a pending request from that requester.

(4) In cases in which the agency requires advance payment or payment due under paragraph (i)(2) or (i)(3) of this section, the request will not be considered received and further work will not be done on it until the required payment is received.

(j) *Other statutes specifically providing for fees.* The fee schedule of this section does not apply to fees charged under any statute that specifically requires an agency to set and collect fees for particular types of records. In cases in which records responsive to requests are maintained for distribution by another agency under such a statutorily based fee schedule program, ACUS will inform the requesters of the steps for obtaining records from those sources so that they may do so most economically.

(k) *Requirements for waiver or reduction of fees.* (1) Requesters may seek a waiver of fees by submitting a written application demonstrating how disclosure of the requested information is in the public interest because it is likely to contribute significantly to public understanding of the operations or activities of the government and is not primarily in the commercial interest of the requester.

(2) The agency will furnish records responsive to a request without charge or at a reduced rate when it determines, based on all available information, that the factors described in paragraphs (k)(2)(i) through (iii) of this section are satisfied:

(i) Disclosure of the requested information would shed light on the operations or activities of the government. The subject of the requested records must concern identifiable operations or activities of the Federal Government with a connection that is direct and clear, not remote or attenuated.

(ii) Disclosure of the requested information is likely to contribute significantly to public understanding of those operations or activities. This factor is satisfied when the following criteria are met:

(A) Disclosure of the requested records must be meaningfully informative about government operations or activities. The disclosure of information that already is in the public domain, in either the same or a substantially identical form, would not be meaningfully informative if nothing new would be added to the public's understanding.

(B) The disclosure must contribute to the understanding of a reasonably broad audience of persons interested in the subject, as opposed to the individual understanding of the requester. A requester's expertise in the subject area as well as the requester's ability and intention to convey information effectively to the public will be considered. The agency will presume that a representative of the news media satisfies this consideration.

(iii) The disclosure must not be primarily in the commercial interest of the requester. To determine whether disclosure of the requested information is primarily in the commercial interest of the requester, the agency will consider the following criteria:

(A) Whether the requester has any commercial interest that would be furthered by the requested disclosure. A commercial interest includes any commercial, trade, or profit interest. Requesters will be given an opportunity to provide explanatory information regarding this consideration.

(B) Whether any identified commercial interest is the primary interest furthered by the request. A waiver or reduction of fees is justified when the requirements of paragraphs (k)(2)(i) and (ii) of this section are satisfied and any commercial interest is not the primary interest furthered by the request. The agency ordinarily will presume that when a news media requester has satisfied factors in paragraphs (k)(2)(i) and (ii) of this section, the request is not primarily in the commercial interest of the requester. Disclosure to data brokers or others who merely compile and market government information for direct economic return will not be presumed primarily to serve the public interest.

(3) Where only some of the records to be released satisfy the requirements for a waiver of fees, a waiver will be granted for those records.

(4) Requests for a waiver or reduction of fees should ordinarily be made when the request is first submitted to the agency and should address the criteria

referenced above. A requester may submit a fee waiver request at a later time so long as the underlying record request is pending or on administrative appeal. When a requester who has committed to pay fees subsequently asks for a waiver of those fees and that waiver is denied, the requester must pay any costs incurred up to the date the fee waiver request was received.

[76 FR 18635, Apr. 5, 2011, as amended at 82 FR 7633, Jan. 23, 2017]

§ 304.10 Preservation of records.

(a) The agency will preserve all correspondence pertaining to the requests that it receives under this subpart, as well as copies of all requested records, until disposition or destruction is authorized by title 44 of the United States Code or the National Archives and Records Administration's General Records Schedule 4.2. Records will not be disposed of while they are the subject of a pending request, appeal, or lawsuit under the FOIA.

(b) In the event that the agency contracts with another agency, entity, or person to maintain records for the agency for the purposes of records management, it will promptly identify such records in its "Freedom of Information Reference Guide" and specify the particular means by which request for such records can be made.

[76 FR 18635, Apr. 5, 2011, as amended at 82 FR 7635, Jan. 23, 2017]

§ 304.11 Other rights and services.

Nothing in this subpart shall be construed to entitle any person, as of right, to any service or to the disclosure of any record to which such person is not entitled under the FOIA.

Subpart B—Protection of Privacy and Access to Individual Records Under the Privacy Act of 1974

AUTHORITY: 5 U.S.C. 552a, 591–96.

§ 304.20 General provisions.

(a) *Purpose and scope.* This subpart contains the rules that the Administrative Conference of the United States ("ACUS" or "the agency") follows under the Privacy Act of 1974 ("the Privacy Act"), 5 U.S.C. 552a, as amended, regarding the protection of, and individual access to, certain records about individuals. These rules should be read together with and are governed by the Privacy Act itself, which provides additional information about records maintained on individuals. The rules in this subpart apply to all records in Privacy Act systems of records maintained by the agency, which are retrieved by an individual's name or personal identifier. They describe the procedures by which individuals may request access to records about themselves, request amendment or correction of those records, and request an accounting of disclosures of those records by the agency. In addition, the agency processes all Privacy Act requests for access to records under the Freedom of Information Act ("FOIA"), 5 U.S.C. 552, *as amended,* following the rules contained in subpart A of this part. Thus, all Privacy Act requests will be subject to exemptions for access to records only applicable under both FOIA and the Privacy Act.

(b) *Definitions.* As used in this subpart:

(1) "Request for access to a record" means a request made under Privacy Act, 5 U.S.C. 552a(d)(1).

(2) "Request for amendment or correction of a record" means a request made under Privacy Act, 5 U.S.C. 552a(d)(2).

(3) "Request for an accounting" means a request made under Privacy Act, 5 U.S.C. 552a(c)(3).

(4) "Requester" means an individual who makes a request for access, a request for amendment or correction, or a request for an accounting under the Privacy Act.

§ 304.21 Requests for access to records.

(a) *How made and addressed.* You may make a request for access to a record about yourself by appearing in person or by sending an e-mail message addressed to *info@acus.gov.* You may also send a written request letter to the agency either by mail addressed to 1120 20th Street, NW., South Lobby, Suite 706, Washington, DC 20036, or by fax delivery to (202) 386–7190. For the quickest possible handling of a mail request, you should mark both your request letter and the envelope "Privacy Act Request."

(b) *Description of records sought.* You must describe the records that you want in enough detail to enable agency personnel to locate the system of records containing them with a reasonable amount of effort. Whenever possible, your request should describe the records sought, the time periods in which you believe they were compiled, and the name or identifying number of each system of records in which you believe they are kept. The agency publishes a notice in the FEDERAL REGISTER that describes its systems of records.

(c) *Agreement to pay fees.* If you make a Privacy Act request for access to records, it will be considered an agreement by you to pay all applicable fees charged under §304.27, up to $50.00. Duplication fees in excess of $50.00 are subject to the requirements of §304.27 of this subpart and the notification requirements in §304.9 of subpart A. The agency ordinarily will confirm this agreement in an acknowledgment letter. When making a request, you may specify a willingness to pay a greater or lesser amount.

(d) *Verification of identity.* When you make a request for access to records about yourself, you must verify your identity. You must state your full name, current address, and date and place of birth. You must sign your request and your signature must either be notarized or submitted by you under 28 U.S.C. 1746, a law that permits statements to be made under penalty of perjury as a substitute for notarization. In order to help the identification and location of requested records, you may also, entirely at your option, include the last four digits of your social security number.

§304.22 Responsibility for responding to requests for access to records.

(a) *In general.* The agency will be responsible for responding to a request in all respects, except in the case of a referral to another agency as is described in paragraphs (b), (c), and (d) of this section. In determining which records are responsive to a request, the agency ordinarily will include only records in its possession and control as of the date upon which it begins its search for them. If any other date is used, the agency will inform the requester of that date.

(b) *Consultations and referrals.* When the agency receives a request for access to a record in its possession and control, it will determine whether another agency of the Federal Government, is better able to determine whether the record is exempt from access under the Privacy Act. If the agency determines that it is the agency best able to process the record in response to the request, then it will do so. If it determines that it is not best able to process the record, then it will either:

(1) Respond to the request regarding that record, after consulting with the agency that is best able to determine whether the record is exempt from access and with any other agency that has a substantial interest in it; or

(2) Refer the responsibility for responding to the request regarding that record to the agency that is best able to determine whether it is exempt from access, or to another agency that originated the record (but only if that agency is subject to the Privacy Act). Ordinarily, the agency that originated a record will be presumed to be best able to determine whether it is exempt from access.

(c) *Notice of referral.* When the agency refers all or any part of the responsibility for responding to a request to another agency, it ordinarily will notify the requester of the referral and inform the requester of the name of the agency to which the request has been referred and of the part of the request that has been referred.

(d) *Timing of responses to consultations and referrals.* All consultations and referrals will be handled according to the date upon which the Privacy Act access request was initially received by the first agency, not any later date.

(e) *Agreements regarding consultations and referrals.* The agency may make agreements with other agencies designed to eliminate the need for consultations or referrals for particular types of records.

§ 304.23 Responses to requests for access to records.

(a) *Acknowledgments of requests.* On receipt of a request, the agency ordinarily will send an acknowledgment letter to the requester that will confirm the requester's agreement to pay fees under § 304.21(c) and provide an assigned request number for further reference. In some cases, the agency may seek further information or clarification from the requester.

(b) *Grants of requests for access.* Once the agency makes a determination to grant a request for access in whole or in part, it will notify the requester in writing. The agency will inform the requester in the notice of any fee charged under § 304.27 and will disclose records to the requester promptly on payment of any applicable fee. If a request is made in person, the agency may disclose records to the requester directly, in a manner not unreasonably disruptive of its operations, on payment of any applicable fee and with a written record made of the grant of the request. If a requester is accompanied by another person, the requester will be required to authorize in writing any discussion of the records in the presence of the other person.

(c) *Adverse determinations of requests for access.* Upon making an adverse determination denying a request for access in any respect, the agency will notify the requester of that determination in writing. Adverse determinations, or denials of requests consist of: a determination to withhold any requested record in whole or in part; a determination that a requested record does not exist or cannot be located; a determination that what has been requested is not a record subject to the Privacy Act; a determination on any disputed fee matter; and a denial of a request for expedited treatment. The notification letter will include:

(1) The name and title or position of the person responsible for the denial;

(2) A brief statement of the reason(s) for the denial, including any Privacy Act exemption(s) applied in denying the request; and

(3) A statement that the denial may be appealed under § 304.24(a) and a description of the requirements of § 304.24(a).

§ 304.24 Appeals from denials of requests for access to records.

(a) *Appeals.* If you are dissatisfied with the response to your request, you may appeal an adverse determination denying your request, in any respect, to the Chairman of the agency. You must make your appeal in writing, by e-mail or letter, and it must be received by the agency within 60 days of the date of the denial of your request. Your appeal letter should provide reasons and supporting information as to why the initial determination was incorrect. The appeal should clearly identify the particular determination (including the assigned request number, if known) that you are appealing. For the quickest possible handling of a mail request, you should mark your appeal letter and the envelope "Privacy Act Appeal." The Chairman of the agency or his or her designee will act on the appeal, except that an appeal ordinarily will not be acted on if the request becomes a matter of FOIA or Privacy Act litigation.

(b) *Responses to appeals.* The decision on your appeal will be made in writing. A decision affirming an adverse determination in whole or in part will include a brief statement of the reason(s) for the affirmance, including any exemption applied, and will inform you of the Privacy Act provisions for court review of the decision. If the adverse determination is reversed or modified on appeal in whole or in part, then you will be notified in a written decision and your request will be reprocessed in accordance with that appeal decision.

(c) *When appeal is required.* As a general rule, if you wish to seek review by a court of any adverse determination or denial of a request, you must first appeal it under this section.

§ 304.25 Requests for amendment or correction of records.

(a) *How made and addressed.* Unless the record is not subject to amendment or correction as stated in paragraph (f) of this section, you may make a request for amendment or correction of an ACUS record about yourself by following same procedures as in § 304.21. Your request should identify each particular record in question, state the amendment or correction that you want, and state why you believe that the record is not accurate, relevant, timely, or complete. You may submit any documentation that you think would be helpful. If you believe that the same record is maintained in more than one system of records, you should state that.

(b) *Agency responses.* Within ten business days of receiving your request for amendment or correction of records, the agency will send you a written acknowledgment of its receipt of your request. The agency will promptly notify you whether your request is granted or denied. If the agency grants your request in whole or in part, it will describe the amendment or correction made and will advise you of your right to obtain a copy of the corrected or amended record, in disclosable form. If the agency denies your request in whole or in part, it will send you a letter that will state:

(1) The reason(s) for the denial; and

(2) The procedure for appeal of the denial under paragraph (c) of this section, including the name and business address of the official who will act on your appeal.

(c) *Appeals.* You may appeal a denial of a request for amendment or correction in the same manner as a denial of a request for access to records (see §304.24(a)) and the same procedures will be followed. The agency will ordinarily act on the appeal within 30 business days of receipt of the appeal, except that the Chairman of the agency may extend the time for response for good cause shown. If your appeal is denied, you will be advised of your right to file a Statement of Disagreement as described in paragraph (d) of this section and of your right under the Privacy Act for court review of the decision.

(d) *Statements of Disagreement.* If your appeal under this section is denied in whole or in part, you have the right to file a Statement of Disagreement that states your reason(s) for disagreeing with the agency's denial of your request for amendment or correction. Statements of Disagreement must be concise, must clearly identify each part of any record that is disputed, and should be no longer than one typed page for each fact disputed. The agency will place your Statement of Disagree-

ment in the system of records in which the disputed record is maintained and will mark the disputed record to indicate that a Statement of Disagreement has been filed and exactly where in the system of records it may be found.

(e) *Notification of amendment/correction or disagreement.* Within 30 business days of the amendment or correction of a record, the agency will notify all persons, organizations, or agencies to which it previously disclosed the record, if an accounting of that disclosure was made, that the record has been amended or corrected. If an individual has filed a Statement of Disagreement, the agency will append a copy of it to the disputed record whenever the record is disclosed and may also append a concise statement of its reason(s) for denying the request to amend or correct the record.

(f) *Records not subject to amendment or correction.* The following records are not subject to amendment or correction:

(1) Transcripts of testimony given under oath or written statements made under oath;

(2) Transcripts of grand jury proceedings, judicial proceedings, or quasi-judicial proceedings, which are the official record of those proceedings; and

(3) Any other record that originated with the courts.

§304.26 Requests for an accounting of record disclosures.

(a) *How made and addressed.* Except where accountings of disclosures are not required to be kept (as stated in paragraph (b) of this section), you may make a request for an accounting of any disclosure that has been made by the agency to another person, organization, or agency of any record about you. This accounting contains the date, nature, and purpose of each disclosure, as well as the name and address of the person, organization, or agency to which the disclosure was made. Your request for an accounting should identify each particular record in question and should be made in writing to the agency, following the procedures in §304.21.

(b) *Where accountings are not required.* The agency is not required to provide accountings to you where they relate to:

(1) Disclosures for which accountings are not required to be kept (i.e., disclosures that are made to officers and employees of the agency and disclosures required under the FOIA); or

(2) Disclosures made to law enforcement agencies for authorized law enforcement activities in response to written requests from a duly authorized representative of any such law enforcement agency specifying portion of the record desired and the law enforcement activity for which the record is sought.

(c) *Appeals.* You may appeal a denial of a request for an accounting in the same manner as a denial of a request for access to records (see § 304.24(a)) and the same procedures will be followed.

§ 304.27 Fees.

The agency will charge fees for duplication of records under the Privacy Act in the same way in which it charges duplication fees under § 304.9 of subpart A. No search or review fee may be charged for any record under the Privacy Act.

§ 304.28 Notice of court-ordered and emergency disclosures.

(a) *Court-ordered disclosures.* When a record pertaining to an individual is required to be disclosed by a court order, the agency will make reasonable efforts to provide notice of such order to the individual. Notice will be given within a reasonable time after the agency's receipt of the order, except that in a case in which the order is not a matter of public record, the notice will be given only after the order becomes public. This notice will be mailed to the individual's last known address and will contain a copy of the order and a description of the information disclosed.

(b) *Emergency disclosures.* Upon disclosing a record pertaining to an individual made under compelling circumstances affecting health or safety, the agency will notify that individual of the disclosure. This notice will be mailed to the individual's last known address and will state the nature of the information disclosed; the person, organization, or agency to which it was disclosed; the date of disclosure; and the compelling circumstances justifying the disclosure.

§ 304.29 Security of systems of records.

(a) *Administrative and physical controls.* The agency will have administrative and physical controls to prevent unauthorized access to its systems of records, to prevent unauthorized disclosure of records, and to prevent physical damage to or destruction of records. The stringency of these controls corresponds to the sensitivity of the records that the controls protect. At a minimum, these controls are designed to ensure that:

(1) Records are protected from public view;

(2) The area in which records are kept is supervised during business hours in order to prevent unauthorized persons from having access to them;

(3) Records are inaccessible to unauthorized persons outside of business hours; and

(4) Records are not disclosed to unauthorized persons or under unauthorized circumstances in oral, written or any other form.

(b) *Restrictive procedures.* The agency will implement practices and procedures that restrict access to records to only those individuals within the agency who must have access to those records in order to perform their duties and that prevent inadvertent disclosure of records.

§ 304.30 Contracts for the operation of record systems.

Any approved contract for the operation of a record system will contain appropriate requirements issued by the General Services Administration in order to ensure compliance with the requirements of the Privacy Act for that record system. The contracting officer of the agency will be responsible for ensuring that the contractor complies with these contract requirements.

§ 304.31 Use and collection of social security numbers and other information.

The agency will ensure that employees authorized to collect information are aware:

(a) That individuals may not be denied any right, benefit, or privilege as a result of refusing to provide their social security numbers, unless the collection is authorized either by a statute or by a regulation issued prior to 1975;

(b) That individuals requested to provide their social security numbers, or any other information collected from them, must be informed, before providing such information, of:

(1) Whether providing social security numbers (or such other information) is mandatory or voluntary;

(2) Any statutory or regulatory authority that authorizes the collection of social security numbers (or such other information);

(3) The principal purpose(s) for which the information is intended to be used;

(4) The routine uses that may be made of the information; and

(5) The effects, in any, on the individual of not providing all or any part of the requested information; and

(c) That, where the information referred to above is requested on a form, the requirements for informing such individuals are set forth on the form used to collect the information, or on a separate form that can be retained by such individuals.

§ 304.32 Employee standards of conduct.

The agency will inform its employees of the provisions of the Privacy Act, including the scope of its restriction against disclosure of records maintained in a system of records without the prior written consent of the individual involved, and the Act's civil liability and criminal penalty provisions. Unless otherwise permitted by law, an employee of the agency will:

(a) Collect from individuals and maintain only the information that is relevant and necessary to discharge the agency's responsibilities;

(b) Collect information about an individual directly from that individual to the greatest extent practicable when the information may result in an adverse determination about an individual's rights, benefits, or privileges under Federal programs;

(c) Inform each individual from whom information is collected of the information set forth in § 304.31(b);

(d) Ensure that the agency maintains no system of records without public notice and also notify appropriate agency officials of the existence or development of any system of records that is not the subject of a current or planned public notice;

(e) Maintain all records that are used by it in making any determination about an individual with such accuracy, relevance, timeliness, and completeness as is reasonably necessary to ensure fairness to the individual in the determination;

(f) Except as to disclosures made to an agency or made under the FOIA, make reasonable efforts, prior to disseminating any record about an individual, to ensure that the record is accurate, relevant, timely, and complete;

(g) Maintain no record describing how an individual exercises his or her First Amendment rights unless such maintenance is expressly authorized by statute or by the individual about whom the record is maintained or is pertinent to and within the scope of an authorized law enforcement activity;

(h) When required by the Privacy Act, maintain an accounting in the specified form of all disclosures of records by the agency to persons, organizations, or agencies;

(i) Maintain and use records with care in order to prevent the unauthorized or inadvertent disclosure of a record to anyone; and

(j) Notify the appropriate agency official of any record that contains information that the Privacy Act does not permit the agency to maintain.

§ 304.33 Preservation of records.

The agency will preserve all correspondence pertaining to the requests that it receives under this subpart, as well as copies of all requested records, until disposition or destruction is authorized by title 44 of the United States Code or the National Archives and Records Administration's General Records Schedule 14. Records will not be disposed of while they are the subject of a pending request, appeal, or lawsuit under the Act.

§ 304.34 **Other rights and services.**

Nothing in this subpart shall be construed to entitle any person, as of right, to any service or to the disclosure of any record to which such person is not entitled under the Privacy Act.

PARTS 305–399 [RESERVED]

CHAPTER IV—MISCELLANEOUS AGENCIES

EDITORIAL NOTE: Federal agencies are required to publish regulations implementing the provisions of the Freedom of Information Act (5 U.S.C. 552(a)), the Privacy Act of 1974 (Pub. L. 93–579, 5 U.S.C. 552a), the Government in the Sunshine Act (Pub. L. 94–409, 5 U.S.C. 552b), and section 504 of the Rehabilitation Act of 1973, as amended by section 119 of the Rehabilitation, Comprehensive Services, and Developmental Disabilities Amendments of 1978 (29 U.S.C. 794). While most agencies have existing chapter assignments in the Code of Federal Regulations, a few agencies do not. Since certain of these agencies are unlikely to be issuing regulations other than those relating to the acts mentioned above, the Director of the Office of the Federal Register has grouped these miscellaneous agencies into this chapter as an efficient means of administering the CFR system.

PARTS 400–424 [RESERVED]

PART 425—PRESIDENT'S COMMISSION ON WHITE HOUSE FELLOWSHIPS

Sec.
425.1 Purpose and scope.
425.2 Procedures for notification of existence of records pertaining to individuals.
425.3 Procedure for requests for access to or disclosure of records pertaining to individuals.
425.4 Correction of records.
425.5 Disclosure of records to agencies or persons other than the individual to whom the record pertains.

AUTHORITY: 5 U.S.C. 552a(f).

SOURCE: 40 FR 52416, Nov. 10, 1975; 40 FR 56651, Dec. 4, 1975, unless otherwise noted.

§ 425.1 Purpose and scope.

This part sets forth the President's Commission on White House Fellowships procedures under the Privacy Act of 1974 as required by 5 U.S.C. 552a(f). Information to applicants regarding the implementation of this Act is contained in the White House Fellowships Application Instructions.

§ 425.2 Procedures for notification of existence of records pertaining to individuals.

(a) The system of records, as defined in the Privacy Act of 1974, maintained by the President's Commission on White House Fellowships is listed annually in the FEDERAL REGISTER as required by that Act. Any person who wishes to know whether a system of records contains a record pertaining to him or her may either appear in person at Room 1308, 1900 E Street, NW., on work days between the hours of 8:30 a.m. and 5 p.m. or may write to the President's Commission on White House Fellowships Administrative Officer, Washington, DC 20415 (Phone 202–382–4661). It is recommended that requests be made in writing.

(b) Requests for notification of the existence of a record should state, if the requester is other than the individual to whom the record pertains, the relationship of the requester to that individual. (Note that requests will not be honored by the Commission pursuant to the Privacy Act unless made: (1) By the individual to whom the record pertains or (2) by such individual's legal guardian if the individual has been declared to be incompetent due to physical or mental incapacity or age by a court of competent jurisdiction.)

(c) The Commission will acknowledge requests for the existence of records within 10 working days from the time it receives the request and will normally notify the requester of the existence or non-existence of records within 30 working days from receipt of request.

(d) No special identity verification is required for individuals who wish to know whether a specific system of records pertains to them.

[40 FR 52416, Nov. 10, 1975; 40 FR 56651, Dec. 4, 1975, as amended at 40 FR 59187, Dec. 22, 1975]

§ 425.3 Procedure for requests for access to or disclosure of records pertaining to individuals.

(a) Any person may request review of records pertaining to him by appearing at Room 1308, 1900 E Street, NW., Washington, DC on work days between the hours of 8:30 a.m. and 5 p.m. or by writing to the Commission on White House Fellowships Administrative Officer, Washington, DC 20415. (See paragraph (b) of this section for identification requirements.) The Commission will strive either to make the record available within 15 working days of the request or to inform the requester of the need for additional identification.

(b) In the case of persons making requests by appearing at the Commission, reasonable identification such as employment identification cards, drivers licenses, or credit cards will normally be accepted as sufficient evidence of identity in the absence of any indications to the contrary.

(c) Charges for copies of records will be at the rate of $0.10 per photocopy of each page. No charge will be made unless the charge as computed above would exceed $3 for each request or related series of requests. If a fee in excess of $25 would be required, the requester shall be notified and the fee must be tendered before the records will be copied. Remittances shall be in the form either of a personal check or bank draft drawn on a bank in the United States, or a money order. Remittances shall be made payable to the order of the Treasury of the United States and mailed or delivered to the Administrative Officer, President's Commission on White House Fellowships, 1900 E Street, NW., Washington, DC 20415.

(d) Individuals will not be denied access to records pertaining to them.

[40 FR 52416, Nov. 10, 1975; 40 FR 56651, Dec. 4, 1975, as amended at 40 FR 59187, Dec. 22, 1975]

§ 425.4 Correction of records.

(a) An individual may request that a record or records pertaining to him or her be amended or corrected. Such requests shall be submitted in writing to the Administrative Officer at the Commission's business address.

(b) The signature of the requester will be sufficient identification for requesting correction of records.

(c) A request for amendment shall contain an exact description of the item or items sought to be amended and specific reasons for the requested amendment, as well as the individual's birthdate for purposes of verification of records.

(d) Within 10 working days after receipt of a request to amend a record, the Administrative Officer shall transmit to the requester a written acknowledgement of receipt of request. No acknowledgement is required if the request can be reviewed and processed with notification to the individual of compliance or denial within the ten-day period. Requester will be notified within 30 days whether or not his or her request has been granted.

(e) If the Administrative Officer determines that the requested amendment is appropriate to insure that the record is:

(1) Relevant and necessary to accomplish the purposes for which the records were collected; and

(2) As accurate, timely, and complete as are reasonably necessary to assure fairness to the requester, the Administrative Officer shall:

(i) Change the record accordingly;

(ii) Advise the requester that the change has been made, thirty days from receipt of written request;

(iii) After an accounting of disclosures has been kept pursuant to 5 U.S.C. 552a(c), advise all previous recipients of the record, who, the Commission believes, still retain a copy thereof, of the fact that the amendment was made and the substance of the amendment.

(f) If, after review of the record, the Administrative Officer determines that the requested amendment is not in conformity with the requirements of the Act, he shall:

(1) Advise the requester in writing within thirty days of written request of such determination together with specific reasons therefor; and

(2) Inform the requester that further review of the request by the Director of the Commission is available if a written request therefor is made within 30 days after date of denial.

(g) Within 30 working days of receipt of a written request for review pursuant to § 425.4(f)(2) the Director shall make an independent review of the record, using the criteria of § 425.4(e) (1) and (2).

(1) If the Director determines that the record should be amended in accordance with the request, the Administrative Officer shall take the actions listed in § 425.4(e)(2) (i), (ii), and (iii).

(2) If the Director, after independent review, determines that the record should not be amended in accordance with the request, the Administrative Officer shall advise the requester:

(i) Of the determination and the reasons therefor;

(ii) Of his or her right to file with the Administrative Officer a concise statement of his or her reasons for disagreeing with the refusal to amend the record;

(iii) That the record will be annotated to indicate to anyone subsequently having access to it that a statement of disagreement has been filed, and that the statement will be made available to anyone to whom the record is disclosed;

(iv) That the Director and the Administrative Officer may, in their discretion, include a brief summary of their reasons for refusing to amend the record whenever such disclosure is made;

(v) That any prior recipients of this disputed record, who, the Commission believes, still retain a copy thereof, will be sent a copy of the statement of disagreement, after an accounting of disclosures has been kept pursuant to 5 U.S.C. 552a(c);

(vi) Of his or her right to seek judicial review of the refusal to amend the record, pursuant to 5 U.S.C. 552a(g)(1)(A).

[40 FR 59187, Dec. 22, 1975]

§425.5 Disclosure of records to agencies or persons other than the individual to whom the record pertains.

Records subject to the Privacy Act that are requested by any person other than the individual to whom they pertain will not be made available except under the following circumstances:

(a) Records may be circulated to appropriate officials incident to placing Fellows in work assignments for the Fellowship year.

(b) An accounting of the date, nature, and purpose of each disclosure of a record as well as the name and address of the person and agency to whom the disclosure was made will be indicated on the record. This accounting is available to the individual to whom the records pertain on written request to the Commission.

[40 FR 52416, Nov. 10, 1975; 40 FR 56651, Dec. 4, 1975, as amended at 40 FR 59187, Dec. 22, 1975]

PART 426—NATIONAL COMMISSION ON MILITARY, NATIONAL, AND PUBLIC SERVICE

Subpart A—Implementation of the Privacy Act of 1974

Subpart B—Disclosure of Records and Information Under the Freedom of Information Act

AUTHORITY: 5 U.S.C. 552a(f).

SOURCE: 83 FR 19409, May 2, 2018, unless otherwise noted.

Subpart A—Implementation of the Privacy Act of 1974

§426.101 Purpose and scope.

The regulations in this part set forth the Commission's procedures under the Privacy Act, as required by 5 U.S.C. 552a(f), with respect to systems of records maintained by the Commission. The rules in this part apply to all records maintained by the Commission that are retrieved by an individual's name or by some identifying number, symbol, or other identifying particular assigned to the individual. These regulations establish procedures by which an individual may exercise the rights granted by the Privacy Act to determine whether a Commission system of records contains a record pertaining to him or her; to gain access to such records; and to request correction or amendment of such records. These rules should be read together with the Privacy Act, which provides additional information about records maintained on individuals.

§426.102 Definitions.

The definitions in subsection (a) of the Privacy Act (5 U.S.C. 552a(a)) apply to this part. In addition, as used in this part:

Business day means a calendar day, excluding Saturdays, Sundays, and legal public holidays.

Chair means the Chair of the Commission, or his or her designee;

Commission means the National Commission on Military, National, and Public Service;

Commission system means a system of records maintained by the Commission;

General Counsel means the General Counsel of the Commission, or his or her designee.

Individual means a citizen of the United States or an alien lawfully admitted for permanent residence.

Privacy Act or *Act* means the Privacy Act of 1974, as amended (5 U.S.C. 552a);

You, your, or other references to the reader of the regulations in this part are meant to apply to the individual to whom a record pertains.

§ 426.103 Inquiries about systems of records or implementation of the Privacy Act.

Inquiries about the Commission's systems of records or implementation of the Privacy Act should be sent to the following address: National Commission on Military, National, and Public Service, Office of the General Counsel, 2530 Crystal Drive, Suite 1000, Box No. 63, Arlington, VA 22202.

§ 426.104 Procedures for accessing records pertaining to an individual.

The following procedures apply to records that are contained in a Commission system:

(a) You may request to be notified if a system of records that you name contains records pertaining to you, and to review any such records, by writing to the Office of the General Counsel (see § 426.103). You also may call the Office of the General Counsel at 703-571-3742 on business days, between the hours of 9 a.m. and 5 p.m., to schedule an appointment to make such a request in person. A request for records should be presented in writing and should identify specifically the Commission system(s) involved. Your request to access records pertaining to you will be treated as a request under both the Privacy Act, as implemented by this part, and the Freedom of Information Act (5

U.S.C. 552), as implemented by subpart B of this part.

(b) Access to the records, or to any other information pertaining to you that is contained in the system, shall be provided if the identification requirements of § 426.105 are satisfied and the records are determined otherwise to be releasable under the Privacy Act and these regulations. The Commission shall provide you an opportunity to have a copy made of any such records about you. Only one copy of each requested record will be supplied, based on the fee schedule in § 426.108.

(c) The Commission will comply promptly with requests made in person at scheduled appointments, if the requirements of this section are met and the records sought are immediately available. The Commission will acknowledge, within 10 business days, mailed requests or personal requests for records that are not immediately available, and the information requested will be provided promptly thereafter.

(d) If you make your request in person at a scheduled appointment, you may, upon your request, be accompanied by a person of your choice to review your records. The Commission may require that you furnish a written statement authorizing discussion of your records in the accompanying person's presence. A record may be disclosed to a representative chosen by you upon your proper written consent.

(e) Medical or psychological records pertaining to you shall be disclosed to you unless, in the judgment of the Commission, access to such records might have an adverse effect upon you. When such a determination has been made, the Commission may refuse to disclose such information directly to you. The Commission will, however, disclose this information to you through a licensed physician designated by you in writing.

(f) If you are unsatisfied with an adverse determination on your request to access records pertaining to you, you may appeal that determination using the procedures set forth in § 426.107(a).

§426.105 Identification required when requesting access to records pertaining to an individual.

The Commission will require reasonable identification of all individuals who request access to records in a Commission system to ensure that records are disclosed to the proper person.

(a) The amount of personal identification required will of necessity vary with the sensitivity of the record involved. In general, if you request disclosure in person, you will be required to show an identification card, such as a driver's license, containing your photograph and sample signature. However, with regard to records in Commission systems that contain particularly sensitive and/or detailed personal information, the Commission reserves the right to require additional means of identification as are appropriate under the circumstances. These means include, but are not limited to, requiring you to sign a statement under oath as to your identity, acknowledging that you are aware of the criminal penalties for requesting or obtaining records under false pretenses or falsifying information (see 5 U.S.C. 552a(i)(3); 18 U.S.C. 1001).

(b) If you request disclosure by mail, the Commission will request such information as may be necessary to ensure that you are properly identified and for a response to be sent. Authorized means to achieve this goal include, but are not limited to, requiring that a mail request include a signed, notarized statement asserting your identity or a statement signed under oath as described in subsection (a) of this section.

§426.106 Procedures for amending or correcting an individual's record.

(a) You are entitled to request amendments to or corrections of records pertaining to you that you believe are not accurate, relevant, timely, or complete, pursuant to the provisions of the Privacy Act, including 5 U.S.C. 552a(d)(2). Such a request should be made in writing and addressed to the Office of the General Counsel (see §426.103).

(b) Your request for amendments or corrections should specify the following:

(1) The particular record that you are seeking to amend or correct;

(2) The Commission system from which the record was retrieved;

(3) The precise correction or amendment you desire, preferably in the form of an edited copy of the record reflecting the desired modification; and

(4) Your reasons for requesting amendment or correction of the record.

(c) The Commission will acknowledge a request for amendment or correction of a record within 10 business days of its receipt, unless the request can be processed and the individual informed of the General Counsel's decision on the request within that 10-day period.

(d) If after receiving and investigating your request, the General Counsel agrees that the record is not accurate, timely, or complete, based on a preponderance of the evidence, then the record will be corrected or amended promptly. The record will be deleted without regard to its accuracy, if the record is not relevant or necessary to accomplish the Commission's function for which the record was provided or is maintained. In either case, you will be informed in writing of the amendment, correction, or deletion. In addition, if accounting was made of prior disclosures of the record, all previous recipients of the record will be informed of the corrective action taken.

(e) If after receiving and investigating your request, the General Counsel does not agree that the record should be amended or corrected, you will be informed promptly in writing of the refusal to amend or correct the record and the reason for this decision. You also will be informed that you may appeal this refusal in accordance with §426.107.

(f) Requests to amend or correct a record governed by the regulations of another agency will be forwarded to such agency for processing, and you will be informed in writing of this referral.

§ 426.107 Procedures for appealing a refusal to amend or correct a record.

(a) You may appeal a refusal to amend or correct a record to the Chair of the Commission. Such appeal must be made in writing within 30 business days of your receipt of the initial refusal to amend or correct your record. Your appeal should be sent to the Office of the General Counsel (see § 426.103), should indicate that it is an appeal, and should include the basis for the appeal.

(b) The Chair will review your request to amend or correct the record, the General Counsel's refusal, and any other pertinent material relating to the appeal. No hearing will be held.

(c) The Chair shall render his or her decision on your appeal within 30 business days of its receipt by the Commission, unless the Chair, for good cause shown, extends the 30-day period. Should the Chair extend the appeal period, you will be informed in writing of the extension and the circumstances of the delay.

(d) If the Chair determines that the record that is the subject of the appeal should be amended or corrected, the record will be so modified, and you will be informed in writing of the amendment or correction. Where an accounting was made of prior disclosures of the record, all previous recipients of the record will be informed of the corrective action taken.

(e) If your appeal is denied, you will be informed in writing of the following:

(1) The denial and the reasons for the denial;

(2) That you may submit to the Commission a concise statement setting forth the reasons for your disagreement as to the disputed record. Under the procedures set forth in paragraph (f) of this section, your statement will be disclosed whenever the disputed record is disclosed; and

(3) That you may seek judicial review of the Chair's determination under 5 U.S.C. 552a(g)(1).

(f) Whenever you submit a statement of disagreement to the Commission in accordance with paragraph (e)(2) of this section, the record will be annotated to indicate that it is disputed. In any subsequent disclosure, a copy of your statement of disagreement will be disclosed with the record. If the Commission deems it appropriate, a concise statement of the Chair's reasons for denying your appeal also may be disclosed with the record. While you will have access to this statement of the Chair's reasons for denying your appeal, such statement will not be subject to correction or amendment. Where an accounting was made of prior disclosures of the record, all previous recipients of the record will be provided a copy of your statement of disagreement, as well as any statement of the Chair's reasons for denying your appeal deemed appropriate.

§ 426.108 Fees charged to locate, review, or copy records.

(a) The Commission will charge no fees for search time or for any other time expended by the Commission to review a record. However, the Commission may charge fees where you request that a copy be made of a record to which you have been granted access. Where a copy of the record must be made in order to provide access to the record (*e.g.*, computer printout where no screen reading is available), the copy will be made available to you without cost.

(b) Copies of records made by photocopy or similar process will be charged to you at the rate of $0.12 per page. Where records are not susceptible to photocopying (*e.g.*, punch cards, magnetic tapes, or oversize materials), you will be charged actual cost as determined on a case-by-case basis. Copying fees will not be charged if the cost of collecting a fee would be equal to or greater than the fee itself. Copying fees for contemporaneous requests by the same individual shall be aggregated to determine the total fee.

(c) Special and additional services provided at your request, such as certification or authentication, postal insurance, and special mailing arrangement costs, will be charged to you at the market rate.

(d) You may request that a copying fee not be charged or, alternatively, be reduced, by submitting a written petition to the Commission's General Counsel (see § 426.103) asserting that you are indigent. If the General Counsel determines, based on the petition, that you are indigent and that the Commission's resources permit a waiver of all or part of the fee, the General Counsel may, in his or her discretion, waive or reduce the copying fee.

(e) All fees shall be paid before any copying request is undertaken.

§426.109 Procedures for maintaining accounts of disclosures.

(a) The Office of the General Counsel shall maintain a log containing the date, nature, and purpose of each disclosure of a record to any person or to another agency. Such accounting also shall contain the name and address of the person or agency to whom each disclosure was made. This log need not include disclosures made to the Commission's employees in the course of their official duties, or pursuant to the provisions of the Freedom of Information Act (5 U.S.C. 552).

(b) The Commission will retain the accounting of each disclosure for at least five years after the disclosure or for the life of the record that was disclosed.

(c) The Commission will make the accounting of disclosures of a record pertaining to you available to you at your request. Such a request should be made in accordance with the procedures set forth in §426.104. This paragraph (c) does not apply to disclosures made for law enforcement purposes under 5 U.S.C. 552a(b)(7).

Subpart B—Disclosure of Records and Information Under the Freedom of Information Act

SOURCE: 83 FR 19415, May 2, 2018, unless otherwise noted.

§426.201 General.

This subpart contains the regulations of the National Commission on Military, National, and Public Service (the "Commission") implementing the Freedom of Information Act ("FOIA"), 5 U.S.C. 552, as amended. These regulations set forth procedures for requesting access to records maintained by the Commission. These regulations should be read together with the text of the FOIA, and the Uniform Freedom of In-

formation Fee Schedule and Guidelines published by the Office of Management and Budget ("OMB Guidelines"). Requests made by individuals for records about themselves under the Privacy Act of 1974, 5 U.S.C. 552a, are processed in accordance with the Commission's Privacy Act regulations as well as under this subpart.

§426.202 Proactive disclosures.

(a) Records that FOIA requires agencies to make available for public inspection in an electronic format may be accessed through the Commission's website at *www.inspire2serve.gov*. The Commission will ensure that its website of posted records and indices is reviewed and updated on an ongoing basis. The Commission has a FOIA Public Liaison who can assist individuals in locating records particular to the Commission. A list of agency FOIA Public Liaisons is available at *http://www.foia.gov/report-makerequest.html*.

(b) The following types of records shall be available routinely on the website, without resort to formal FOIA request procedures, unless such records fall within one of the exemptions listed at 5 U.S.C. 552(b) of the Act:

(1) Any formal report issued by the Commission;

(2) Testimonies and presentations submitted to the Commission;

(3) Schedules for public meetings and hearings of the Commission along with transcripts or notes of such public meetings and hearings;

(4) Press statements;

(5) Substantive rules of general applicability adopted by the Commission, procedural rules governing the Commission's general operations that may affect the public, and statements of general policy or interpretation of general applicability formulated and adopted by the Commission; and

(6) Copies of all records, regardless of form or format, that have been released previously to any person under 5 U.S.C. 552(a)(3), and that the Commission determines have become or are likely to become the subject of subsequent requests for substantially the same records. When the Commission receives three or more requests for substantially the same records, then the Commission shall make the released

records available in the Commission's reading room and on the Commission's website.

(c) The Commission shall also maintain a public reading room, at the Commission's offices, containing records available for public inspection that cannot be produced in electronic form. The reading room shall be available for use on workdays during the hours of 9 a.m. to 4 p.m. Requests for appointments to review the materials in the public reading room should be directed to the FOIA Public Liaison.

(d) Based upon applicable exemptions in 5 U.S.C. 552(b), the Commission may redact certain information contained in any matter described in this section before making such information available for inspection or publishing it. The justification for the redaction shall be explained in writing, and the extent of such redaction shall be indicated on the portion of the record which is made available or published, unless including that indication would harm an interest protected by the exemptions under which the redaction is made. The location of the information deleted must also be indicated on the record, if technically feasible.

§ 426.203　**Requirements for making requests.**

(a) *In general.* Many documents are available on the Commission's website and the Commission encourages requesters to visit the website before making a request for records pursuant to this subpart. Except for records already available on the website or subject to the FOIA exemptions and exclusions, the Commission shall promptly provide records to any person in response to a request that conforms to the rules and procedures of this section. Requesters may contact the agency's FOIA Public Liaison to discuss the records they seek and to receive assistance in describing the records.

(b) *Form of request.* For records not available on the website, requesters wishing to obtain information from the Commission should submit a written request to the Commission. It may be submitted by mail or via the internet (website or email). A request by mail must be addressed to: FOIA Request, National Commission on Military, Na-

tional, and Public Service, 2530 Crystal Drive, Suite 1000, Box No. 63, Arlington, VA 22202. As there may be delays in mail delivery, it is advisable to send the request via email to *FOIA@inspire2serve.gov*. The Commission will communicate with the requester by email unless he or she specifies otherwise. Requesters may specify the preferred form or format for the records sought, and the Commission will accommodate the request if the record is readily reproducible in that form or format.

(c) *Contents of request.* Requests must include the following:

(1) The requester's full name, mailing address, a telephone number at which the requester can be reached during normal business hours, and an email address for the requester, if the requester has one;

(2) A description of the records sought in enough detail to allow the records to be located with a reasonable amount of effort. To the extent possible, requesters should include specific information, such as the date, title or name, author, recipient, and subject matter of the records sought. If known, the requester must include any file designations or descriptions for the records requested;

(3) If submitting the request as an educational institution, a non-commercial scientific institution, or a representative of the news media, information to support being placed in that category of requester as they are defined in § 426.210(b);

(4) A fee waiver request, if applicable (see § 426.210(f));

(5) A statement explaining why expedited processing is necessary, if it is being requested (see § 426.205(c)); and

(6) Where the request is making a request for records about himself or herself, verification of the individual's identity (please see the Commission's Privacy Act regulations at 1 CFR, chapter IV, part 426, subpart A).

(d) *Date received.* The Commission shall deem itself to have received a request on the date that it receives a request containing the information required by paragraph (c) of this section. If after receiving a request, the Commission determines that it does not reasonably describe the records sought, the agency must inform the requester what additional information is needed or why the request is otherwise insufficient. Requesters who are attempting to reformulate or modify such a request may discuss their request with the FOIA Public Liaison.

§426.204 Responsibility for responding to requests.

(a) *In general.* In determining which records are responsive to a request, an agency ordinarily will include only records in its possession as of the date that it begins its search. If any other date is used, the agency must inform the requester of that date. A record that is excluded from the requirements of the FOIA pursuant to 5 U.S.C. 552(c), is not considered responsive to a request.

(b) *Authority to grant or deny requests.* The Chief FOIA Officer or designee is authorized to grant or to deny any requests for records.

(c) *Consultation, referral, and coordination.* When reviewing records in response to a request, the Commission will determine whether another agency of the Federal Government is better able to determine whether the record is exempt from disclosure under the FOIA. As to any such record, the Commission will proceed in one of the following ways:

(1) *Consultation.* When records originated within the Commission, but contain within them information of interest to another agency or other Federal Government office, the Commission will typically consult with that other entity prior to making a release determination.

(2) *Referral.* When the Commission believes that a different agency is best able to determine whether to disclose the record, the Commission typically should refer the responsibility for responding to the request regarding that record to that agency. Ordinarily, the agency that originated the record is presumed to be the best agency to make the disclosure determination. Whenever an agency refers any part of the responsibility for responding to a request to another agency, it must document the referral, maintain a copy of the record that it refers, and notify the requester of the referral, the name of

the agency, and the FOIA agency contact.

(3) *Coordination.* The standard referral procedure is not appropriate where disclosure of the identity of the agency to which the referral would be made could harm an interest protected by an applicable exemption, such as the exemptions that protect personal privacy or national security interests. In such instances, in order to avoid harm to an interest protected by an applicable exemption, the agency that received the request should coordinate with the originating agency to seek its views on the disclosability of the record. The release determination for the record that is the subject of the coordination should then be conveyed to the requester by the agency that originally received the request.

(d) *Timing of response to consultations and referrals.* All consultations and referrals received by the Commission will be handled according to the date that the first agency received the perfected FOIA request.

§426.205 Timing of responses to requests.

(a) *In general.* The Commission ordinarily will respond to requests according to their order of receipt. The following timing and steps are the normal process:

(1) *Acknowledgment.* The Commission will provide an acknowledgment notice with an individualized tracking number, the date of receipt of the request, a confirmation of a waiver or reduction of fees (if requested), and a summary of the records requested to each requester within 10 working days after receiving a request that has all of the requisite information.

(2) *Response time.* Ordinarily, the Commission shall have 20 work days from when a request is received to determine whether to grant or deny a request for records. The 20-day time period shall not be tolled by the Commission except that the Commission may:

(i) Make one reasonable demand to the requester for clarifying information about the request and toll the 20-day time period while awaiting clarifying information; or

(ii) Notify the requester of the fee assessment for the request and toll the

20-day time period while awaiting the requester's response.

(3) *Appeal.* The Commission will make a decision with respect to an appeal of a full or partial denial of a request for records within 20 work days after receipt of the appeal.

(b) *Multi-Track processing.* The Commission uses a multi-track system to process FOIA requests, so that a FOIA request is processed based on its complexity. Each request will be assigned to the Standard, Complex, or Expedited track.

(1) *Standard Track.* Requests that are routine and require little search time, review, or analysis are assigned to the Standard Track. The Commission will respond to these requests in the order in which they are received and make every effort to respond no later than 20 working days after receipt of the request.

(2) *Complex Track.* Requests that are non-routine are assigned to the Complex Track if the response may be voluminous; requires an unusually high level of effort for search, review, or duplication; or causes an undue disruption to the day-to-day activities of the Commission in carrying out its statutory responsibilities. The requester will be notified if the request is assigned to the Complex Track and will be given an estimate of the time for response. The Commission will respond to Complex Track requests as soon as practicable, and may discuss with the requester the possibility of reformulating the request to reduce processing time.

(3) *Expedited Track.* Requests for expedited processing that meet the standards set forth in paragraph (c) of this section, will be assigned to the Expedited track. In such cases, the process described in paragraph (c) will be followed.

(c) *Expedited processing.* A request for expedited processing must accompany the initial request for records, and the request should be clearly marked "Expedited Processing Requested." It must be a certified, written statement of compelling need for expedited processing, stating that the facts are true and correct. The Commission shall decide whether to grant the request within 10 calendar days of its receipt, and

shall notify the requester in writing. If the Commission grants this request, then the Commission will give the expedited request priority over non-expedited requests and shall process it as soon as practicable. Denials of expedited processing requests can be appealed using the same procedures as denials of other FOIA requests. In determining whether processing should be expedited, the Chief FOIA Officer may consider whether:

(1) Failure to obtain the requested records on an expedited basis could reasonably be expected to pose an imminent threat to a person's life or physical safety;

(2) With respect to a request made by a person primarily engaged in disseminating information, there is an urgency to inform the public about actual or alleged Federal Government activity; or

(3) A reasonable expectation of an imminent loss of a substantial due process right.

(d) *Unusual circumstances.* If the Commission determines that "unusual circumstances" exist, as that term is defined in the FOIA, the time limits for responding to requests and appeals may be extended by no more than 10 work days by providing written notice of the extension to the requester. The requester will be given an opportunity to limit the scope of the request or to arrange with the Commission an alternative time frame for processing the request. A FOIA Officer shall include with the notice of extension a brief statement of the reason for the extension, the date the FOIA Officer expects to make a determination, and the availability of the FOIA Public Liaison to assist the requester, and the requester's right to seek dispute resolution services from the Office of Government Information Services (OGIS) of the National Archives and Records Administration.

§ 426.206 Response to requests.

(a) *Acknowledgements of requests.* The Commission will send an acknowledgement of the request in writing and assign it an individualized tracking number if it will take longer than 10 working days to process. Upon request, the Commission will provide an estimated date by which the Commission expects to provide a response to the requester. If a request involves a voluminous amount of material, or searches in multiple locations, the agency may provide interim responses, releasing the records on a rolling basis.

(b) *Grant of request.* If a FOIA Officer grants a request, in full or in part, the Commission shall promptly provide the requester written notice of the decision, what fees apply under section 10 of this subpart, and the availability of its FOIA Public Liaison to offer assistance. The requester will be notified whether the request has been assigned to the Standard, Complex, or Expedited track, pursuant to §426.205(b).

(c) *Request denial.* If the Chief FOIA Officer denies a request in any respect, the Commission will notify the requester of that determination in writing. A denial of request includes decisions that: Fees will not be waived, no expedited processing will be done, there are no responsive records subject to FOIA, the requested record does not exist or has been destroyed, the requested record is exempt in whole or in part, or the request does not reasonably describe the records sought. The written notice will include:

(1) The name and title or position of the person responsible for the denial;

(2) A brief statement of the reasons for the denial, including any FOIA exemption applied by the agency in denying the request;

(3) A description of the material withheld, such as the approximate number of pages or some other reasonable form of estimation;

(4) A statement that the denial may be appealed under section 8(a) of this subpart, and a description of the appeal requirements; and

(5) A statement notifying the requester of the assistance available from the agency's FOIA Public Liaison and the dispute resolution services offered by OGIS.

(d) *Redactions.* When a portion of a record is withheld, the amount of information redacted and the claimed exemption will be noted at the place in the record where the redaction was made.

§426.207 Confidential commercial information.

(a) *Definitions.*

Confidential commercial information means commercial or financial information obtained by the Commission from a submitter that may be protected from disclosure under Exemption 4 of the FOIA, 5 U.S.C. 552(b)(4).

Submitter means any person or entity, including a corporation, State, or foreign government, but not including another Federal Government entity, that provides confidential commercial information, either directly or indirectly to the Federal Government.

(b) *Designation of confidential commercial information.* A submitter of confidential commercial information must use good faith efforts to designate by appropriate markings, at the time of submission, any portion of its submission that it considers to be protected from disclosure under Exemption 4. These designations expire 10 years after the date of the submission unless the submitter requests and provides justification for a longer designation period.

(c) *When notice to submitters is required.* (1) The Commission must promptly provide written notice to the submitter of confidential commercial information whenever records containing such information are requested under the FOIA if the agency determines that it may be required to disclose the records, provided the requested information has been designated in good faith by the submitter or the Commission has a reason to believe that the requested information may be protected from disclosure under Exemption 4.

(2) The notice must either describe the commercial information requested or include a copy of the requested records or portions of records containing the information. In cases involving a voluminous number of submitters, the Commission may post or publish a notice in a place or manner reasonably likely to inform the submitters of the proposed disclosure, instead of sending individual notifications.

(d) *Exceptions to submitter notice requirements.* The notice requirements of this section do not apply if:

(1) The Commission determines that the information is exempt under the FOIA, and therefore will not be disclosed;

(2) The information has been lawfully published or has been officially made available to the public;

(3) Disclosure of the information is required by a statute other than the FOIA or by a regulation issued in accordance with the requirements of Executive Order 12,600 of June 23, 1987; or

(4) The designation made by the submitter under paragraph (b) of this section appears obviously frivolous. In such case, the Commission must give the submitter written notice of any final decision to disclose the information within a reasonable number of days prior to a specified disclosure date.

(e) *Opportunity to object to disclosure.* (1) The Commission must specify a reasonable time period within which the submitter must respond to the notice referenced above.

(2) If a submitter has any objections to disclosure, it should provide the Commission a detailed written statement that specifies all grounds for withholding the particular information under any exemption of the FOIA. In order to rely on Exemption 4 as basis for nondisclosure, the submitter must explain why the information constitutes a trade secret or commercial or financial information that is confidential.

(3) A submitter who fails to respond within the time period specified in the notice will be considered to have no objection to disclosure of the information. The Commission is not required to consider any information received after the date of any disclosure decision. Any information provided by a submitter under this subpart may itself be subject to disclosure under the FOIA.

(4) The Commission must consider a submitter's objections and specific grounds for nondisclosure in deciding whether to disclose the requested information.

(f) *Notice of intent to disclose.* Whenever the Commission decides to disclose information over the objection of a submitter, the agency must provide the submitter written notice, which must include:

(1) A statement of the reasons why each of the submitter's disclosure objections was not sustained;

(2) A description of the information to be disclosed or copies of the records as the Commission intends to release them; and

(3) A specified disclosure date, which must be a reasonable time after the notice.

(g) *Notice of FOIA lawsuit.* Whenever a requester files a lawsuit seeking to compel the disclosure of confidential commercial information, the Commission must promptly notify the submitter.

(h) *Requester notification.* The Commission must notify the requester whenever it provides the submitter with notice and an opportunity to object to disclosure; whenever it notifies the submitter of its intent to disclose the requested information; and whenever a submitter files a lawsuit to prevent the disclosure of the information.

§ 426.208   Appeals.

(a) *Grounds for administrative appeals.* A requester may appeal an initial determination of the Commission, including but not limited to a determination:

(1) To deny access to records in whole or in part (as provided in § 426.206(c));

(2) To assign a particular fee category to the requester (as provided in § 426.209(d));

(3) To deny a request for a reduction or waiver of fees (as provided in § 426.209(f));

(4) That no records could be located that are responsive to the request (as provided in § 426.206(c)); or

(5) To deny a request for expedited processing (as provided in § 426.205(c)).

(b) *Initiating appeals.* Requesters not satisfied with the FOIA Officer's decision may make a written request appealing the decision within 90 days of the date of the FOIA Officer's decision. Any appeal requests should be clearly marked with the words "Freedom of Information Act Appeal." Appeals may be made through the Commission's email, *FOIA@inspire2serve.gov;* website, *www.inspire2serve.gov,* or through the mail, and may be addressed to: FOIA

Appeals, National Commission on Military, National, and Public Service, 2530 Crystal Drive, Suite 1000, Box No. 63, Arlington, VA 22202. As there may be delays in mail delivery, it is advisable to send the request via email. The request should set out the name and contact information of the requester, specify the date of the initial request and the initial determination, and set forth why the appeal should be granted.

(c) *Adjudication of appeals.* Appeals will be processed in the order of their receipt. An appeal ordinarily will not be adjudicated if the request become a matter of FOIA litigation. Before seeking review by a court of an agency's adverse determination, a requester generally must first submit a timely administrative appeal.

(d) *Appeal decisions.* The Commission's Chair or his designee shall decide whether to affirm or reverse the initial determination (in whole or in part), and shall notify the requester of this decision in writing within 20 work days, pursuant to §426.205(c). If the appeal is denied (in whole or in part), the Commission will notify the requester in writing of the decision, the reasons for the denial (including the FOIA exemptions relied upon), the name and title of the official responsible for the determination on appeal, and the provisions for judicial review and dispute resolution services offered by the OGIS. If the appeal is granted in full or in part, the Chief FOIA Officer will notify the requester in writing and promptly process the request.

(e) *Dispute resolution.* Dispute resolution is a voluntary process. If the Commission agrees to participate in the dispute resolution services provided by OGIS, it will actively engage as a partner to the process in an attempt to resolve the dispute. Requesters may seek dispute resolution by contacting the FOIA Public Liaison or OGIS at: Office of Government Information Services, National Archives and Records Administration, 8601 Adelphi Road, OGIS, College Park, MD 20740; email: *ogis@nara.gov;* telephone: (202) 741–5770; facsimile: (202) 741–5769; toll free telephone: (877) 684–6448.

§426.209   **Preservation of records.**

The Commission will preserve all correspondence pertaining to the requests that it receives under this subpart, as well as copies of all requested records, until disposition or destruction is authorized pursuant to title 44 of the United States Code or the General Records Schedule 4.2 of the National Archives and Records Administration. The Commission will not dispose of or destroy records while they are the subject of a pending request, appeal, or lawsuit under the FOIA.

§426.210   **Fees.**

(a) *In general.* The Commission shall charge the requester for processing a request under the FOIA in accordance with the provisions of this section and with the OMB Guidelines. For purposes of assessing fees, the FOIA establishes three categories of requesters: Commercial use requesters, non-commercial scientific or educational institutions or news media requesters, and all other requesters. Different fees are assessed depending on the category. Requesters may seek a fee waiver, and the Commission will consider fee waiver requests in accordance with the requirements in paragraph (f) of this section. To resolve any fee issues that arise under this section, the Commission will contact a requester for additional information. No fees shall be charged if the amount of fees incurred in processing the request is below $25. The Commission ordinarily will collect all applicable fees before sending copies of records to a requester. Requesters must pay fees by check or money order made payable to the Treasury of the United States, or by another method as determined by the Commission.

(b) *Definitions.* For purposes of this section:

Commercial use request means a request that asks for information for a use or a purpose that furthers a commercial, trade, or profit interest, which can include furthering those interests through litigation. The Commission's decision to place a requester in the commercial use category will be made on a case-by-case basis based on the requester's intended use of the information. The Commission will notify requesters of their placement in this category.

Direct costs means those expenses that the Commission incurs in searching for and duplicating (and, in the case of commercial use requests, reviewing) records in order to respond to a FOIA request. For example, direct costs include the salary of the employee performing the work (*i.e.*, the basic rate of pay for the employee, plus 16 percent of that rate to cover benefits) and the cost of operating computers and other electronic equipment, such as photocopiers and scanners. Direct costs do not include overhead expenses such as the costs of space, and of heating or lighting a facility.

Duplication means reproducing a copy of a record, or of the information contained in it, necessary to respond to a FOIA request. Copies can take the form of paper, audiovisual materials, or electronic records, among others.

Educational institution means any school that operates a program of scholarly research. A requester in this fee category must show that the request is made in connection with his or her role at the educational institution. The Commission may seek verification from the requester that the request is in furtherance of scholarly research and the Commission will advise requesters of their placement in this category.

Example 1. A request from a professor of geology at a university for records relating to soil erosion, written on letterhead of the Department of Geology, would be presumed to be from an educational institution.

Example 2. A request from the same professor of geology seeking drug information from the Food and Drug Administration in furtherance of a murder mystery he is writing would not be presumed to be an institutional request, regardless of whether it was written on institutional stationery.

Example 3. A student who makes a request in furtherance of their coursework or other school-sponsored activities and provides a copy of a course syllabus or other reasonable documentation to indicate the research purpose for the request, would qualify as part of this fee category.

Noncommercial scientific institution means an institution that is not operated on a "commercial" basis, as defined in this paragraph (b) and that is operated solely for the purpose of conducting scientific research the results of which are not intended to promote any particular product or industry. A requester in this category must show that the request is authorized by and is made under the auspices of a qualifying institution and that the records are sought to further scientific research and are not for a commercial use. The Commission will advise requesters of their placement in this category.

Representative of the news media means any person or entity that gathers information of potential interest to a segment of the public, uses its editorial skills to turn the raw materials into a distinct work, and distributes that work to an audience. The term "news" means information that is about current events or that would be of current interest to the public. Examples of news media entities include television or radio stations that broadcast news to the public at large and publishers of periodicals that disseminate news and make their products available through a variety of means to the general public, including news organizations that disseminate solely on the internet. A request for records supporting the news-dissemination function of the requester will not be considered to be for a commercial use. "Freelance" journalists who demonstrate a solid basis for expecting publication through a news media entity will be considered as a representative of the news media. A publishing contract would provide the clearest evidence that publication is expected; however, the Commission can also consider a requester's past publication record in making this determination. The Commission will advise requesters of their placement in this category.

Review means the examination of a record located in response to a request in order to determine whether any portion of it is exempt from disclosure. Review time includes processing any record for disclosure, such as doing all that is necessary to prepare the record for disclosure, including the process of redacting the record and marking the appropriate exemptions. Review costs are properly charged even if a record ultimately is not disclosed. Review time also includes time spent both obtaining and considering any formal objection to disclosure made by a confidential commercial information submitter under §426.207 of this subpart, but it does not include time spent resolving general legal or policy issues regarding the application of exemptions.

Search means the process of looking for and retrieving records or information responsive to a request. Search time includes page-by-page or line-by-line identification of information within records and the reasonable efforts expended to locate and retrieve information from electronic records.

(c) *Fees chargeable for specific services.* In responding to FOIA requests, the Commission will charge the following fees unless a waiver or reduction of fees has been granted under paragraph (f) of this section. No additional costs will be added to charges calculated under this section.

(1) *Duplicating records.* The Commission shall assess requester fees for the cost of copying records. The charge will be $0.12 per page, up to 8½ x 14, made by photocopy or similar process. The charge will be the actual cost for duplicating photographs, films, and other materials. Where paper documents must be scanned so they can be sent electronically, the requester must pay the direct costs associated with scanning those materials. The Commission will honor a requester's preference for receiving a record in a particular form or format where the agency can readily reproduce it in the form or format requested.

(2) *Search services.* The Commission shall charge a requester for all time spent by its employees searching for records that are responsive to a request, even if no responsive records are found or the records are exempt from disclosure. For non-electronic searches, the Commission shall charge for search time at the salary rate (basic pay plus 16 percent) of the employee who conducts the search. For electronic records, the Commission shall charge the requester for the actual direct cost of the search, including computer search time, runs, and the operator's salary.

(3) *Review of records.* The Commission shall only charge review fees to requesters who make commercial use requests. Review fees will be assessed in connection with the initial review of the record, but no charge will be made for review at the administrative appeal stage. However, if a particular exemption is deemed to no longer apply, any costs associated with an agency's re-review of the records in order to consider the use of other exemptions may be assess as review fees. The Commission shall charge a requester for time spent reviewing records at the salary rate(s) (*i.e.*, basic pay plus 16 percent) of the employees who conduct the review.

(4) *Inspection of records in the reading room.* Fees for all services provided shall be charged whether or not copies are made available to the requester for inspection. However, no fee shall be charged for monitoring a requester's inspection of records in the physical reading room.

(5) *Other services.* Although not required to provide special services, if the Commission chooses to do so as a matter of administrative discretion, the requested services are charged at the actual cost to the Commission. Examples of such services include certifying that records are true copies or sending records by express mail.

(d) *Fees applicable to each category of requester.* The Commission shall apply the fees set forth in this paragraph, for each category described in paragraph (c) of this section, to FOIA requests processed by the Commission.

(1) *Commercial use.* A requester seeking records for commercial use shall be charged the full direct cost of searching for, reviewing, and duplicating the records they request as set forth in paragraph (c) of this section. The Commission is not required to consider a waiver request based upon the assertion that disclosure would be in the public interest from a commercial use requester.

(2) *Educational and non-commercial scientific uses.* A requester seeking records for educational or non-commercial scientific use shall be charged only for the cost of duplicating the records they request, except that the Commission shall provide the first 100 pages of duplication (or cost equivalent for other

media) free of charge. To be eligible, the requester must show that the records are not sought for a commercial use, but rather in furtherance of scholarly or scientific research.

(3) *News media uses.* A requester seeking records under the news media use category shall be charged only the cost of duplicating the records they request, except that the Commission shall provide the requester with the first 100 pages of duplication (or cost equivalent for the other media) free of charge.

(4) *Other requests.* A requester seeking records for any other use shall be charged the full direct cost of searching for and duplicating records that are responsive to the request, as set out in paragraph (b) of this section, except that the Commission shall provide the first 100 pages of duplication and the first two hours of search time free of charge.

(e) *Other circumstances when fees are not charged.* Notwithstanding paragraphs (c) and (d) of this section, the Commission may not charge a requester a fee for processing a FOIA request if the total fee is equal to or less than $25. Additionally, the Commission may not charge a requester a search or duplication fee if the Commission fails to comply with any time limit under § 426.205 or § 426.208, unless:

(1) A court has determined that exceptional circumstances exist, as defined by the FOIA, then a failure to comply with such time limit shall be excused for the length of time provided by the court order;

(2) The Commission has determined that unusual circumstances, as defined by the FOIA, apply and the Commission provides timely written notice to the requester in accordance with § 426.205(d), then the time limit shall be excused for an additional 10 days; or

(3) The Commission has determined that unusual circumstances apply; more than 5,000 pages are necessary to respond to the request; the Commission has provided a timely written notice to the requester in accordance with § 426.205(d), and the Commission has discussed with the requester via written mail, electronic mail, or telephone (or made not less than three good-faith attempts to do so) how the requester could effectively limit the scope of the

request. Then the Commission may charge a requester all applicable fees.

(f) *Waiver or reduction of fees.* (1) A requester may request a waiver or reduction of fees otherwise applicable to a FOIA request in writing during the initial FOIA request. The waiver must demonstrate that the fee reduction or waiver is in the public interest because it furnishes information that is likely to contribute significantly to public understanding of the operations or activities of the government, and the information is not primarily in the commercial interest of the requester.

(2) To determine whether the requester has satisfied the waiver request requirements, the Commission shall consider whether the subject of the requested records has a direct connection to government operations or activities; the disclosable portion of the requested records is meaningfully informative, and is not already in the public domain; the disclosure would contribute to the understanding of a reasonably broad audience, as opposed to the individual requester; and the public's understanding would be significantly enhanced by the disclosure. The Commission shall also consider whether the requester, or any person on whose behalf the requester may be acting, has a commercial interest that would be furthered by the disclosure, and whether the public interest is greater in magnitude than that of any identified commercial interest in disclosure.

(3) Where only some of the records to be released satisfy the requirements for a waiver or reduction of fees, a waiver or reduction shall be granted for those records.

(4) The Commission shall notify the requester in writing regarding its determination to reduce or waive fees.

(5) If the Commission denies a request to reduce or waive fees, then the Commission shall advise the requester, in the denial notification letter, that the requester may incur fees as a result of processing the request. In the denial notification letter, the Commission shall advise the requester that the Commission will not proceed to process the request further unless the requester, in writing, directs the Commission to do so and either agrees to

pay any fees that may apply to processing the request or specifies an upper limit (of not less than $25) that the requester is willing to pay to process the request. If the Commission does not receive this written direction and agreement within 30 days of the date of the denial notification letter, then the Commission shall deem the FOIA request to be withdrawn.

(6) If the Commission denies a request to reduce or waive fees, then the requester shall have the right to submit an appeal in accordance with §426.208. The Commission shall communicate this appeal right as part of its denial notification to the requester.

(g) *Notice of estimated fees.* (1) When an agency determines or estimates that the fees to be assessed in accordance with this section will exceed $25, the agency must notify the requester of the actual or estimated amount of the fees, including a breakdown of the fees for search, review or duplication, unless the requester has indicated a willingness to pay fees as high as those anticipated. If only a portion of the fee can be estimated readily the Commission will advise the requester accordingly. The notice will specify what duplication and search time the requester is entitled to and how they have been accounted for in the estimate.

(2) If the agency notifies the requester that the actual or estimated fees are in excess of $25, the request will not be considered received and further work will not be completed until the requester commits in writing to pay the actual or estimated total fee, or designates some amount of fees the requester is willing to pay, or in the case of a noncommercial use requester who has not yet been provided with the statutory entitlements, designates that the requester seeks only that which can be provided by the statutory entitlements. The requester must provide the commitment or designation in writing, and must, when applicable designate an exact dollar amount the requester is willing to pay. Agencies are not required to accept payments in installments.

(3) If the requester has indicated a willingness to pay some designated amount of fees, but the Commission estimates that the total fee will exceed that amount, the Commission will toll the processing of the request when it notifies the requester of the estimated fees in excess of the amount the requester has indicated a willingness to pay. The Commission will inquire whether the requester wishes to revise the amount of fees the requester is willing to pay or modify the request. Once the requester responds, the time to respond will resume from where it was at the date of the notification.

(4) The FOIA Public Liaison will be available to assist any requester in reformulating a request to meet the requester's needs at a lower cost.

(h) *Advance payment.* (1) For requests other than those described in paragraphs (h)(2) and (3) of this section, the Commission will not require the requester to make an advance payment before work is commenced or continued on a request. Payment owed for work already completed (*i.e.*, payment before copies are sent to a requester) is not an advance payment.

(2) When the Commission determines or estimates that a total fee to be charged under this section will exceed $250, it may require that the requester make an advance payment up to the amount of the entire anticipated fee before beginning to process the request. An agency may elect to process the request prior to collecting fees when it receives a satisfactory assurance of full payment from a requester with a history of prompt payment.

(3) If a requester previously has failed to pay a fee within 30 calendar days of the date of the billing, the requester shall be required to pay the full amount owed plus any applicable interest, and to make an advance payment of the full amount of the estimated fee before the Commission begins to process a new request.

(4) In cases in which an agency requires advance payment, the request will not be considered received and further work will not be completed until the required payment is received. If the requester does not pay the advance payment within 30 calendar days after the date of the agency's fee determination, the request will be closed.

(i) *Charging interest.* The Commission may charge interest on any unpaid bill starting on the 31st day following the date of billing the requester. Interest charges will be assessed at the rate provided in 31 U.S.C. 3717 and will accrue from the billing date until payment is received by the Commission. The Commission will follow the provisions of the Debt Collection Act of 1982 (Pub. L. 97-365, 96 Stat. 1749), as amended, and its administrative procedures.

(j) *Aggregating requests.* If the Commission reasonably determines that a requester or a group of requesters acting together is attempting to divide a request into a series of requests for the purpose of avoiding fees, the Commission may aggregate those requests and charge accordingly. The Commission may presume that multiple requests involving related matters submitted within a 30 calendar day period have been made in order to avoid fees. For requests separated by a longer period, the Commission will aggregate them only where there is a reasonable basis for determining that aggregation is warranted in view of all the circumstances involved. The Commission shall not aggregate multiple requests involving unrelated matters.

(k) *Other statutes specifically providing for fees.* The fee schedule of this section does not apply to fees charged under any statute that specifically requires an agency to set and collect fees for particular types of records. In instances where records responsive to a request are subject to a statutorily-based fee schedule program, the Commission must inform the requester of the contact information for that program.

§ 426.211 Other rights and services.

Nothing in this subpart shall be construed to entitle any person, as of right, to any service or to the disclosure of any record to which such person is not entitled under the FOIA.

PART 457—ENFORCEMENT OF NONDISCRIMINATION ON THE BASIS OF HANDICAP IN PROGRAMS OR ACTIVITIES CONDUCTED BY THE NATIONAL CAPITAL PLANNING COMMISSION

AUTHORITY: 29 U.S.C. 794.

SOURCE: 51 FR 22887, 22896, June 23, 1986, unless otherwise noted.

§ 457.101 Purpose.

This part effectuates section 119 of the Rehabilitation, Comprehensive Services, and Developmental Disabilities Amendments of 1978, which amended section 504 of the Rehabilitation Act of 1973 to prohibit discrimination on the basis of handicap in programs or activities conducted by Executive agencies or the United States Postal Service.

§ 457.102 Application.

This part applies to all programs or activities conducted by the agency.

§ 457.103 Definitions.

For purposes of this part, the term—

Assistant Attorney General means the Assistant Attorney General, Civil Rights Division, United States Department of Justice.

Auxiliary aids means services or devices that enable persons with impaired sensory, manual, or speaking skills to have an equal opportunity to participate in, and enjoy the benefits of, programs or activities conducted by the agency. For example, auxiliary aids useful for persons with impaired vision include readers, brailled materials, audio recordings, telecommunications devices and other similar services and devices. Auxiliary aids useful for persons with impaired hearing include telephone handset amplifiers, telephones compatible with hearing aids, telecommunication devices for deaf persons (TDD's), interpreters, notetakers, written materials, and other similar services and devices.

Complete complaint means a written statement that contains the complainant's name and address and describes the agency's alleged discriminatory action in sufficient detail to inform the agency of the nature and date of the alleged violation of section 504. It shall be signed by the complainant or by someone authorized to do so on his or her behalf. Complaints filed on behalf of classes or third parties shall describe or identify (by name, if possible) the alleged victims of discrimination.

Facility means all or any portion of buildings, structures, equipment, roads, walks, parking lots, rolling stock or other conveyances, or other real or personal property.

Handicapped person means any person who has a physical or mental impairment that substantially limits one or more major life activities, has a record of such an impairment, or is regarded as having such an impairment.

As used in this definition, the phrase:

(1) *Physical or mental impairment* includes—

(i) Any physiological disorder or condition, cosmetic disfigurement, or anatomical loss affecting one or more of the following body systems: Neurological; musculoskeletal; special sense organs; respiratory, including speech organs; cardiovascular; reproductive; digestive; genitourinary; hemic and lymphatic; skin; and endocrine; or

(ii) Any mental or psychological disorder, such as mental retardation, organic brain syndrome, emotional or mental illness, and specific learning disabilities. The term "physical or mental impairment" includes, but is not limited to, such diseases and conditions as orthopedic, visual, speech, and hearing impairments, cerebral palsy, epilepsy, muscular dystrophy, multiple sclerosis, cancer, heart disease, diabetes, mental retardation, emotional illness, and drug addiction and alcoholism.

(2) *Major life activities* includes functions such as caring for one's self, performing manual tasks, walking, seeing, hearing, speaking, breathing, learning, and working.

(3) *Has a record of such an impairment* means has a history of, or has been misclassified as having, a mental or physical impairment that substantially limits one or more major life activities.

(4) *Is regarded as having an impairment* means—

(i) Has a physical or mental impairment that does not substantially limit major life activities but is treated by the agency as constituting such a limitation;

(ii) Has a physical or mental impairment that substantially limits major life activities only as a result of the attitudes of others toward such impairment; or

(iii) Has none of the impairments defined in subparagraph (1) of this definition but is treated by the agency as having such an impairment.

Historic preservation programs means programs conducted by the agency that have preservation of historic properties as a primary purpose.

Historic properties means those properties that are listed or eligible for listing in the National Register of Historic Places or properties designated as historic under a statute of the appropriate State or local government body.

Qualified handicapped person means—

(1) With respect to preschool, elementary, or secondary education services provided by the agency, a handicapped person who is a member of a class of persons otherwise entitled by statute, regulation, or agency policy to receive education services from the agency.

(2) With respect to any other agency program or activity under which a person is required to perform services or to achieve a level of accomplishment, a handicapped person who meets the essential eligibility requirements and who can achieve the purpose of the program or activity without modifications in the program or activity that the agency can demonstrate would result in a fundamental alteration in its nature;

(3) With respect to any other program or activity, a handicapped person

who meets the essential eligibility requirements for participation in, or receipt of benefits from, that program or activity; and

(4) *Qualified handicapped person* is defined for purposes of employment in 29 CFR 1613.702(f), which is made applicable to this part by § 457.140.

Section 504 means section 504 of the Rehabilitation Act of 1973 (Pub. L. 93–112, 87 Stat. 394 (29 U.S.C. 794)), as amended by the Rehabilitation Act Amendments of 1974 (Pub. L. 93–516, 88 Stat. 1617), and the Rehabilitation, Comprehensive Services, and Developmental Disabilities Amendments of 1978 (Pub. L. 95–602, 92 Stat. 2955). As used in this part, section 504 applies only to programs or activities conducted by Executive agencies and not to federally assisted programs.

Substantial impairment means a significant loss of the integrity of finished materials, design quality, or special character resulting from a permanent alteration.

§§ 457.104–457.109   [Reserved]

§ 457.110   Self-evaluation.

(a) The agency shall, by August 24, 1987, evaluate its current policies and practices, and the effects thereof, that do not or may not meet the requirements of this part, and, to the extent modification of any such policies and practices is required, the agency shall proceed to make the necessary modifications.

(b) The agency shall provide an opportunity to interested persons, including handicapped persons or organizations representing handicapped persons, to participate in the self-evaluation process by submitting comments (both oral and written).

(c) The agency shall, until three years following the completion of the self-evaluation, maintain on file and make available for public inspection:

(1) A description of areas examined and any problems identified, and

(2) A description of any modifications made.

§ 457.111   Notice.

The agency shall make available to employees, applicants, participants, beneficiaries, and other interested persons such information regarding the provisions of this part and its applicability to the programs or activities conducted by the agency, and make such information available to them in such manner as the head of the agency finds necessary to apprise such persons of the protections against discrimination assured them by section 504 and this regulation.

§§ 457.112–457.129   [Reserved]

§ 457.130   General prohibitions against discrimination.

(a) No qualified handicapped person shall, on the basis of handicap, be excluded from participation in, be denied the benefits of, or otherwise be subjected to discrimination under any program or activity conducted by the agency.

(b)(1) The agency, in providing any aid, benefit, or service, may not, directly or through contractual, licensing, or other arrangements, on the basis of handicap—

(i) Deny a qualified handicapped person the opportunity to participate in or benefit from the aid, benefit, or service;

(ii) Afford a qualified handicapped person an opportunity to participate in or benefit from the aid, benefit, or service that is not equal to that afforded others;

(iii) Provide a qualified handicapped person with an aid, benefit, or service that is not as effective in affording equal opportunity to obtain the same result, to gain the same benefit, or to reach the same level of achievement as that provided to others;

(iv) Provide different or separate aid, benefits, or services to handicapped persons or to any class of handicapped persons than is provided to others unless such action is necessary to provide qualified handicapped persons with aid, benefits, or services that are as effective as those provided to others;

(v) Deny a qualified handicapped person the opportunity to participate as a member of planning or advisory boards; or

(vi) Otherwise limit a qualified handicapped person in the enjoyment of any right, privilege, advantage, or opportunity enjoyed by others receiving the aid, benefit, or service.

(2) The agency may not deny a qualified handicapped person the opportunity to participate in programs or activities that are not separate or different, despite the existence of permissibly separate or different programs or activities.

(3) The agency may not, directly or through contractual or other arrangments, utilize criteria or methods of administration the purpose or effect of which would—

(i) Subject qualified handicapped persons to discrimination on the basis of handicap; or

(ii) Defeat or substantially impair accomplishment of the objectives of a program or activity with respect to handicapped persons.

(4) The agency may not, in determining the site or location of a facility, make selections the purpose or effect of which would—

(i) Exclude handicapped persons from, deny them the benefits of, or otherwise subject them to discrimination under any program or activity conducted by the agency; or

(ii) Defeat or substantially impair the accomplishment of the objectives of a program or activity with respect to handicapped persons.

(5) The agency, in the selection of procurement contractors, may not use criteria that subject qualified handicapped persons to discrimination on the basis of handicap.

(6) The agency may not administer a licensing or certification program in a manner that subjects qualified handicapped persons to discrimination on the basis of handicap, nor may the agency establish requirements for the programs or activities of licensees or certified entities that subject qualified handicapped persons to discrimination on the basis of handicap. However, the programs or activities of entities that are licensed or certified by the agency are not, themselves, covered by this part.

(c) The exclusion of nonhandicapped persons from the benefits of a program limited by Federal statute or Executive order to handicapped persons or the exclusion of a specific class of handicapped persons from a program limited by Federal statute or Executive order to a different class of handicapped persons is not prohibited by this part.

(d) The agency shall administer programs and activities in the most integrated setting appropriate to the needs of qualified handicapped persons.

§§457.131–457.139 [Reserved]

§457.140 Employment.

No qualified handicapped person shall, on the basis of handicap, be subjected to discrimination in employment under any program or activity conducted by the agency. The definitions, requirements, and procedures of section 501 of the Rehabilitation Act of 1973 (29 U.S.C. 791), as established by the Equal Employment Opportunity Commission in 29 CFR part 1613, shall apply to employment in federally conducted programs or activities.

§§457.141–457.148 [Reserved]

§457.149 Program accessibility: Discrimination prohibited.

Except as otherwise provided in §457.150, no qualified handicapped person shall, because the agency's facilities are inaccessible to or unusable by handicapped persons, be denied the benefits of, be excluded from participation in, or otherwise be subjected to discrimination under any program or activity conducted by the agency.

§457.150 Program accessibility: Existing facilities.

(a) *General.* The agency shall operate each program or activity so that the program or activity, when viewed in its entirety, is readily accessible to and usable by handicapped persons. This paragraph does not—

(1) Necessarily require the agency to make each of its existing facilities accessible to and usable by handicapped persons;

(2) In the case of historic preservation programs, require the agency to take any action that would result in a substantial impairment of significant historic features of an historic property; or

(3) Require the agency to take any action that it can demonstrate would result in a fundamental alteration in

the nature of a program or activity or in undue financial and administrative burdens. In those circumstances where agency personnel believe that the proposed action would fundamentally alter the program or activity or would result in undue financial and administrative burdens, the agency has the burden of proving that compliance with § 457.150(a) would result in such alteration or burdens. The decision that compliance would result in such alteration or burdens must be made by the agency head or his or her designee after considering all agency resources available for use in the funding and operation of the conducted program or activity, and must be accompanied by a written statement of the reasons for reaching that conclusion. If an action would result in such an alteration or such burdens, the agency shall take any other action that would not result in such an alteration or such burdens but would nevertheless ensure that handicapped persons receive the benefits and services of the program or activity.

(b) *Methods*—(1) *General.* The agency may comply with the requirements of this section through such means as redesign of equipment, reassignment of services to accessible buildings, assignment of aides to beneficiaries, home visits, delivery of services at alternate accessible sites, alteration of existing facilities and construction of new facilities, use of accessible rolling stock, or any other methods that result in making its programs or activities readily accessible to and usable by handicapped persons. The agency is not required to make structural changes in existing facilities where other methods are effective in achieving compliance with this section. The agency, in making alterations to existing buildings, shall meet accessibility requirements to the extent compelled by the Architectural Barriers Act of 1968, as amended (42 U.S.C. 4151–4157), and any regulations implementing it. In choosing among available methods for meeting the requirements of this section, the agency shall give priority to those methods that offer programs and activities to qualified handicapped persons in the most integrated setting appropriate.

(2) *Historic preservation programs.* In meeting the requirements of § 457.150(a) in historic preservation programs, the agency shall give priority to methods that provide physical access to handicapped persons. In cases where a physical alteration to an historic property is not required because of § 457.150(a)(2) or (a)(3), alternative methods of achieving program accessibility include—

(i) Using audio-visual materials and devices to depict those portions of an historic property that cannot otherwise be made accessible;

(ii) Assigning persons to guide handicapped persons into or through portions of historic properties that cannot otherwise be made accessible; or

(iii) Adopting other innovative methods.

(c) *Time period for compliance.* The agency shall comply with the obligations established under this section by October 21, 1986, except that where structural changes in facilities are undertaken, such changes shall be made by August 22, 1989, but in any event as expeditiously as possible.

(d) *Transition plan.* In the event that structural changes to facilities will be undertaken to achieve program accessibility, the agency shall develop, by February 23, 1987 a transition plan setting forth the steps necessary to complete such changes. The agency shall provide an opportunity to interested persons, including handicapped persons or organizations representing handicapped persons, to participate in the development of the transition plan by submitting comments (both oral and written). A copy of the transition plan shall be made available for public inspection. The plan shall, at a minimum—

(1) Identify physical obstacles in the agency's facilities that limit the accessibility of its programs or activities to handicapped persons;

(2) Describe in detail the methods that will be used to make the facilities accessible;

(3) Specify the schedule for taking the steps necessary to achieve compliance with this section and, if the time period of the transition plan is longer than one year, identify steps that will

be taken during each year of the transition period; and

(4) Indicate the official responsible for implementation of the plan.

§ 457.151 Program accessibility: New construction and alterations.

Each building or part of a building that is constructed or altered by, on behalf of, or for the use of the agency shall be designed, constructed, or altered so as to be readily accessible to and usable by handicapped persons. The definitions, requirements, and standards of the Architectural Barriers Act (42 U.S.C. 4151–4157), as established in 41 CFR 101–19.600 to 101–19.607, apply to buildings covered by this section.

§§ 457.152–457.159 [Reserved]

§ 457.160 Communications.

(a) The agency shall take appropriate steps to ensure effective communication with applicants, participants, personnel of other Federal entities, and members of the public.

(1) The agency shall furnish appropriate auxiliary aids where necessary to afford a handicapped person an equal opportunity to participate in, and enjoy the benefits of, a program or activity conducted by the agency.

(i) In determining what type of auxiliary aid is necessary, the agency shall give primary consideration to the requests of the handicapped person.

(ii) The agency need not provide individually prescribed devices, readers for personal use or study, or other devices of a personal nature.

(2) Where the agency communicates with applicants and beneficiaries by telephone, telecommunication devices for deaf person (TDD's) or equally effective telecommunication systems shall be used.

(b) The agency shall ensure that interested persons, including persons with impaired vision or hearing, can obtain information as to the existence and location of accessible services, activities, and facilities.

(c) The agency shall provide signage at a primary entrance to each of its inaccessible facilities, directing users to a location at which they can obtain information about accessible facilities. The international symbol for accessibility shall be used at each primary entrance of an accessible facility.

(d) This section does not require the agency to take any action that it can demonstrate would result in a fundamental alteration in the nature of a program or activity or in undue financial and administrative burdens. In those circumstances where agency personnel believe that the proposed action would fundamentally alter the program or activity or would result in undue financial and administrative burdens, the agency has the burden of proving that compliance with § 457.160 would result in such alteration or burdens. The decision that compliance would result in such alteration or burdens must be made by the agency head or his or her designee after considering all agency resources available for use in the funding and operation of the conducted program or activity, and must be accompanied by a written statement of the reasons for reaching that conclusion. If an action required to comply with this section would result in such an alteration or such burdens, the agency shall take any other action that would not result in such an alteration or such burdens but would nevertheless ensure that, to the maximum extent possible, handicapped persons receive the benefits and services of the program or activity.

§§ 457.161–457.169 [Reserved]

§ 457.170 Compliance procedures.

(a) Except as provided in paragraph (b) of this section, this section applies to all allegations of discrimination on the basis of handicap in programs or activities conducted by the agency.

(b) The agency shall process complaints alleging violations of section 504 with respect to employment according to the procedures established by the Equal Employment Opportunity Commission in 29 CFR part 1613 pursuant to section 501 of the Rehabilitation Act of 1973 (29 U.S.C. 791).

(c) The Executive Director shall be responsible for coordinating implementation of this section. Complaints may be sent to Equal Employment Opportunity Director, National Capital Planning Commission, 1325 G Street NW., Washington, DC 20576.

(d) The agency shall accept and investigate all complete complaints for which it has jurisdiction. All complete complaints must be filed within 180 days of the alleged act of discrimination. The agency may extend this time period for good cause.

(e) If the agency receives a complaint over which it does not have jurisdiction, it shall promptly notify the complainant and shall make reasonable efforts to refer the complaint to the appropriate government entity.

(f) The agency shall notify the Architectural and Transportation Barriers Compliance Board upon receipt of any complaint alleging that a building or facility that is subject to the Architectural Barriers Act of 1968, as amended (42 U.S.C. 4151–4157), or section 502 of the Rehabilitation Act of 1973, as amended (29 U.S.C. 792), is not readily accessible to and usable by handicapped persons.

(g) Within 180 days of the receipt of a complete complaint for which it has jurisdiction, the agency shall notify the complainant of the results of the investigation in a letter containing—

(1) Findings of fact and conclusions of law;

(2) A description of a remedy for each violation found; and

(3) A notice of the right to appeal.

(h) Appeals of the findings of fact and conclusions of law or remedies must be filed by the complainant within 90 days of receipt from the agency of the letter required by § 457.170(g). The agency may extend this time for good cause.

(i) Timely appeals shall be accepted and processed by the head of the agency.

(j) The head of the agency shall notify the complainant of the results of the appeal within 60 days of the receipt of the request. If the head of the agency determines that additional information is needed from the complainant, he or she shall have 60 days from the date of receipt of the additional information to make his or her determination on the appeal.

(k) The time limits cited in paragraphs (g) and (j) of this section may be extended with the permission of the Assistant Attorney General.

(l) The agency may delegate its authority for conducting complaint investigations to other Federal agencies, except that the authority for making the final determination may not be delegated to another agency.

[51 FR 22887, 22896, June 23, 1986, as amended at 51 FR 22888, June 23, 1986]

§§ 457.171–457.999 [Reserved]

PART 500—ENFORCEMENT OF NONDISCRIMINATION ON THE BASIS OF HANDICAP IN PROGRAMS OR ACTIVITIES CONDUCTED BY THE NATIONAL COMMISSION FOR EMPLOYMENT POLICY

AUTHORITY: 29 U.S.C. 794.

SOURCE: 51 FR 22888, 22896, June 23, 1986, unless otherwise noted.

§ 500.101 Purpose.

This part effectuates section 119 of the Rehabilitation, Comprehensive Services, and Developmental Disabilities Amendments of 1978, which amended section 504 of the Rehabilitation Act of 1973 to prohibit discrimination on the basis of handicap in programs or activities conducted by Executive agencies or the United States Postal Service.

§ 500.102 Application.

This part applies to all programs or activities conducted by the agency.

§500.103 Definitions.

For purposes of this part, the term—

Assistant Attorney General means the Assistant Attorney General, Civil Rights Division, United States Department of Justice.

Auxiliary aids means services or devices that enable persons with impaired sensory, manual, or speaking skills to have an equal opportunity to participate in, and enjoy the benefits of, programs or activities conducted by the agency. For example, auxiliary aids useful for persons with impaired vision include readers, brailled materials, audio recordings, telecommunications devices and other similar services and devices. Auxiliary aids useful for persons with impaired hearing include telephone handset amplifiers, telephones compatible with hearing aids, telecommunication devices for deaf persons (TDD's), interpreters, notetakers, written materials, and other similar services and devices.

Complete complaint means a written statement that contains the complainant's name and address and describes the agency's alleged discriminatory action in sufficient detail to inform the agency of the nature and date of the alleged violation of section 504. It shall be signed by the complainant or by someone authorized to do so on his or her behalf. Complaints filed on behalf of classes or third parties shall describe or identify (by name, if possible) the alleged victims of discrimination.

Facility means all or any portion of buildings, structures, equipment, roads, walks, parking lots, rolling stock or other conveyances, or other real or personal property.

Handicapped person means any person who has a physical or mental impairment that substantially limits one or more major life activities, has a record of such an impairment, or is regarded as having such an impairment.

As used in this definition, the phrase:

(1) *Physical or mental impairment* includes—

(i) Any physiological disorder or condition, cosmetic disfigurement, or anatomical loss affecting one or more of the following body systems: Neurological; musculoskeletal; special sense organs; respiratory, including speech organs; cardiovascular; reproductive; digestive; genitourinary; hemic and lymphatic; skin; and endocrine; or

(ii) Any mental or psychological disorder, such as mental retardation, organic brain syndrome, emotional or mental illness, and specific learning disabilities. The term *physical or mental impairment* includes, but is not limited to, such diseases and conditions as orthopedic, visual, speech, and hearing impairments, cerebral palsy, epilepsy, muscular dystrophy, multiple sclerosis, cancer, heart disease, diabetes, mental retardation, emotional illness, and drug addiction and alcoholism.

(2) *Major life activities* includes functions such as caring for one's self, performing manual tasks, walking, seeing, hearing, speaking, breathing, learning, and working.

(3) *Has a record of such an impairment* means has a history of, or has been misclassified as having, a mental or physical impairment that substantially limits one or more major life activities.

(4) *Is regarded as having an impairment* means—

(i) Has a physical or mental impairment that does not substantially limit major life activities but is treated by the agency as constituting such a limitation;

(ii) Has a physical or mental impairment that substantially limits major life activities only as a result of the attitudes of others toward such impairment; or

(iii) Has none of the impairments defined in subparagraph (1) of this definition but is treated by the agency as having such an impairment.

Historic preservation programs means programs conducted by the agency that have preservation of historic properties as a primary purpose.

Historic properties means those properties that are listed or eligible for listing in the National Register of Historic Places or properties designated as historic under a statute of the appropriate State or local government body.

Qualified handicapped person means—

(1) With respect to preschool, elementary, or secondary education services provided by the agency, a handicapped person who is a member of a class of persons otherwise entitled by statute,

regulation, or agency policy to receive education services from the agency.

(2) With respect to any other agency program or activity under which a person is required to perform services or to achieve a level of accomplishment, a handicapped person who meets the essential eligibility requirements and who can achieve the purpose of the program or activity without modifications in the program or activity that the agency can demonstrate would result in a fundamental alteration in its nature;

(3) With respect to any other program or activity, a handicapped person who meets the essential eligibility requirements for participation in, or receipt of benefits from, that program or activity; and

(4) *Qualified handicapped person* is defined for purposes of employment in 29 CFR 1613.702(f), which is made applicable to this part by § 500.140.

Section 504 means section 504 of the Rehabilitation Act of 1973 (Pub. L. 93–112, 87 Stat. 394 (29 U.S.C. 794)), as amended by the Rehabilitation Act Amendments of 1974 (Pub. L. 93–516, 88 Stat. 1617), and the Rehabilitation, Comprehensive Services, and Developmental Disabilities Amendments of 1978 (Pub. L. 95–602, 92 Stat. 2955). As used in this part, section 504 applies only to programs or activities conducted by Executive agencies and not to federally assisted programs.

Substantial impairment means a significant loss of the integrity of finished materials, design quality, or special character resulting from a permanent alteration.

§§ 500.104–500.109 [Reserved]

§ 500.110 Self-evaluation.

(a) The agency shall, by August 24, 1987, evaluate its current policies and practices, and the effects thereof, that do not or may not meet the requirements of this part, and, to the extent modification of any such policies and practices is required, the agency shall proceed to make the necessary modifications.

(b) The agency shall provide an opportunity to interested persons, including handicapped persons or organizations representing handicapped persons, to participate in the self-evaluation process by submitting comments (both oral and written).

(c) The agency shall, until three years following the completion of the self-evaluation, maintain on file and make available for public inspection:

(1) a description of areas examined and any problems identified, and

(2) a description of any modifications made.

§ 500.111 Notice.

The agency shall make available to employees, applicants, participants, beneficiaries, and other interested persons such information regarding the provisions of this part and its applicability to the programs or activities conducted by the agency, and make such information available to them in such manner as the head of the agency finds necessary to apprise such persons of the protections against discrimination assured them by section 504 and this regulation.

§§ 500.112–500.129 [Reserved]

§ 500.130 General prohibitions against discrimination.

(a) No qualified handicapped person shall, on the basis of handicap, be excluded from participation in, be denied the benefits of, or otherwise be subjected to discrimination under any program or activity conducted by the agency.

(b)(1) The agency, in providing any aid, benefit, or service, may not, directly or through contractual, licensing, or other arrangements, on the basis of handicap—

(i) Deny a qualified handicapped person the opportunity to participate in or benefit from the aid, benefit, or service;

(ii) Afford a qualified handicapped person an opportunity to participate in or benefit from the aid, benefit, or service that is not equal to that afforded others;

(iii) Provide a qualified handicapped person with an aid, benefit, or service that is not as effective in affording equal opportunity to obtain the same result, to gain the same benefit, or to reach the same level of achievement as that provided to others;

(iv) Provide different or separate aid, benefits, or services to handicapped persons or to any class of handicapped persons than is provided to others unless such action is necessary to provide qualified handicapped persons with aid, benefits, or services that are as effective as those provided to others;

(v) Deny a qualified handicapped person the opportunity to participate as a member of planning or advisory boards; or

(vi) Otherwise limit a qualified handicapped person in the enjoyment of any right, privilege, advantage, or opportunity enjoyed by others receiving the aid, benefit, or service.

(2) The agency may not deny a qualified handicapped person the opportunity to participate in programs or activities that are not separate or different, despite the existence of permissibly separate or different programs or activities.

(3) The agency may not, directly or through contractual or other arrangments, utilize criteria or methods of administration the purpose or effect of which would—

(i) Subject qualified handicapped persons to discrimination on the basis of handicap; or

(ii) Defeat or substantially impair accomplishment of the objectives of a program or activity with respect to handicapped persons.

(4) The agency may not, in determining the site or location of a facility, make selections the purpose or effect of which would—

(i) Exclude handicapped persons from, deny them the benefits of, or otherwise subject them to discrimination under any program or activity conducted by the agency; or

(ii) Defeat or substantially impair the accomplishment of the objectives of a program or activity with respect to handicapped persons.

(5) The agency, in the selection of procurement contractors, may not use criteria that subject qualified handicapped persons to discrimination on the basis of handicap.

(6) The agency may not administer a licensing or certification program in a manner that subjects qualified handicapped persons to discrimination on the basis of handicap, nor may the agency establish requirements for the programs or activities of licensees or certified entities that subject qualified handicapped persons to discrimination on the basis of handicap. However, the programs or activities of entities that are licensed or certified by the agency are not, themselves, covered by this part.

(c) The exclusion of nonhandicapped persons from the benefits of a program limited by Federal statute or Executive order to handicapped persons or the exclusion of a specific class of handicapped persons from a program limited by Federal statute or Executive order to a different class of handicapped persons is not prohibited by this part.

(d) The agency shall administer programs and activities in the most integrated setting appropriate to the needs of qualified handicapped persons.

§§ 500.131–500.139 [Reserved]

§ 500.140 Employment.

No qualified handicapped person shall, on the basis of handicap, be subjected to discrimination in employment under any program or activity conducted by the agency. The definitions, requirements, and procedures of section 501 of the Rehabilitation Act of 1973 (29 U.S.C. 791), as established by the Equal Employment Opportunity Commission in 29 CFR part 1613, shall apply to employment in federally conducted programs or activities.

§§ 500.141–500.148 [Reserved]

§ 500.149 Program accessibility: Discrimination prohibited.

Except as otherwise provided in § 500.150, no qualified handicapped person shall, because the agency's facilities are inaccessible to or unusable by handicapped persons, be denied the benefits of, be excluded from participation in, or otherwise be subjected to discrimination under any program or activity conducted by the agency.

§ 500.150 Program accessibility: Existing facilities.

(a) *General.* The agency shall operate each program or activity so that the program or activity, when viewed in its entirety, is readily accessible to and usable by handicapped persons. This paragraph does not—

(1) Necessarily require the agency to make each of its existing facilities accessible to and usable by handicapped persons;

(2) In the case of historic preservation programs, require the agency to take any action that would result in a substantial impairment of significant historic features of an historic property; or

(3) Require the agency to take any action that it can demonstrate would result in a fundamental alteration in the nature of a program or activity or in undue financial and administrative burdens. In those circumstances where agency personnel believe that the proposed action would fundamentally alter the program or activity or would result in undue financial and administrative burdens, the agency has the burden of proving that compliance with § 500.150(a) would result in such alteration or burdens. The decision that compliance would result in such alteration or burdens must be made by the agency head or his or her designee after considering all agency resources available for use in the funding and operation of the conducted program or activity, and must be accompanied by a written statement of the reasons for reaching that conclusion. If an action would result in such an alteration or such burdens, the agency shall take any other action that would not result in such an alteration or such burdens but would nevertheless ensure that handicapped persons receive the benefits and services of the program or activity.

(b) *Methods*—(1) *General.* The agency may comply with the requirements of this section through such means as redesign of equipment, reassignment of services to accessible buildings, assignment of aides to beneficiaries, home visits, delivery of services at alternate accessible sites, alteration of existing facilities and construction of new facilities, use of accessible rolling stock, or any other methods that result in making its programs or activities readily accessible to and usable by handicapped persons. The agency is not required to make structural changes in existing facilities where other methods are effective in achieving compliance with this section. The agency, in making alterations to existing buildings, shall meet accessibility requirements to the extent compelled by the Architectural Barriers Act of 1968, as amended (42 U.S.C. 4151–4157), and any regulations implementing it. In choosing among available methods for meeting the requirements of this section, the agency shall give priority to those methods that offer programs and activities to qualified handicapped persons in the most integrated setting appropriate.

(2) *Historic preservation programs.* In meeting the requirements of § 500.150(a) in historic preservation programs, the agency shall give priority to methods that provide physical access to handicapped persons. In cases where a physical alteration to an historic property is not required because of § 500.150(a)(2) or (a)(3), alternative methods of achieving program accessibility include—

(i) Using audio-visual materials and devices to depict those portions of an historic property that cannot otherwise be made accessible;

(ii) Assigning persons to guide handicapped persons into or through portions of historic properties that cannot otherwise be made accessible; or

(iii) Adopting other innovative methods.

(c) *Time period for compliance.* The agency shall comply with the obligations established under this section by October 21, 1986, except that where structural changes in facilities are undertaken, such changes shall be made by August 22, 1989, but in any event as expeditiously as possible.

(d) *Transition plan.* In the event that structural changes to facilities will be undertaken to achieve program accessibility, the agency shall develop, by February 23, 1987 a transition plan setting forth the steps necessary to complete such changes. The agency shall provide an opportunity to interested persons, including handicapped persons or organizations representing handicapped persons, to participate in the development of the transition plan by submitting comments (both oral and written). A copy of the transition plan shall be made available for public inspection. The plan shall, at a minimum—

(1) Identify physical obstacles in the agency's facilities that limit the accessibility of its programs or activities to handicapped persons;

(2) Describe in detail the methods that will be used to make the facilities accessible;

(3) Specify the schedule for taking the steps necessary to achieve compliance with this section and, if the time period of the transition plan is longer than one year, identify steps that will be taken during each year of the transition period; and

(4) Indicate the official responsible for implementation of the plan.

§ 500.151 **Program accessibility: New construction and alterations.**

Each building or part of a building that is constructed or altered by, on behalf of, or for the use of the agency shall be designed, constructed, or altered so as to be readily accessible to and usable by handicapped persons. The definitions, requirements, and standards of the Architectural Barriers Act (42 U.S.C. 4151–4157), as established in 41 CFR 101–19.600 to 101–19.607, apply to buildings covered by this section.

§§ 500.152–500.159 **[Reserved]**

§ 500.160 **Communications.**

(a) The agency shall take appropriate steps to ensure effective communication with applicants, participants, personnel of other Federal entities, and members of the public.

(1) The agency shall furnish appropriate auxiliary aids where necessary to afford a handicapped person an equal opportunity to participate in, and enjoy the benefits of, a program or activity conducted by the agency.

(i) In determining what type of auxiliary aid is necessary, the agency shall give primary consideration to the requests of the handicapped person.

(ii) The agency need not provide individually prescribed devices, readers for personal use or study, or other devices of a personal nature.

(2) Where the agency communicates with applicants and beneficiaries by telephone, telecommunication devices for deaf person (TDD's) or equally effective telecommunication systems shall be used.

(b) The agency shall ensure that interested persons, including persons with impaired vision or hearing, can obtain information as to the existence and location of accessible services, activities, and facilities.

(c) The agency shall provide signage at a primary entrance to each of its inaccessible facilities, directing users to a location at which they can obtain information about accessible facilities. The international symbol for accessibility shall be used at each primary entrance of an accessible facility.

(d) This section does not require the agency to take any action that it can demonstrate would result in a fundamental alteration in the nature of a program or activity or in undue financial and adminstrative burdens. In those circumstances where agency personnel believe that the proposed action would fundamentally alter the program or activity or would result in undue financial and administrative burdens, the agency has the burden of proving that compliance with § 500.160 would result in such alteration or burdens. The decision that compliance would result in such alteration or burdens must be made by the agency head or his or her designee after considering all agency resources available for use in the funding and operation of the conducted program or activity, and must be accompanied by a written statement of the reasons for reaching that conclusion. If an action required to comply with this section would result in such an alteration or such burdens, the agency shall take any other action that would not result in such an alteration or such burdens but would nevertheless ensure that, to the maximum extent possible, handicapped persons receive the benefits and services of the program or activity.

§§ 500.161–500.169 **[Reserved]**

§ 500.170 **Compliance procedures.**

(a) Except as provided in paragraph (b) of this section, this section applies to all allegations of discrimination on the basis of handicap in programs or activities conducted by the agency.

(b) The agency shall process complaints alleging violations of section 504 with respect to employment according to the procedures established by the Equal Employment Opportunity Commission in 29 CFR part 1613 pursuant to section 501 of the Rehabilitation Act of 1973 (29 U.S.C. 791).

(c) The Director shall be responsible for coordinating implementation of this section. Complaints may be sent to Director, National Commission for Employment Policy, Suite 300, 1522 K Street NW., Washington, DC 20005.

(d) The agency shall accept and investigate all complete complaints for which it has jurisdiction. All complete complaints must be filed within 180 days of the alleged act of discrimination. The agency may extend this time period for good cause.

(e) If the agency receives a complaint over which it does not have jurisdiction, it shall promptly notify the complainant and shall make reasonable efforts to refer the complaint to the appropriate government entity.

(f) The agency shall notify the Architectural and Transportation Barriers Compliance Board upon receipt of any complaint alleging that a building or facility that is subject to the Architectural Barriers Act of 1968, as amended (42 U.S.C. 4151–4157), or section 502 of the Rehabilitation Act of 1973, as amended (29 U.S.C. 792), is not readily accessible to and usable by handicapped persons.

(g) Within 180 days of the receipt of a complete complaint for which it has jurisdiction, the agency shall notify the complainant of the results of the investigation in a letter containing—

(1) Findings of fact and conclusions of law;

(2) A description of a remedy for each violation found; and

(3) A notice of the right to appeal.

(h) Appeals of the findings of fact and conclusions of law or remedies must be filed by the complainant within 90 days of receipt from the agency of the letter required by § 500.170(g). The agency may extend this time for good cause.

(i) Timely appeals shall be accepted and processed by the head of the agency.

(j) The head of the agency shall notify the complainant of the results of the appeal within 60 days of the receipt of the request. If the head of the agency determines that additional information is needed from the complainant, he or she shall have 60 days from the date of receipt of the additional information to make his or her determination on the appeal.

(k) The time limits cited in paragraphs (g) and (j) of this section may be extended with the permission of the Assistant Attorney General.

(l) The agency may delegate its authority for conducting complaint investigations to other Federal agencies, except that the authority for making the final determination may not be delegated to another agency.

[51 FR 22888, 22896, June 23, 1986, as amended at 51 FR 22888, June 23, 1986]

§§ 500.171–500.999   [Reserved]

CHAPTER V   [RESERVED]

CHAPTER VI—NATIONAL CAPITAL PLANNING COMMISSION

PART 600 [RESERVED]

PART 601—IMPLEMENTATION OF THE NATIONAL ENVIRONMENTAL POLICY ACT

Subpart A—General

Subpart B—Lead and Cooperating Agencies

Subpart C—NEPA Submission Schedules

Subpart D—Initiating the NEPA Process

Subpart E—Environmental Assessments

Subpart F—Environmental Impact Statements

Subpart G—Dispute Resolution

AUTHORITY: 42 U.S.C. 4371; 40 CFR 1507.3

SOURCE: 82 FR 45424, Sept. 29, 2017; 82 FR 48609, Oct. 19, 2017, unless otherwise noted.

Subpart A—General

§ 601.1 Purpose.

This part establishes rules that supplement the Council on Environmental Quality's (CEQ) National Environmental Policy Act (NEPA) regulations that the National Capital Planning Commission (NCPC or Commission) and its applicants shall follow to ensure:

(a) Compliance with NEPA, as amended (42 U.S.C. 4321 *et seq.*) and CEQ regulations for implementing the procedural provisions of NEPA (40 CFR parts 1501 through 1508).

(b) Compliance with other laws, regulations, and Executive Orders identified by NCPC as applicable to a particular application.

§ 601.2 Policies.

Consistent with 40 CFR 1500.1 and 1500.2, it shall be the policy of the NCPC to:

(a) Comply with the procedures and policies of NEPA and other related laws, regulations, and orders applicable to Commission actions.

(b) Provide applicants sufficient guidance to ensure plans and projects comply with the rules of this part and other laws, regulations, and orders applicable to Commission actions.

(c) Integrate NEPA into its decision-making process at the earliest possible stage.

(d) Integrate the requirements of NEPA and other planning and environmental reviews required by law including, without limitation, the National Historic Preservation Act, 54 U.S.C.

306108 (NHPA), to ensure all such procedures run concurrently.

(e) Use the NEPA process to identify and assess the reasonable alternatives to proposed actions that will avoid or minimize adverse effects on the quality of the human environment in the National Capital Region.

(f) Use all practicable means to protect, restore, and enhance the quality of the human environment including the built and socioeconomic environments and historic properties within the National Capital Region.

(g) Streamline the NEPA process and Environmental Impact Statements (EIS) to the maximum extent possible.

(h) Use the NEPA process to assure orderly and effective NCPC decision-making and to foster meaningful public involvement in NCPC's decisions.

§ 601.3   Definitions.

For purposes of this part, the following definitions shall apply:

Administrative Record means a compilation of all materials (written and electronic) that were before the agency at the time it made its final decision. An Administrative Record documents an agency's decision-making process and the basis for the decision.

Categorical Exclusion or *CATEX* means, as defined by 40 CFR 1508.4, a category of actions which do not individually or cumulatively have a significant effect on the human environment except under Extraordinary Circumstances and which have been found to have no such effect in procedures adopted by a Federal Agency (NCPC) in implementation of CEQ's regulations and for which, therefore, neither an Environmental Assessment (EA) nor an EIS is required.

Central Area means the geographic area in the District of Columbia comprised of the Shaw School and Downtown Urban Renewal Areas or such other area as the District of Columbia and NCPC shall subsequently jointly determine.

Chairman means the Chairman of the National Capital Planning Commission appointed by the President, pursuant to 40 U.S.C. 8711(c).

Commemorative Works Act or *CWA* means the Federal law codified at 40 U.S.C. 8901 *et seq.* that sets forth the requirements for the location and development of new memorials and monuments on land under the jurisdiction of the National Park Service (NPS) or the General Services Administration (GSA) in the District of Columbia and its Environs.

Commission means the National Capital Planning Commission created by 40 U.S.C. 8711.

Comprehensive Plan means The Comprehensive Plan for the National Capital: Federal Elements prepared and adopted by the Commission pursuant to 40 U.S.C. 8721(a).

Cooperating Agency means, as defined in 40 CFR 1508.5, any Federal Agency other than a Lead Agency that has jurisdiction by law or special expertise with respect to a proposal (or reasonable alternative) for legislation or other major action significantly affecting the quality of the human environment; a state or local agency of similar qualifications; or when the effects are on a reservation, an Indian Tribe when agreed to by the Lead Agency.

Cumulative impact means, as defined in 40 CFR 1508.7, the impact on the environment that results from the incremental impact of an action when added to other past, present, and reasonably foreseeable future actions regardless of what agency (Federal or Non-Federal) or person undertakes such other actions. Cumulative impacts can result from individually minor, but collectively significant, actions taking place over a period of time.

Emergency Circumstances means a sudden and serious occurrence or situation requiring immediate attention to protect the lives and safety of the public and protect property and ecological resources and functions from imminent harm.

Environmental Assessment or *EA* means, as defined in 40 CFR 1508.9, a concise document for which a Federal Agency is responsible that serves to briefly provide sufficient evidence and analysis for determining whether to prepare an EIS or a FONSI; aid an agency's compliance with NEPA when no EIS is necessary; facilitate preparation of an EIS when one is necessary; and includes a brief discussion of the need for the proposal, alternatives as required by section 102(2)(E) of NEPA, the environmental impacts of the proposed action and alternatives, and a listing of agencies and persons consulted.

Environmental Document means, as set forth in 40 CFR 1508.10, an Environmental Assessment, and Environmental Impact Statement, and for purposes of these regulations, a Categorical Exclusion determination.

Environmental Impact Statement or *EIS* means, as defined in 40 CFR 1508.11, a detailed written statement as required by 42 U.S.C. 4332(2)(C).

Environs means the territory surrounding the District of Columbia included in the National Capital Region pursuant to 40 U.S.C. 8702(a)(1).

Executive Director means the Executive Director employed by the National Capital Planning Commission pursuant to 40 U.S.C. 8711(d).

Executive Director's Recommendation or *EDR* means a concise written report and recommendation prepared by NCPC staff under the direction of NCPC's Executive Director regarding a proposed action that is transmitted to the Commission for its consideration.

Extraordinary Circumstances means special circumstances that when present negate an agency's ability to categorically exclude a project and require an agency to undertake further NEPA review.

Federal Agency means the executive agencies of the Federal government as defined in 5 U.S.C. 105.

Finding of No Significant Impact or *FONSI* means, as defined at 40 CFR 1508.13, a document prepared by NCPC or a Federal Agency applicant that briefly presents the reasons why an action, not otherwise excluded (40 CFR 1508.4), will not have a significant effect on the human environment and for which an EIS will not be prepared. It shall include the EA or a summary of it and shall note any other EAs or EISs related to it (40 CFR 1501.7(a)(5)). If the EA is included in the FONSI, the FONSI need not repeat any of the discussion in the EA but may include the EA by reference.

Lead Agency means, as defined in 40 CFR 1508.16, the agency or agencies preparing or having primary responsibility for preparing an EA or an EIS.

Memorandum of Agreement or *MOA* means for purposes of implementing the regulations in this part, a written agreement entered into between a Lead, Co-lead, Cooperating Agency, or a Non-Federal Agency to facilitate implementation of NEPA and preparation of the requisite environmental documentation. A MOA can be written at a programmatic level to apply to all projects involving NCPC and particular applicant or on a project-by-project basis.

Mitigation means, as defined in 40 CFR 1508.20, avoiding an impact altogether by not taking a certain action or parts of an action; minimizing impacts by limiting the degree or magnitude of the action and its implementation; rectifying the impact by repairing, rehabilitating, or restoring the affected environment; reducing or eliminating the impact over time by preservation and maintenance operations during the life of the action; and compensating for the impact by replacing or providing substitute resources or environments.

Monumental Core means the general area encompassed by the U.S. Capitol grounds, the National Mall, the Washington Monument grounds, the White House grounds, the Ellipse, West Potomac Park, East Potomac Park, the Southwest Federal Center, the Federal Triangle area, President's Park, the Northwest Rectangle, Arlington Cemetery and the Pentagon area, and Joint Base Myer-Henderson Hall.

National Capital Planning Act means the July 1952 legislative enactment, codified at 40 U.S.C. 8701 *et seq.* that created the present day National Capital Planning Commission and conferred authority upon it to serve as the planning authority for the Federal government in the National Capital Region.

National Capital Region means, as defined in 40 U.S.C. 8702(2), the District of Columbia; Montgomery and Prince Georges Counties in Maryland; Arlington Fairfax, Loudon, and Prince William Counties in Virginia; and all cities in Maryland or Virginia in the geographic area bounded by the outer boundaries of the combined area of the counties listed.

Non-Federal Agency for purposes of the National Environmental Policy Act and the regulations in this part means those applicants outside the definition of Federal Agency that prepare plans for or undertake projects on land within the National Capital Region subject to NCPC's jurisdiction. Non-Federal Agencies include, without limitation, the Smithsonian Institution, the John F. Kennedy Center for the Performing Arts, the National Gallery of Art, the United States Institute of Peace, the Government of the District of Columbia, private parties undertaking development on Federal land, and the Maryland National Capital Parks and Planning Commission. In most instances, the Non-Federal Agency has legal jurisdiction over the project and special expertise relative to the project's components.

Notice of Availability or *NOA* means a public notice or other means of public communication that announces the availability of an EA or an EIS for public review.

Notice of Intent or *NOI* means, as defined in 40 CFR 1508.22, a notice published in the FEDERAL REGISTER that an EIS will be prepared and considered. The notice shall briefly describe the proposed action and possible alternatives; describe the agency's proposed Public Scoping process including whether, when, and where any Public Scoping meeting will be held; and state the name and address of a person within the agency who can answer questions about the proposed action and the EIS. For purposes of NCPC implementation of NEPA, NCPC may determine, at its sole discretion, to publish an NOI that an EA will be prepared and considered.

Purpose and need as described in 40 CFR 1502.13 means the underlying purpose and need for agency action to which the agency is responding in proposing the alternatives including the proposed action.

Programmatic NEPA Review means a broad or high level NEPA review that assesses the environmental impacts of proposed policies, plans or programs, or projects for which subsequent project or site-specific NEPA analysis will be conducted. A Programmatic NEPA Review utilizes a tiering approach.

Record of Decision or *ROD* means a concise public record of an agency's decision in cases requiring an EIS that is prepared in accordance with 40 CFR 1505.2.

Scope means, as defined in 40 U.S.C. 1508.25, the range of actions (connected, cumulative and similar); alternatives (no action, other reasonable courses of action; and Mitigation measures not included in the proposed action); and impacts (direct, indirect and cumulative) considered in an EIS or an EA. The process of defining and determining the scope of issues to be addressed in an EIS or EA with public involvement shall be referred to as *Public Scoping.* Internal scoping activities shall be referred to by the word scoping without capitalization.

Submission Guidelines means the formally-adopted document which describes the application process and application requirements for projects requiring review by the Commission.

Tiering means, as defined in 40 CFR 1508.28, an approach where Federal Agency applicants, NCPC on behalf of Non-Federal Agency applicants, or NCPC for its own projects initially consider the broad, general impacts of a proposed program, plan, policy, or large scale project—or at the early stage of a phased proposal—and then conduct subsequent narrower, decision focused reviews.

Subpart B—Lead and Cooperating Agencies

§ 601.4 Designation of Lead Agency.

(a) A Federal Agency applicant shall serve as the Lead Agency and prepare an EA or an EIS for:

(1) An application that requires Commission approval; and

(2) An application for action on a master plan that includes future projects that require Commission approval; provided that:

(i) The applicant intends to submit individual projects covered by the master plan to the Commission within five years of the date of Commission action on the master plan; and

(ii) The applicant intends to use the master plan EA or EIS to satisfy its NEPA obligation for specific projects referenced in the master plan.

(b) NCPC shall serve as Lead Agency and prepare an EA or an EIS for:

(1) An application submitted by a Non-Federal Agency that requires Commission approval;

(2) An application submitted by a Non-Federal Agency for action on a master plan that includes future projects that require Commission approval; provided that:

(i) The Non-Federal Agency applicant intends to submit individual projects covered by the master plan to the Commission within five years of the date of Commission action on the master plan; and

(ii) The Non-Federal Agency applicant intends to use the master plan EA or EIS to satisfy its NEPA obligation for a specific project referenced in the master plan; and

(3) An application for approval of land acquisitions undertaken pursuant to 40 U.S.C. 8731–8732.

§ 601.5 Lead Agency obligations.

(a) The obligations of a Federal Agency applicant designated as the Lead Agency in accordance with § 601.4(a) shall include, without limitation, the following:

(1) Act as Lead Agency as defined in 40 CFR 1501.5 for the NEPA process.

(2) Integrate other environmental reviews and other applicable regulatory requirements to include, without limitation, Section 106 of the NHPA.

(3) Allow NCPC, to participate as a Co-lead or Cooperating Agency, as appropriate, and consult with Commission staff as early as possible in the planning process to obtain guidance with respect to the goals, objectives, standards, purpose, need, and alternatives for the NEPA analysis.

(4) Invite affected Federal, state, regional and local agencies to participate as a Cooperating Agency in the NEPA process.

(5) Consult with the affected agencies as early as possible in the planning process to obtain guidance on the goals, objectives, standards, purpose, need, and alternatives for the NEPA analysis.

(6) Work with Cooperating Agencies and stakeholders in the following manner:

(i) Keep them informed on the project schedule and substantive matters; and

(ii) Allow them an opportunity to review and comment within reasonable time frames on, without limitation, Public Scoping notices; technical reports; public materials (including responses to comments received from the public); potential Mitigation measures; the draft EA or EIS; and the draft FONSI or ROD.

(7) Prepare the appropriate Environmental Document consistent with the applicant's NEPA regulations, the requirements of this part, and CEQ regulations. If the Lead Agency applies a CATEX and NCPC as Cooperating Agency does not have a corresponding CATEX that it can apply, the Lead Agency shall prepare an EA to satisfy NCPC's NEPA requirement.

(8) Determine in its Environmental Document whether an action will have an adverse environmental impact or would limit the choice of reasonable alternatives under 40 CFR 1505.1(e) and take appropriate action to ensure that the objectives and procedures of NEPA are achieved.

(9) Prepare, make available for public review, and issue a FONSI or ROD.

(10) Ensure that the draft and final EIS comply with the requirements of 40 CFR 1506.5(c) and include a disclosure statement executed by any contractor (or subcontractor) under contract to prepare the EIS document and that the disclosure appears as an appendix to the EIS.

(11) Compile, maintain, and produce the Administrative Record.

(12) Provide periodic reports on implementation of Mitigation measures to NCPC and other Cooperating Parties consistent with a schedule established in the Environmental Document. All such reports shall be posted on NCPC's Web site.

(13) For an application that has yet to obtain final Commission approval, re-evaluate and update Environmental Documents that are five or more years old as measured from the time of their adoption when either or both of the following criteria apply:

(i) There are substantial changes to the proposed action that are relevant to environmental concerns.

(ii) There are significant new circumstances or information that are relevant to environmental concerns and have a bearing on the proposed action or its impacts.

(14) Consult with NCPC on the outcome of the re-evaluation of its Environmental Document; provided that if NCPC disagrees with the Lead Agency's conclusion on the need to update its Environmental Document, NCPC may, at its sole discretion, either prepare its own Environmental Document or decline to consider the application.

(b) When NCPC serves as Lead Agency in accordance with § 601.4(b), in addition to the obligations listed in paragraphs (a)(1) through (14) of this section, NCPC shall:

(1) Require Non-Federal Agency applicants other than the District of Columbia and the Maryland National Capital Parks and Planning Commission to enter into a MOA with NCPC. In the MOA, and in subsequent implementation thereof, the Non-Federal Agency shall commit to providing all necessary assistance to facilitate and ensure NCPC's compliance with its NEPA obligation.

(2) The MOA may be prepared as a programmatic MOA that addresses a uniform approach for the treatment of all applications from a particular Non-Federal Agency applicant or address a specific Non-Federal Agency application. The request to enter into a project specific MOA shall be made after a determination is made as to the inability to utilize a CATEX.

(3) A MOA with a Non-Federal Agency shall specify, without limitation, roles and responsibilities; project information necessary to prepare the proper Environmental Document; project timelines and submission schedules; the submission of periodic reports on implementation of Mitigation measures, principal contacts and contact information; and a mechanism for resolving disputes.

(4) Upon adoption of the MOA, NCPC shall publish the MOA in the FEDERAL REGISTER and post it on NCPC's Web site.

§ 601.6 Resolving disputes over Lead Agency status.

(a) In the event of a dispute with a Federal Agency applicant over Co-Lead Agency status, the parties shall use their best efforts to cooperatively resolve disputes at the working levels of their respective agencies and, if necessary, by elevating such disputes within their respective agencies.

(b) If internal resolution at higher agency levels proves unsuccessful, at NCPC's sole discretion, one of the following actions shall be pursued: The parties shall request CEQ's determination on which agency shall serve as Lead, or NCPC shall prepare its own Environmental Document, or NCPC shall decline to take action on the underlying application.

(c) Disputes other than those relating to the designation of Lead Agency status or Cooperating Agency status as described in § 601.7(b), shall be governed by the requirements of subpart G of this part.

§ 601.7 Cooperating Agencies.

(a) When a Federal Agency applicant serves as the Lead Agency, NCPC shall act as a Cooperating Agency. As a Cooperating Agency, NCPC shall, without limitation, undertake the following:

(1) Act as a Cooperating Agency as described in 40 CFR 1501.6.

(2) Assist in the preparation of and sign a MOA with terms agreeable to NCPC if requested by the Lead Agency. At the Lead Agency's discretion, the MOA may be prepared as a programmatic MOA that addresses a uniform approach for the treatment of all applications where NCPC serves as a Cooperating Agency or address a specific application. The request to enter into a project specific MOA shall be made after a determination is made by the Lead Agency on the inability to utilize a CATEX.

(3) Participate in the NEPA process by providing comprehensive, timely reviews of and comments on key NEPA materials including, without limitation, Public Scoping notices; technical reports; documents (including responses to comments received from the public); the draft and final EA or EIS; and the Draft FONSI or ROD.

(4) Supply available data, assessments, and other information that may be helpful in the preparation of the Environmental Document or the Administrative Record in a timely manner.

(5) Make an independent evaluation of the Federal Agency applicant's Environmental Document and take responsibility for the scope and contents of the EIS or EA when it is sufficient as required by 40 CFR 1506.5.

(6) Prepare and, following Commission final approval of an application, sign a FONSI or ROD. Alternatively, if NCPC concurs with the a Federal Agency's FONSI or ROD, NCPC may co-sign the Federal Agency's document following the Commission's final approval of an application if co-signing is consistent with the Federal Agency's NEPA regulations.

(7) Provide documentation requested and needed by the Lead Agency for the Administrative Record.

(b) In the event a Federal Agency applicant fails to allow NCPC to participate in a meaningful manner as a Cooperating Agency, the parties shall agree to use their best efforts to cooperatively resolve the issue at the working levels of their respective agencies, and, if necessary, by elevating the issue within their respective agencies. If internal resolution at higher agency levels is unsuccessful, the parties may agree to seek mediation. Alternatively, NCPC may prepare its own Environmental Document either as a stand-alone document or a supplement to the Federal Agency applicant's Environmental Document or take no action on the underlying application.

Subpart C—NEPA Submission Schedules

§601.8 NEPA submission schedule for applications governed by the National Capital Planning Act.

(a) *NEPA compliance requirements.* Federal Agency applicants, and NCPC for non-Federal Agency applications, shall comply with NEPA for the following types of projects:

(1) Projects requiring Commission approval; and

(2) Master plans requiring Commission action with future projects requir-ing subsequent Commission approval; provided that:

(i) The applicant intends to submit individual projects depicted in the master plan to the Commission within five years of the date of Commission action on the master plan; and

(ii) The applicant intends to use the master plan EA or EIS to satisfy its NEPA obligation for specific projects referenced in the master plan.

(b) *Timing of NEPA compliance.* When Federal Agency and Non-Federal Agency applicants submit projects of the type described in paragraph (a) of this section, the Federal Agency applicant or NCPC for a Non-Federal agency application shall submit the requisite Environmental Documentation timed to coincide with the Commission's review stages as set forth in paragraphs (c) through (f) of this section.

(c) *Concept review.* The NEPA Public Scoping process shall have been initiated by the Federal Agency applicant or NCPC for a Non-Federal Agency application before the applicant submits an application for concept review. Alternatively, if the Federal Agency applicant or NCPC is contemplating use of a CATEX, the initiation of the Public Scoping process may be deferred until the final decision on use of a CATEX is made. Any NEPA information available at the time of concept review shall be submitted by the Federal Agency applicant or NCPC for a Non-Federal Agency application to facilitate effective Commission concept review.

(d) *Preliminary review.* A Draft Environmental Document shall be issued or published before the applicant submits an application for preliminary review. The NEPA information shall be provided to the Commission to facilitate the Commission's preliminary review and the provision of meaningful Commission comments and direction.

(e) *Final review.* (1) At the time a Non-Federal Agency submits an application for final approval, the determination (FONSI or ROD) resulting from the Environmental Document shall be submitted by NCPC in a form consistent with the rules of this part. At the time a Federal Agency applicant submits an application to the

103

Commission for final review, the Federal Agency applicant shall submit a determination (FONSI or ROD) in a form consistent with the applicant's NEPA regulations. As a Cooperating Agency, NCPC may co-sign the Federal Agency's FONSI or ROD following final Commission approval if co-signing is consistent with the Federal Agency's NEPA regulations. Alternatively, NCPC may prepare and sign its own independent document in accordance with the requirements of §§ 601.16(a) or 601.25(a) through (c).

(2) If at the time of final review, the Commission denies a Federal Agency applicant's project and requests changes thereto, the Federal Agency applicant shall proceed in a manner consistent with applicable law. The Federal Agency applicant may pursue, among others, the option of revising the project in a manner responsive to the Commission's comments. If the Federal Agency pursues this option, it shall review and consider the need for possible changes to its Environmental Document and its FONSI or ROD. Upon resubmission of a revised application for final review, the applicant shall submit a revised Environmental Document and a revised FONSI or ROD if in its judgement revised documents are necessary. If NCPC and the applicant disagree regarding the need for a revised Environmental Document and FONSI or ROD, the parties shall work together to resolve their differences. The final decision regarding the need for a revised Environmental Document and a revised FONSI or ROD shall be made by the Commission's Executive Committee.

(f) *Deviations from the submission schedule for Emergency Circumstances.* (1) This paragraph (f) applies when the following three conditions exist: NCPC is the Lead Agency; Emergency Circumstances exist; and an Extraordinary Circumstance as set forth in § 601.11 is present that precludes use of a CATEX.

(2) When the three conditions described above exist, NCPC shall undertake one of the following actions:

(i) When Emergency Circumstances render it necessary to take an action that requires an EA, the Executive Director shall prepare a concise, focused EA consistent with CEQ guidance. At the earliest opportunity, the Commission shall grant approval for the EA.

(ii) Where Emergency Circumstances make it necessary for the Commission to take an action with significant environmental impact without observing the provisions of these regulations, NCPC shall consult with CEQ about alternative arrangements. NCPC will limit such arrangements to actions necessary to control the immediate impacts of the emergency. Other actions remain subject to NEPA review.

§ 601.9 NEPA submission schedule for applications governed by the Commemorative Works Act.

(a) *Timing of NEPA compliance.* When, pursuant to the Commemorative Works Act, the National Park Service (NPS) or the General Services Administration (GSA) submits an application to the Commission for approval of a site and design for a commemorative work, NPS or GSA shall be required to comply with NEPA and submit the NEPA documentation timed to coincide with the Commission's review stages as set forth in paragraphs (b) through (e) of this section.

(b) *Concept site review.* (1) The NEPA Scoping Process shall have been initiated by NPS or GSA before the appropriate agency submits an application to the Commission for concept site review. Available NEPA documentation for all concept sites shall be included in the application to facilitate effective Commission concept review.

(2) The Commission shall provide comments to NPS or GSA on the multiple sites to assist the applicant in selecting a preferred site.

(c) *Concept design review for preferred sites.* (1) The NEPA Public Scoping Process shall have been initiated before NPS or GSA submits an application to the Commission for concept design review. Available NEPA documentation shall be included in the application to facilitate effective Commission concept review.

(2) The Commission shall provide comments to NPS or GSA on the preferred site(s) and the concept designs for each site to facilitate selection of a preferred site and refinement of the memorial design for that site. The

Commission may establish guidelines for the applicant to follow in preparing its preliminary and final commemorative work design to avoid, minimize or mitigate environmental impacts including adverse effects on historic properties. If the Commission imposes guidelines to avoid, minimize or mitigate adverse impacts, the applicant shall address the guidelines in its Environmental Document.

(d) *Preliminary site and design review.* (1) NPS or GSA shall have issued or published its Draft Environmental Document for the site selection process and the memorial design and shall have initiated the requisite public comment period before the applicant submits an application for preliminary site and design approval. The NEPA information shall be provided to the Commission to facilitate the Commission's preliminary review and the provision of meaningful Commission comments and directions.

(2) The Commission shall take an action on the preliminary site and design and provide comments to the applicant on the preliminary design to assist the applicant's preparation of a final design.

(e) *Final site and design review.* (1) At the time NPS or GSA submits an application to the Commission for final site and design review, the determination (FONSI or ROD) resulting from the Environmental Document shall be submitted by the applicant in a form consistent with its NEPA regulations. As a Cooperating Agency, NCPC may co-sign the applicant's FONSI or ROD following final Commission approval if co-signing is consistent with the applicant's NEPA regulations. Alternatively, NCPC may prepare and sign its own independent document in accordance with the requirements of §601.16(a) or §601.25(a) through (c).

(2) If at the time of final review, the Commission denies the NPS or GSA project and requests changes thereto, the applicant shall proceed in a manner consistent with applicable law. The Federal Agency applicant may pursue, among others, the option of revising the project in a manner responsive to the Commission's comments. If the Federal Agency pursues this option, it shall review and consider the need for

possible changes to its Environmental Document and its FONSI or ROD. Upon resubmission of a revised application for final review, the applicant shall submit a revised Environmental Document and a revised FONSI or ROD if in its judgement revised documents are necessary. If NCPC and the applicant disagree regarding the need for a revised Environmental Document and FONSI or ROD, the parties shall work together to resolve their differences. The final decision regarding the need for a revised Environmental Document and a revised FONSI or ROD shall be made by the Commission's Executive Committee.

Subpart D—Initiating the NEPA Process

§601.10 Characteristics of Commission actions eligible for a Categorical Exclusion.

(a) A Categorical Exclusion is a type of action that does not individually or cumulatively have a significant effect on the human environment and which has been found to have no such effect by NCPC.

(b) Actions that generally qualify for application of a Categorical Exclusion and do not require either an EA or an EIS exhibit the following characteristics:

(1) Minimal or no effect on the human environment;

(2) No significant change to existing environmental conditions;

(3) No significant cumulative environmental impacts; and

(4) Similarity to actions previously assessed in an EA concluding in a FONSI and monitored to confirm the FONSI.

§601.11 Extraordinary Circumstances.

(a) Before applying a CATEX listed in §601.12, the Executive Director shall determine if a project or plan requires additional environmental review or analysis due to the presence of Extraordinary Circumstances. If any of the Extraordinary Circumstances listed in paragraphs (b)(1) through (11) of this section are present, the Executive Director shall not apply a CATEX and ensure that the proper Environmental

Document (EA or EIS) shall be prepared and made available to the Commission before the Commission takes action on the matter.

(b) Extraordinary Circumstances that negate the application of a CATEX include:

(1) A reasonable likelihood of significant impact on public health or safety.

(2) A reasonable likelihood of significant environmental impacts on sensitive resources unless the impacts have been or will be avoided, minimized, or mitigated to non-significant levels through another process to include, without limitation, Section 106 of the NHPA. Environmentally sensitive resources include without limitation:

(i) Proposed federally listed, threatened or endangered species or their designated critical habitats.

(ii) Properties listed or eligible for listing on the National Register of Historic Places.

(iii) Areas having special designation or recognition based on Federal law or an Executive Order, to include without limitation, National Historic Landmarks, floodplains, wetlands, and National Parks.

(iv) Cultural, scientific or historic resources.

(3) A reasonable likelihood of effects on the environment that are risky, highly uncertain, or unique.

(4) A reasonable likelihood of violating an Executive Order, or Federal, state or local law or requirements imposed for the protection of the environment.

(5) A reasonable likelihood of causing a significant increase in surface transportation congestion, disruption of mass transit, and interference with pedestrian and bicycle movements.

(6) A reasonable likelihood of significantly degrading air quality or violating air quality control standards under the Clean Air Act (42 U.S.C. 7401–7671q).

(7) A reasonable likelihood of significantly impacting water quality, public water supply systems, or state or local water quality control standards under the Clean Water Act (33 U.S.C. 1251 *et seq.*) and the Safe Drinking Act (42 U.S.C. 300f).

(8) A reasonable likelihood of a disproportionately high and adverse effect on low income and minority populations.

(9) A reasonable likelihood of degrading existing unsatisfactory environmental conditions.

(10) A reasonable likelihood of establishing a precedent for future action or making a decision in principle about future actions with potentially significant environmental effects.

(11) Any other circumstance that makes the action sufficiently unique in its potential impacts on the human environment that further environmental analysis and review is appropriate.

(c) The Executive Director shall include in his/her EDR, or the documentation of a delegated action, his/her decision to apply a Categorical Exclusion including consideration of possible Extraordinary Circumstances or not apply a Categorical Exclusion because of Extraordinary Circumstances.

§ 601.12 National Capital Planning Commission Categorical Exclusions.

(a) Commission actions that may be categorically excluded and normally do not require either an EA or an EIS are listed in paragraphs (a)(1) through (13) of this section. An action not specifically included in the list is not eligible for a Categorical Exclusion even if it appears to meet the general criteria listed in § 601.10(b).

(1) Approval of the installation or restoration of onsite primary or secondary electrical distribution systems including minor solar panel arrays.

(2) Approval of the installation or restoration of minor site elements, such as but not limited to identification signs, sidewalks, patios, fences, curbs, retaining walls, landscaping, and trail or stream improvements. Additional features include water distribution lines and sewer lines which involve work that is essentially replacement in kind.

(3) Approval of the installation or restoration of minor building elements, such as, but not limited to windows, doors, roofs, building signs, and rooftop equipment and green roofs.

(4) Adoption of a Federal Element of the Comprehensive Plan or amendment

thereto or broad based policy or feasibility plans prepared and adopted by the Commission in response to the Comprehensive Plan.

(5) Approval of the installation of communication antennae on Federal buildings and co-location of communication antennae on Federal property consistent with GSA Bulletin FMR D–242, Placement of Commercial Antennas on Federal Property.

(6) Approval of Federal and District government agency proposals for new construction, building expansion, or improvements to existing facilities, when all of the following apply:

(i) The new structure and proposed use are in compliance with local planning and zoning and any applicable District of Columbia, state, or Federal requirements.

(ii) The site and the scale of construction are consistent with those of existing adjacent or nearby buildings.

(iii) The proposed use will not substantially increase the number of motor vehicles in the vicinity of the facility.

(iv) There is little to no evidence of unresolved resource conflicts or community controversy related to environmental concerns or other environmental issues.

(7) Approval of transfers of jurisdiction pursuant to 40 U.S.C. 8124 that are not anticipated to result in changes in land-use and that have no potential for environmental impact.

(8) Approval of a minor modification to a General Development Plan applicable to lands acquired pursuant to the Capper-Cramton Act, 46 Stat. 482 (1930), as amended, when non-significant environmental impacts are anticipated.

(9) Reorganization of NCPC.

(10) Personnel actions, including, but not limited to, investigations; performance reviews; award of personal service contracts, promotions and awards; reductions in force, reassignments and relocations; and employee supervision and training.

(11) Legal activities including, but not limited to, legal advice and opinions; litigation or other methods of dispute resolution; and procurement of outside legal services.

(12) Procurement of goods and services, transactions, and other types of activities related to the routine and continuing administration, management, maintenance and operations of the Commission or its facilities.

(13) Adoption and issuance of rules, directives, official policies, guidelines, and publications or recommendations of an educational, financial, informational, legal, technical or procedural nature.

(b) The Executive Director shall include in his/her EDR, or the documentation of a delegated action, his/her decision to apply a Categorical Exclusion and the rationale for this decision.

Subpart E—Environmental Assessments

§601.13 Characteristics of Commission actions eligible for an Environmental Assessment.

(a) An EA is a concise document with sufficient information and analysis to enable the Executive Director to determine whether to issue a FONSI or prepare an EIS.

(b) Commission actions that generally require an EA exhibit the following characteristics:

(1) Minor but likely insignificant degradation of environmental quality;

(2) Minor but likely insignificant cumulative impact on environmental quality; and

(3) Minor but likely insignificant impact on protected resources.

§601.14 Commission actions generally eligible for an Environmental Assessment.

Commission actions that typically require preparation of an EA include without limitation:

(a) Approval of final plans for Federal public buildings in the District of Columbia, and the provisions for open space in and around the same, pursuant to 40 U.S.C. 8722(d) and D.C. Code 2–1004(c).

(b) Approval of final plans for District of Columbia public buildings and the open space around them within the Central Area pursuant to 40 U.S.C. 8722(e) and D.C. Code 2–1004(d).

(c) Recommendations to a Federal or District of Columbia agency on any master plan or master plan modification submitted to the Commission that include proposed future projects that require Commission approval pursuant to 40 U.S.C. 8722(d)–(e) and D.C. Code 2–1004(c)–(d) within a five-year time-frame.

(d) Approval of a final site and design for a commemorative work authorized under the Commemorative Works Act pursuant to 40 U.S.C. 8905.

(e) Approval of transfers of jurisdiction over properties within the District of Columbia owned by the United States or the District among or between Federal and District authorities, pursuant to 40 U.S.C. 8124, unless such transfers met the criteria of § 601.12(a)(7).

§ 601.15 Process for preparing an Environmental Assessment.

An EA prepared by NCPC as the Lead Agency for a project requiring Commission approval shall comply with the following requirements:

(a) The EA shall include, without limitation, a brief discussion of the proposed action; the purpose and need for the proposed action; the environmental impacts of the proposed action; the environmental impacts of the alternatives considered; Mitigation measures, if necessary; and a list of agencies and persons consulted in preparation of the assessment.

(b) The NCPC shall involve to the extent practicable applicants; Federal and District of Columbia agencies; the public; and stakeholders in the preparation of an EA.

(c) The NCPC, at the sole discretion of the Executive Director, may undertake Public Scoping for an action requiring an EA. The Public Scoping shall generally commence after issuance of a public notice in a media source with widespread circulation and the NCPC Web site of NCPC's intent to prepare an EA. The notice shall include the date, time and location of the Public Scoping meeting.

(d) The NCPC may solicit public review and comment of a Draft EA. The public comment period generally shall be thirty (30) calendar days. The public comment period shall begin when the Executive Director announces the availability of the Draft EA on the NCPC Web site (*www.ncpc.gov*). The NCPC, at its sole discretion, may decline to circulate a draft EA for non-controversial projects.

§ 601.16 Finding of No Significant Impact.

(a) If NCPC is the Lead Agency and the final EA supports a FONSI, NCPC shall prepare and execute a FONSI. The FONSI shall be prepared following closure of the discretionary public comment period on a Draft EA, or if no public comment period is deemed necessary, at the conclusion of the preparation of an EA. The FONSI shall briefly state the reasons why the proposed action will not have a significant effect on the environment and include the EA or a summary thereof, any Mitigation commitments, and a schedule for implementing the Mitigation commitments. The FONSI shall be signed following the Commission final approval of the applicant's project.

(b) If NCPC is not the Lead Agency, it shall evaluate the adequacy of the Lead Agency's FONSI. If NCPC determines the FONSI to be adequate, NCPC shall proceed as follows. If consistent with the Federal Agency's NEPA regulations, NCPC may co-sign the Lead Agency's FONSI following the Commission final approval of the application. Alternatively, NCPC may prepare and execute its own FONSI consistent with the requirements of paragraph (a) of this section and sign the FONSI following the Commission's final approval of the project.

(c) In certain limited circumstances described in 40 CFR 1501.4(e)(2)(i) and (ii), a FONSI prepared by NCPC shall be available for public review for thirty (30) days before NCPC makes it final determination. NCPC shall also publish all FONSIs on its Web site seven (7) calendar days before the Commission takes action on the underlying application.

(d) If the Commission determines a Lead Agency's EA does not support a FONSI, either the Lead Agency shall prepare an EIS, or the Commission shall not approve or consider further the underlying application.

§ 601.17 Supplemental Environmental Assessments.

(a) The NCPC shall prepare a supplemental EA if five or more years have elapsed since adoption of the EA and:

(1) There are substantial changes to the proposed action that are relevant to environmental concerns; or

(2) There are significant new circumstances or information that are relevant to environmental concerns and have a bearing on the proposed action or its impacts.

(b) The NCPC may supplement a Draft or Final EA at any time to further the purposes of NEPA.

(c) The NCPC shall prepare, circulate, and file a supplement to a Draft or Final EA, and adopt a FONSI in accordance with the requirements of §§ 601.15 and 601.16. If NCPC is not the Lead Agency, it shall proceed as outlined in § 601.16(b) and (c).

Subpart F—Environmental Impact Statements

§ 601.18 Requirement for and timing of an Environmental Impact Statement.

Prior to the Commission's approval of a major Federal action significantly affecting the quality of the human environment, the Executive Director shall prepare an EIS for a Non-Federal Agency application.

§ 601.19 Context, intensity, and significance of impacts.

(a) As required by 40 CFR 1508.27(a) and (b), NCPC's determination of whether an EIS is required and whether impacts are significant shall be made with consideration to the context and intensity of the impacts associated with a proposed action.

(b) The significance of an action is determined in the context of its effects on society as a whole, the National Capital Region and its Environs, the particular interests affected, and the specific locality or area within which the proposed action is located. The context will vary from project to project and will be based on the type, attributes, and characteristics of a particular proposal.

(c) The significance of an action is also determined based on the severity of impacts imposed by the proposal. Severity shall be determined based on an evaluation of a proposal in the manner outlined in 40 CFR 1508.27(b)(1) through (10). The evaluation shall also be informed by the relevant policies of "The Comprehensive Plan for the National Capital: Federal Elements" and other applicable Commission plans and programs. Proposed actions that conflict with or delay achievement of the goals and objectives of Commission plans and programs are generally more likely to be found to have significant impacts than proposals that are consistent with Commission plans and programs.

(d) Proposed actions shall also be deemed significant and require an EIS if they exhibit at least one of the following characteristics:

(1) The proposed action results in a substantial change to the Monumental Core.

(2) The proposed action causes substantial alteration to the important historical, cultural, and natural features of the National Capital and its Environs.

(3) The proposed action is likely to be controversial because of its impacts on the human environment.

§ 601.20 Streamlining Environmental Impact Statements.

The NCPC as Lead Agency shall use all available techniques to minimize the length of an EIS. Such techniques include, without limitation, drafting an EIS in clear, concise language; preparing an analytic vs. encyclopedic EIS; reducing emphasis on background information; using the scoping process to emphasize significant issues and de-emphasize non-significant issues; incorporating relevant information by reference; using a programmatic EIS and tiering to eliminate duplication in subsequent EISs; and following the format guidelines of § 601.22.

§ 601.21 Programmatic Environmental Impact Statements and tiering.

(a) The NCPC shall prepare a programmatic Environmental Document (Programmatic EA or PEA or Programmatic EIS or PEIS) to assess the impacts of proposed projects and plans when there is uncertainty regarding the timing, location and environmental impacts of subsequent implementing actions. At the time NCPC undertakes a site or project specific action within the parameters of the PEA or PEIS, NCPC shall tier its Environmental Document by summarizing information in the PEIS or PEA, as applicable, and concentrate on the issues applicable to the specific action.

(b) A PEIS or PEA prepared by NCPC shall be governed by the CEQ regulations and the rules of this part.

§601.22 Contents of an Environmental Impact Statement.

(a) When NCPC serves as Lead Agency for an EIS, the following information shall be included in the EIS:

(1) A cover sheet. The cover sheet shall be one-page and include a list of responsible and Cooperating Agencies; the title of the proposed action that is the subject of the EIS; the name, address, and telephone number of the NCPC point of contact; the designation as to whether the statement is draft, final, or draft or final supplement; a one paragraph abstract of the EIS; and the date by which comments must be received.

(2) A summary. The summary shall accurately summarize the information presented in the EIS. The summary shall focus on the main conclusions, areas of controversy, and the issues to be resolved.

(3) A table of contents. The table of contents shall allow a reader to quickly locate subject matter in the EIS—either by topic area and/or alternatives analyzed.

(4) The purpose and need. A statement of the purpose of and need for the action briefly stating the underlying purpose and need to which the agency is responding.

(5) The identification of alternatives including the proposed action. This section shall provide a brief description and supporting documentation for all alternatives including the proposed action; the no action alternative; all reasonable alternatives including those not within the jurisdiction of the agency; alternatives considered but eliminated and the reason for their elimination; the agency's preferred alternative, if one exists; the environ-

mentally preferred alternative; and Mitigation measures not already included in the proposed action.

(6) The identification of the affected environment. This section shall provide a succinct description of the environment to be affected by the proposed action and the alternatives considered. This section shall include, if applicable, other activities in the area affected by or related to the proposed action.

(7) The identification of environmental consequences. This section shall focus on the environmental impacts of the alternatives including the proposed action, any adverse environmental effects which cannot be avoided should the proposal be implemented, the relationship between short-term uses of the environment and the maintenance and enhancement of long-term productivity, and any irreversible commitments of resources which would be involved if the proposal is implemented. The impacts shall be discussed in terms of direct, indirect and cumulative effects and their significance, as well as any appropriate means to mitigate adverse impacts. The discussion shall also include issues and impact topics considered but dismissed to reveal non-impacted resources. Resource areas and issues requiring consideration shall include those identified in the scoping process, and, without limitation, the following:

(i) Possible conflicts between the proposed action and the land use plans, policies, or controls (local, state, or Indian tribe) for the area concerned.

(ii) Natural and biological resources including topography, hydrology, soils, flora, fauna, floodplains, wetlands, and endangered species.

(iii) Air quality.

(iv) Noise.

(v) Water resources including wastewater treatment and storm water management.

(vi) Utilities including energy requirements and conservation.

(vii) Solid waste and hazardous waste generation/removal.

(viii) Community facilities.

(ix) Housing.

(x) Transportation network.

(xi) Socio-cultural and economic environments.

(xii) Environmental Justice and the requirements of Executive Order 12898 (Federal Actions to Address Environmental Justice in Minority Populations).

(xiii) Urban quality and design of the built environment including visual resources and aesthetics.

(xiv) Historic and cultural resources to include documentation of the results of the Section 106 Consultation process.

(xv) Public health and safety.

(8) A list of preparers. This list shall include all pertinent organizations, agencies, individuals, and government representatives primarily responsible for the preparation of the EIS and their qualifications.

(9) An index. The index shall be structured to reasonably assist the reader of the Draft or Final EIS in identifying and locating major topic areas or elements of the EIS information. The level of detail of the index shall provide sufficient focus on areas of interest to any reader not just the most important topics.

(10) An appendix. The appendix shall consist of material prepared in connection with an EIS (as distinct from material which is incorporated by reference) and material which substantiates any analysis fundamental to the EIS. The material in the appendix shall be analytical and relevant to the decision to be made. The appendix shall be posted on NCPC's Web site.

(b) [Reserved]

§ 601.23 The Environmental Impact Statement process.

(a) The NCPC shall involve the applicant, Federal and District of Columbia agencies, members of the public and stakeholders in the preparation of an EIS. Public participation shall be required as part of the Public Scoping process and review of the Draft EIS. The NCPC shall also consult with agencies having jurisdiction by law or expertise. Agencies with "jurisdiction by law" are those with ultimate jurisdiction over a project and whose assistance may be required on certain issues and those with other kinds of regulatory or advisory authority with respect to the action or its effects on particular environmental resources.

(b) To determine the scope of an EIS through a Public Scoping process, NCPC shall proceed as follows:

(1) Disseminate a NOI in accordance with 40 CFR 1501.7 and 1506.6.

(2) Publish a NOI in the FEDERAL REGISTER and on NCPC's Web site which shall begin the Public Scoping process.

(3) Include the date, time, and location of a Public Scoping meeting in the NOI. The public meeting shall be announced at least thirty (30) calendar days in advance of its scheduled date.

(4) Hold Public Scoping meeting(s) in facilities that are accessible to the disabled; include translators if requested in advance; include signers or interpreters for the hearing impaired if requested in advance; and allow special arrangements for consultation with affected Indian tribes or other Native American groups who have environmental concerns that cannot be shared in a public forum.

(5) Consider all comments received during the announced comment period regarding the analysis of alternatives, the affected environment, and identification of potential impacts.

(6) Apply the provisions of this section to a Supplemental EIS if the Executive Director of NCPC, in his/her sole discretion, determines a Public Scoping process is required for a Supplemental EIS.

(c) A Draft EIS shall be available to the public for their review and comment, for a period of generally forty-five (45) calendar days. The public comment period shall begin when NCPC shares a copy of the Draft EIS with EPA in anticipation of EPA's publication of an NOA. The NCPC shall hold at least one public meeting during the public comment period on a Draft EIS. The public meeting shall be announced at least thirty (30) calendar days in advance of its scheduled occurrence. The announcement shall identify the subject of the Draft EIS and include public meeting date, time, and location.

§ 601.24 Final Environmental Impact Statement.

(a) The NCPC shall prepare a Final EIS following the public comment period and the public meeting(s) on the

Draft EIS. The Final EIS shall respond to oral and written comments received during the Draft EIS public comment period.

(b) The Commission shall take final action on an application following a thirty (30) day Commission-sponsored review period of the Final EIS. The thirty (30) day period shall start when the EPA publishes a NOA for the Final EIS in the FEDERAL REGISTER.

§ 601.25 Record of Decision.

(a) If NCPC is the Lead Agency and decides to recommend approval of a proposed action covered by an EIS, it shall prepare and sign a ROD stating the Commission's decision and any Mitigation measures required by the Commission.

(1) The ROD shall include among others:

(i) A statement of the decision.

(ii) The identification of alternatives considered in reaching a decision specifying the alternatives that were considered to be environmentally preferable. The ROD shall discuss preferences among alternatives based on relevant factors including economic and technical planning considerations and the Commission's statutory mission. The ROD shall identify those factors balanced to reach a decision and the influence of various factors on the decision.

(iii) A statement as to whether all practicable means to avoid or minimize environmental harm from the alternative selected has been adopted, and if not, why they are not.

(iv) A monitoring and enforcement program that summarizes Mitigation measures.

(v) Date of issuance.

(vi) Signature of the Chairman.

(2) The contents of the draft ROD proposed for Commission adoption shall be summarized in the EDR and a full version of the draft document shall be included as an Appendix to the EDR. The Draft ROD, independently of the EDR, shall be made available to the public for review fourteen (14) calendar days prior to the Commission's consideration of the proposed action for which the EIS was prepared.

(3) The Commission shall arrive at its decision about the proposed action for

which NCPC serves as the Lead Agency and its environmental effects in a public meeting of record as identified by the Commission's monthly agenda.

(b) If NCPC is not the Lead Agency, following the Commission final approval of a project to which a ROD pertains, and consistent with the Federal Agency's NEPA regulations, NCPC may take one of the following actions. It may either co-sign the Lead Agency's ROD following Commission approval of the project if NCPC agrees with its contents and conclusions or it shall prepare, sign, and sign and adopt its own ROD in accordance with the requirements of paragraphs (a)(1) through (3) of this section.

(c) If the Commission determines a Lead Agency's EIS fails to support a ROD, the Lead Agency shall revise its EIS, or, alternatively, the Commission shall not approve or give any further consideration to underlying application.

§ 601.26 Supplemental Environmental Impact Statement.

(a) The NCPC shall prepare a supplemental EIS if five or more years has elapsed since adoption of the EIS and:

(1) There are substantial changes to the proposed action that are relevant to environmental concerns; or

(2) There are significant new circumstances or information that are relevant to environmental concerns and have a bearing on the proposed action or its impacts.

(b) The NCPC may supplement a Draft or Final EIS at any time, to further the purposes of NEPA.

(c) The NCPC shall prepare, circulate, and file a supplement to a Draft or Final EIS in in accordance with the requirements of §§ 601.22 through 601.24 except that Public Scoping is optional for a supplemental EIS.

(d) The NCPC shall prepare a ROD for a Supplemental EIS. The ROD's contents, the procedure for public review, and the manner in which it shall be adopted shall be as set forth in § 601.25.

§ 601.27 Legislative Environmental Impact Statement.

(a) Consistent with 40 CFR 1506.8, the Executive Director shall prepare an EIS for draft legislation initiated by

NCPC for submission to Congress. The EIS for the proposed legislation shall be included as part of the formal transmittal of NCPC's legislative proposal to Congress.

(b) The requirements of this section shall not apply to legislation Congress directs NCPC to prepare.

Subpart G—Dispute Resolution

§ 601.28 Dispute resolution.

Any disputes arising under this part, shall be resolved, unless otherwise otherwise provided by law or regulation by the parties through interagency, good faith negotiations starting at the working levels of each agency, and if necessary, by elevating such disputes within the respective Agencies. If resolution at higher levels is unsuccessful, the parties may participate in mediation.

§ 601.29 [Reserved]

PART 602—NATIONAL CAPITAL PLANNING COMMISSION FREEDOM OF INFORMATION ACT REGULATIONS

AUTHORITY: 5 U.S.C. 552, as amended.

SOURCE: 82 FR 44037, Sept. 20, 2017, unless otherwise noted.

§ 602.1 Purpose.

This part contains the rules the National Capital Planning Commission (NCPC or Commission) shall follow in processing third party Requests for Records concerning the activities of the NCPC under the Freedom of Information Act (FOIA), 5 U.S.C. 552, as amended. Requests made by a U.S. citizen or an individual lawfully admitted for permanent residence to access his or her own records under the Privacy Act, 5 U.S.C. 522a are processed under this part and in accordance with part 603 of Title 1 of the Code of Federal Regulations (CFR) to provide the greatest degree of access while safeguarding an individual's personal privacy. Information routinely provided to the public as part of regular NCPC activity shall be provided to the public without regard to this part.

§ 602.2 Policy.

(a) It is the NCPC's policy to facilitate the broadest possible availability and dissemination of information to the public through use of the NCPC's Web site, *www.ncpc.gov*, and physical distribution of materials not available electronically. The NCPC staff shall be available to assist the public in obtaining information formally by using the procedures herein or informally in a manner not inconsistent with the rule set forth in this part.

(b) To the maximum extent possible, the NCPC shall make available agency Records of interest to the public that are appropriate for disclosure.

§ 602.3 Definitions.

For purposes of this part, the following definitions shall apply:

Act and FOIA mean the Freedom of Information Act, 5 U.S.C. 552, as amended.

Adverse Determination or Determination shall include a determination to withhold, in whole or in part, Records requested in a FOIA Request; the failure to respond to all aspects of a Request; the determination to deny a request for a Fee Waiver; or the determination to deny a request for expedited processing. The term shall also encompass a challenge to NCPC's determination that Records have not been described adequately, that there are no responsive Records, or that an adequate Search has been conducted.

Agency Record or Record means any documentary material which is either created or obtained by a federal agency (Agency) in the transaction of Agency business and under Agency control. Agency Records may include without limitation books; papers; maps; charts; plats; plans; architectural drawings; photographs and microfilm; machine readable materials such as magnetic tape, computer disks and electronic data storage devices; electronic records including email messages; and audiovisual material such as still pictures, sound, and video recordings. This definition generally does not cover records of Agency staff that are created and maintained primarily for a staff member's convenience, exempt from Agency creation or retention requirements, and withheld from distribution to other Agency employees for their official use.

Confidential Commercial Information means commercial or financial information obtained by the NCPC from a Submitter that may be protected from disclosure under Exemption 4 of the FOIA. Exemption 4 of the FOIA protects trade secrets and commercial or financial information obtained from a person which information is privileged or confidential.

Controlled Unclassified Information means unclassified information that does not meet the standards for National Security Classification under Executive Order 13536, as amended, but is pertinent to the national interests of the United States or to the important interests of entities outside the federal government, and under law or policy requires protection from unauthorized disclosure, special handling safeguards, or prescribed limits on exchange or dissemination.

Commercial Use Request means a FOIA Request from or on behalf of one who seeks information for a use or purpose that furthers the commercial, trade, or profit interests of the Requester or the person on whose behalf the Request is made.

Direct Costs means those expenditures that the NCPC incurs in searching for, duplicating, and reviewing documents to respond to a FOIA Request. Direct Costs include, for example, the salary of the employee performing the work (the basic rate of pay for the employee plus 16 percent of the rate to cover benefits) and the cost of operating duplicating machinery. Direct Costs do not include overhead expenses such as costs of space, and heating or lighting the facility in which the Records are stored.

Duplication means the process of making a copy of a document necessary to respond to a FOIA Request in a form that is reasonably usable by a Requester. Copies can take the form of, among others, paper copy, audio-visual materials, or machine readable documents (*i.e.*, computer disks or electronic data storage devices).

Educational Institution means a preschool, a public or private elementary or secondary school, an institution of undergraduate higher education, an institution of graduate higher education, an institution of professional education, and an institution of vocational education, which operates a program or programs of scholarly research. To be classified in this category, a Requester must show that the Request is authorized by and is made under the auspices of a qualifying institution and that the records are not sought for a commercial use but are sought to further scholarly research.

Expedited Processing means giving a FOIA Request priority because a Requester has shown a compelling need for the Records.

Fee Waiver means a waiver in whole or in part of fees if a Requester can demonstrate that certain statutory requirements are satisfied including that the information is in the public interest and is not requested primarily for commercial purposes.

FOIA Public Liaison means an NCPC official who is responsible for assisting in reducing delays, increasing transparency and understanding the status of Requests, and assisting in the resolution of disputes.

FOIA Request or Request means a written Request made by an entity or member of the public for an Agency Record submitted via the U.S. Postal Service mail or other delivery means to include without limitation electronic-mail (email) or facsimile.

Frequently Requested Documents means documents that have been Requested at least three times under the FOIA. It also includes documents the NCPC anticipates would likely be the subject of multiple Requests.

Multi-track Processing means placing requests in multiple tracks based on the amount of work or time (or both) needed to process the request. Simple Requests requiring relatively minimal work and/or review are placed in one processing track, more complex Requests are placed in one or more other tracks, and expedited Requests are placed in a separate track. Requests in each track are processed on a first-in/first-out basis.

Noncommercial Scientific Institution means an institution that is not operated for commerce, trade or profit, but is operated solely for the purpose of conducting scientific research the results of which are not intended to promote any particular product or industry. To be in this category, a Requester must show that the Request is authorized by and is made under the auspices of a qualifying institution and that the Records are not sought for commercial use but are sought to further scientific research.

Privacy Act Request means, in accordance with NCPC's Privacy Act Regulations (1 CFR part 603) a written (paper copy with an original signature) request made by an individual for information about himself/herself that is contained in a Privacy Act system of records. The Privacy Act applies only to U.S. citizens and aliens lawfully admitted for permanent residence such that only individuals satisfying these criteria may make Privacy Act Requests.

Reading Room Materials means Records, paper or electronic, that are required to be made available to the public under 5.U.S.C. 552(a)(2) as well as other Records that the NCPC, at its discretion, makes available to the public for inspection and copying without requiring the filing of a FOIA Request.

Representative of the News Media means any person or entity that gathers information of potential interest to a segment of the population, uses his/her/its editorial skills to turn raw material into a distinct work, and distributes that work to an audience. News media entities include television or radio stations broadcasting to the public at large; publishers of periodicals that qualify as disseminators of news and make their products available for purchase or subscription by the general public; and alternative media to include electronic dissemination through telecommunication (internet) services. To be in this category, a Requester must not be seeking the Requested Records for a commercial use. A *Freelance Journalist* is a Representative of the News Media who is able to demonstrate a solid basis for expecting publication through a news organization, even though not actually employed by that news organization. A publication contract or past evidence of a specific freelance assignment from a news organization may indicate a solid basis for expecting publication.

Requester means an entity or member of the public submitting a FOIA Request.

Requester Category means one of the five categories NCPC places Requesters in for the purpose of determining whether the Requester will be charged for Search, Review and Duplication, and includes Commercial Use Requests, Educational Institutions, Noncommercial Scientific Institutions, Representatives of the News Media, and all other Requesters.

Review means the examination of Records to determine whether any portion of the located Record is eligible to be withheld. It also includes processing any Records for disclosure, *i.e.*, doing all that is necessary to excise the record and otherwise prepare the Record for release. Review does not include time spent resolving general legal or policy issues regarding the application of exemptions.

Search means the process of looking for material, by manual or electronic means that is responsive to a FOIA Request. The term also includes page-by-page or line-by-line identification of material within documents.

Submitter means any person or entity outside the federal government from whom the NCPC directly or indirectly obtains commercial or financial information. The term includes, among others, corporations, banks, state and local governments, and agencies of foreign governments who provide information to the NCPC.

Unusual Circumstances means, for purposes of § 602.7(c), and only to the extent reasonably necessary to the proper processing of a particular Request:

(1) The need to Search for and collect the Requested Agency Records from establishments that are separate from the Commission's offices;

(2) The need to Search for, collect and appropriately examine and Review a voluminous amount of separate and distinct Agency Records which are demanded in a single Request; or

(3) The need for consultation with another Agency having a substantial interest in the determination of the FOIA Request.

Workday means a regular Federal workday. It does not include Saturdays, Sundays, and legal public holidays.

§ 602.4   Information available without a FOIA Request.

(a) The NCPC shall maintain an electronic library at *www.ncpc.gov* that makes Reading Room Materials capable of production in electronic form available for public inspection and downloading. The NCPC shall also maintain an actual public reading room containing Reading Room Materials incapable of production in electronic form at NCPC's offices. The actual reading room shall be available for use on Workdays during the hours of 9:00 a.m. to 4:00 p.m. Requests for appointments to review Reading Room Materials in the actual public reading room should be directed to the NCPC's Information Resources Specialist identified on the NCPC Web site (*www.ncpc.gov*).

(b) The following types of Records shall be available routinely without resort to formal FOIA Request procedures unless such Records fall within one of the exemptions listed at 5 U.S.C. 552(b) of the Act:

(1) Commission agendas;

(2) Plans and supporting documentation submitted by applicants to the Commission to include environmental and historic preservation reports prepared for a plan or project;

(3) Executive Director's Recommendations;

(4) Commission Memoranda of Action;

(5) Transcripts of Commission proceedings;

(6) The Comprehensive Plan for the National Capital: Federal Elements and other plans prepared by the NCPC;

(7) Federal Capital Improvements Plan for the National Capital Region following release of the President's Budget;

(8) Policies adopted by the Commission;

(9) Correspondence between the Commission and the Congress, other federal and local government agencies, and the public; and

(10) Frequently Requested Documents.

§ 602.5   FOIA Request requirements.

(a) The NCPC shall designate a Chief Freedom of Information Act Officer who shall be authorized to grant or deny any Request for a Record of the NCPC.

(b) Requests for a Record or Records that is/are not available in the actual or electronic reading rooms shall be directed to the Chief Freedom of Information Act Officer.

(c) All FOIA Requests shall be made in writing. If sent by U.S. mail, Requests should be sent to NCPC's official business address contained on the NCPC Web site. If sent via email, they should be directed to *FOIA@ncpc.gov*. To expedite internal handling of FOIA Requests, the words Freedom of Information Act Request shall appear prominently on the transmittal envelope or the subject line of a Request sent via email or facsimile.

(d) The FOIA Request shall:

(1) State that the Request is made pursuant to the FOIA;

(2) Describe the Agency Record(s) Requested in sufficient detail including, without limitation, any specific information known such as date, title or name, author, recipient, or time frame for which you are seeking Records, to enable the NCPC personnel to locate the Requested Agency Records;

(3) State, pursuant to the fee schedule set forth in § 602.14, a willingness to pay all fees associated with the FOIA Request or the maximum fee the Requester is willing to pay to obtain the Requested Records, unless the Requester is seeking a Fee Waiver or placement in a certain Requester Category;

(4) State, if desired, the preferred form or format of disclosure of Agency Records with which the NCPC shall endeavor to comply unless compliance would damage or destroy an original Agency Record or reproduction is costly and/or requires the acquisition of new equipment; and

(5) Provide a phone number, email address or mailing address at which the Requester can be reached to facilitate the handling of the Request.

(e) If a FOIA Request is unclear, overly broad, involves an extremely voluminous amount of Records or a burdensome Search, or fails to state a willingness to pay the requisite fees or the maximum fee which the Requester is willing to pay, the NCPC shall endeavor to contact the Requester to define the subject matter, identify and clarify the Records being sought, narrow the scope of the Request, and obtain assurances regarding payment of fees. The timeframe for a response set forth in §602.6(a) shall be tolled (stopped temporarily) and the NCPC will not begin processing a Request until the NCPC obtains the information necessary to clarify the Request and/or clarifies issues pertaining to the fee.

(f) NCPC shall designate a FOIA Public Liaison to assist a Requester in making a Request or to assist a Requester in correcting a Request that does not reasonably describe the Records sought or to correct other deficiencies described in paragraph (e) of this section that necessitate follow-up with the Requester.

§602.6 FOIA response requirements.

(a) The Freedom of Information Act Officer, upon receipt of a FOIA Request made in compliance with these rules, shall determine whether to grant or deny the Request. The Freedom of Information Officer shall notify the Requester in writing within 20 Workdays of receipt of a perfected Request of his/her determination and the reasons therefore and of the right to appeal any Adverse Determination to the head of the NCPC.

(b) In cases involving Unusual Circumstances, the agency may extend the 20 Workday time limit by written notice to the Requester. The written notice shall set forth the reasons for the extension and the date on which a determination is expected to be dispatched. No such notice shall specify a date that would result in an extension of more than 10 Working Days unless the agency affords the Requester an opportunity to modify his/her Request or arranges an alternative timeframe with the Requester for completion of the NCPC's processing. The agency shall also advise the Requester of his/her right to seek assistance from the FOIA Public Liaison or OGIS to resolve time limit disputes arising under this paragraph.

(c) NCPC shall deny a Request based on an exemption contained in the FOIA and withhold information from disclosure pursuant to an exemption only if NCPC reasonably foresees that disclosure would harm an interest protected by an exemption or if disclosure is prohibited by law. If a Request is denied based on an exemption, NCPC's response shall comply with the requirements of paragraph (d) below.

(d) If a Request is denied in whole or in part, the Chief FOIA Officer's written determination shall include, if technically feasible, the precise amount of information withheld, and the exemption under which it is being withheld unless revealing the exemption would harm an interested protected by the exemption. NCPC shall release any portion of a withheld Record that reasonably can be segregated from the exempt portion of the Record.

§602.7 Multi-track processing.

The NCPC may use multiple tracks for processing FOIA Requests based on the complexity of Requests and those for which expedited processing is Requested. Complexity shall be determined based on the amount of work and/or time needed to process a Request and/or the number of pages of responsive Records. If the NCPC utilizes Multi-track Processing, it shall advise a Requester when a Request is placed in a slower track of the limits associated with a faster track and afford the Requester the opportunity to limit the scope of its Request to qualify for faster processing.

§ 602.8 Expedited processing.

(a) The NCPC shall provide Expedited Processing of a FOIA Request if the person making the Request demonstrates that the Request involves:

(1) Circumstances in which the lack of expedited treatment could reasonably be expected to pose an imminent threat to the life or physical safety of an individual;

(2) An urgency to inform the public about an actual or alleged federal government activity, if made by a person primarily engaged in disseminating information;

(3) The loss of substantial due process rights; or

(4) A matter of widespread and exceptional media interest in which there exists possible questions about the government's integrity which affect public confidence.

(b) A Request for Expedited Processing may be made at the time of the initial FOIA Request or at a later time.

(c) A Requester seeking Expedited Processing must submit a detailed statement setting forth the basis for the Expedited Processing Request. The Requester must certify in the statement that the need for Expedited Processing is true and correct to the best of his/her knowledge. To qualify for Expedited Processing, a Requester relying upon the category in paragraph (a)(2) of this section must establish:

(1) He/She is a full time Representative of the News Media or primarily engaged in the occupation of information dissemination, though it need not be his/her sole occupation;

(2) A particular urgency to inform the public about the information sought by the FOIA Request beyond the public's right to know about the government activity generally; and

(3) The information is of the type that has value that will be lost if not disseminated quickly such as a breaking news story. Information of historical interest only or information sought for litigation or commercial activities will not qualify nor would a news media deadline unrelated to breaking news.

(d) Within 10 calendar days of receipt of a Request for expedited processing, the NCPC shall decide whether to grant or deny the Request and notify the Requester of the decision in writing. If a Request for Expedited Processing is granted, the Request shall be given priority and shall be processed in the expedited processing track as fast as practicable. If a Request for Expedited Processing is denied, any appeal of that decision shall be acted on expeditiously.

§ 602.9 Consultations and referrals.

(a) If a Requester seeks a Record in which another agency of the Federal Government is better able to determine whether the record is exempt from disclosure under the FOIA, NCPC shall either respond to the FOIA Request after consultation with the Agency best able to determine if the Requested Record(s) is/are subject to disclosure or refer the responsibility for responding to the FOIA Request to the Agency responsible for originating the Record(s). Generally, the Agency originating a Record will be presumed by the NCPC to be the Agency best qualified to render a decision regarding disclosure or exemption except for Agency Records submitted to the NCPC pursuant to its authority to review Agency plans and/or projects.

(b) Upon referral of Records to another Agency, the NCPC shall notify the Requester in writing of the referral, inform the Requester of the name of the Agency to which all or part of the responsive records have been referred, provide the Requester a description of the part of the Request referred, and advise the Requester of a point of contact within the receiving Agency.

(c) The timeframe for a response to a FOIA Request requiring consultation or referral shall be based on the date the FOIA Request was initially received by the NCPC and not any later date.

§ 602.10 Classified and Controlled Unclassified Information.

(a) For Requests for an Agency Record that has been classified or may be appropriate for classification by another Agency pursuant to an Executive Order concerning the classification of Records, the NCPC shall refer the responsibility for responding to the FOIA Request to the Agency that either classified the Record, should consider classifying the Record, or has primary interest in the Record, as appropriate.

(b) Whenever a Request is made for a Record that is designated Controlled Unclassified Information by another Agency, the NCPC shall refer the FOIA Request to the Agency that designated the Record as Controlled Unclassified Information. Decisions to disclose or withhold information designated as Controlled Unclassified Information shall be made based on the applicability of the statutory exemptions contained in the FOIA, not on a Controlled Unclassified Information marking or designation.

§602.11 Confidential Commercial Information.

(a) Confidential Commercial Information obtained by the NCPC from a Submitter shall be disclosed under the FOIA only in accordance with the requirements of this section.

(b) A Submitter of Confidential Commercial Information shall use good-faith efforts to designate, by appropriate markings, either at the time of submission or at a reasonable time thereafter, any portions of its submission that it considers to be protected from disclosure under Exemption 4 of the FOIA. These designations will expire ten years after the date of the submission unless the Submitter requests, and provides justification for, a longer designation period.

(c) Notice shall be given to a Submitter of a FOIA Request for potential Confidential Commercial Information if:

(1) The requested information has been designated in good faith by the Submitter as Confidential Commercial Information eligible for protection from disclosure under Exemption 4 of the FOIA; or

(2) The NCPC has reason to believe the requested information is Confidential Commercial Information protected from disclosure under Exemption 4 of the FOIA.

(d) Subject to the requirements of paragraphs (c) and (g) of this section, the NCPC shall provide a Submitter with prompt written notice of a FOIA Request or administrative appeal that seeks the Submitter's Confidential Commercial Information. The notice shall give the Submitter an opportunity to object to disclosure of any specified portion of that Confidential Commercial Information pursuant to paragraph (e) of this section. The notice shall either describe the Confidential Commercial Information Requested or include copies of the Requested Records or portions thereof containing the Confidential Commercial Information. When notice to a large number of Submitters is required, NCPC may provide notification by posting or publishing the notice in a place reasonably likely to accomplish the intent of the notice requirement such as a newspaper, newsletter, the NCPC Web site, or the FEDERAL REGISTER.

(e) The NCPC shall allow a Submitter a reasonable time to respond to the notice described in paragraph (d) of this section and shall specify within the notice the time period for response. If a Submitter has any objection to disclosure, it shall submit a detailed written statement. The statement must specify all grounds for withholding any portion of the Confidential Commercial Information under any exemption of the FOIA and, in the case of Exemption 4, it must show why the Confidential Commercial Information is a trade secret or commercial or financial information that is privileged or confidential. If the Submitter fails to respond to the notice within the specified time, the NCPC shall consider this failure to respond as no objection to disclosure of the Confidential Commercial Information on the part of the Submitter, and NCPC shall proceed to release the requested information. A statement provided by the Submitter that is not received by NCPC until after the NCPC's disclosure decision has been made shall not be considered by the NCPC. Information provided by a Submitter under this paragraph may itself be subject to disclosure under the FOIA.

(f) The NCPC shall consider a Submitter's objections and specific grounds for nondisclosure in deciding whether to disclose Confidential Commercial Information. Whenever the NCPC decides to disclose Confidential Commercial Information over the objection of a Submitter, the NCPC shall give the Submitter written notice, which shall include:

(1) A statement of the reason(s) why each of the Submitter's disclosure objections was not sustained;

(2) A description of the Confidential Commercial Information to be disclosed; and

(3) A specified disclosure date, which shall be a reasonable time subsequent to the notice.

(g) The notice requirements of paragraphs (c) and (d) of this section shall not apply if:

(1) The NCPC determines that the Confidential Commercial Information is exempt under FOIA;

(2) The Confidential Commercial Information has been published lawfully or has been officially made available to the public;

(3) The Confidential Commercial Information's disclosure is required by statute (other than the FOIA) or by a regulation issued in accordance with the requirements of Executive Order 12600 (Predisclosure Notification Procedures for Confidential Commercial Information); or

(4) The designation made by the Submitter under paragraph (b) of this section appears obviously frivolous in which case the NCPC shall, within a reasonable time prior to a specified disclosure date, give the Submitter written notice of any final decision to disclose the Confidential Commercial Information.

(h) Whenever a Requester files a lawsuit seeking to compel the disclosure of Confidential Commercial Information, the NCPC shall promptly notify the Submitter.

(i) Whenever the NCPC provides a Submitter with notice and an opportunity to object to disclosure under paragraph (d) of this section, the NCPC shall also notify the Requester. Whenever the NCPC notifies a Submitter of its intent to disclose Requested Information under paragraph (f) of this section, the NCPC shall also notify the Requester. Whenever a Submitter files a lawsuit seeking to prevent the disclosure of Confidential Commercial Information, the NCPC shall notify the Requester.

§ 602.12 Appeals of Adverse Determinations.

(a) An appeal of an Adverse Determination shall be made in writing to the Chairman of the Commission (Chairman). An appeal may be submitted via U.S. mail or other type of manual delivery service or via email or facsimile within 90 Workdays of the date of a notice of an Adverse Determination. To facilitate handling of an appeal, the words Freedom of Information Act Appeal shall appear prominently on the transmittal envelope or the subject line of a Request sent via electronic-mail or facsimile.

(b) An appeal of an Adverse Determination shall include a detailed statement of the legal, factual or other basis for the Requester's objections to an Adverse Determination; a daytime phone number or email address where the Requester can be reached if the NCPC requires additional information or clarification regarding the appeal; copies of the initial Request and the NCPC's written response; and for an Adverse Determination of a Request for Expedited Processing or a Fee Waiver, a demonstration of compliance with the requirements of §§ 602.8(a) and (c) or 602.15(a) through (c) respectively.

(c) The Chairman shall respond to an appeal of an Adverse Determination in writing within 20 Workdays of receipt.

(1) If the Chairman grants the appeal, the Chairman shall notify the Requester, and the NCPC shall make available copies of the Requested Records promptly thereafter upon receipt of the appropriate fee determined in accordance with § 602.13.

(2) If the Chairman denies the appeal in whole or in part, the letter to the Requester shall state

(i) The reason(s) for the denial, including the FOIA exemptions(s) applied;

(ii) A statement that the decision is final;

(iii) A notice of the Requester's right to seek judicial review of the denial in the District Court of the United States in either the locale in which the Requester resides, the locale in which the Requester has his/her principal place of business, or in the District of Columbia; and

(iv) A notice that the Requester may seek dispute resolution services from either the NCPC FOIA Public Liaison or the Office of Government Information Services (OGIS) to resolve disputes between a Requester and the NCPC as a non-exclusive alternative to litigation. Contact information for OGIS can be obtained from the OGIS Web site at *ogis@nara.gov*.

(d) The NCPC shall not act on an appeal of an Adverse Determination if the underlying FOIA Request becomes the subject of FOIA litigation.

(e) A party seeking court review of an Adverse Determination must first appeal the decision under this section to NCPC.

§602.13 Fees.

(a) NCPC shall charge fees for processing FOIA requests in accordance with the provisions of this section and OMB Guidelines.

(b) For purposes of assessing fees, NCPC shall categorize Requesters into three categories: Commercial Use Requesters; Noncommercial Scientific Institutions, Educational Institutions, and News Media Requesters; and all other Requesters. Different fees shall be charged depending upon the category into which a Requester falls. If fees apply, a Requesters may seek a fee waiver in accordance with the requirements of §602.15.

(c) Search Fees shall be charged as follows:

(1) NCPC shall not charge Search fees to Requests made by Educational Institutions, Noncommercial Scientific Institutions, or Representatives of the New Media. NCPC shall charge Search fees to all other Requesters subject to the restrictions of paragraph (f)(5) of this section even if NCPC fails to locate any responsive Records or if the NCPC withholds Records located based on a FOIA exemption.

(2) For each quarter hour spent by personnel searching for Requested Records, including electronic searches that do not require new programming, the Search fees shall be calculated based on the average hourly General Schedule (GS) base salary, plus the District of Columbia locality payment, plus 16 percent for benefits of employees in the following three categories: Staff Assistant (assigned at the GS 9–11 grades); Professional Personnel (assigned at the GS 11–13 grades); and Managerial Staff (assigned at the 14–15 grades). For a Staff Assistant the quarter hour fee to Search for and retrieve a Requested Record shall be $9.00. If a Search and retrieval cannot be performed entirely by a Staff Assistant, and the identification of Records within the scope of a Request requires the use of Professional Personnel, the fee shall be $12.00 for each quarter hour of Search time spent by Professional Personnel. If the time of Managerial Personnel is required, the fee shall be $18.00 for each quarter hour of Search time spent by Managerial Personnel.

(3) For a computer Search of Records, Requesters shall be charged the Direct Costs of creating a computer program, if necessary, and/or conducting the Search. Direct Costs for a computer Search shall include the cost that is directly attributable to the Search for responsive Records and the costs of the operator's salary for the time attributable to the Search.

(d) Duplication fees shall be charged to all Requesters, subject to the limitations of paragraph (f)(5) of this section. For a paper photocopy of a Record (no more than one copy of which shall be supplied), the fee shall be 10 cents per page for single or double sided copies, 90 cents per page for 8½ by 11 inch color copies, and $1.50 per page for color copies up to 11 x 17 inches per page. For copies produced by computer, and placed on an electronic data saving device or provided as a printout, the NCPC shall charge the Direct Costs, including operator time, of producing the copy. For other forms of Duplication, the NCPC shall charge the Direct Costs of that Duplication.

(e) Review fees shall be charged to only those Requesters who make a Commercial Use Request. Review fees will be charged only for the NCPC initial Review of a Record to determine whether an exemption applies to a particular Record or portion thereof. No charge will be made for Review at the administrative appeal level for an exemption already applied. However, Records or portions thereof withheld under an exemption that is subsequently determined not applicable upon appeal may be reviewed again to determine whether any other exemption not previously considered applies. If the NCPC determines a different exemption applies, the costs of that Review are chargeable. Review fees will be charged at the same rates as those charged for a Search under paragraph (c)(2) of this section.

(f) The following limitations on fees shall apply:

(1) If NCPC fails to comply with the time limits in which to respond to a request, NCPC shall not charge Search fees or, in the case of Educational Institutions, Noncommercial Scientific Institutions, or Representatives of the News Media, duplication fees, except as described in paragraphs (f)(2)–(4) of this section.

(2) If NCPC has determined that unusual circumstances as defined by the FOIA apply, and the agency provided timely written notice to the Requester in accordance with the FOIA, a failure to comply with the time limit shall be excused for an additional 10 days.

(3) If NCPC determines that Unusual Circumstances exist, and more than 5000 pages of responsive records are necessary to respond to the Request, NCPC may charge Search fees. NCPC may also charge duplication fees in the case of Educational Institutions, Noncommercial Scientific Institutions, or Representatives of the News Media. The provisions of this paragraph shall only apply if NCPC provides timely written notice of the Unusual Circumstances to the Requester and discusses with the Requester via mail, e-mail or phone (or made at least three good faith efforts to do so) how to effectively limit the scope of the Request.

(4) If a court has determined that exceptional circumstances exist, as defined by the FOIA, a failure to comply with the time limits shall be excused for the length of time provided by the court order.

(5) No Search or Review fees shall be charged for a quarter-hour period unless more than half of that period is required for Search or Review.

(6) Except for Requesters of a Commercial Use Request, the NCPC shall provide without charge the first two hours of Search (or the cost equivalent) and the first 100 pages of Duplication (or the cost equivalent);

(7) Except for Requesters of a Commercial Use Request, no fee shall be charged for a Request if the total fee calculated under this section equals $50.00 or less.

(8) Requesters other than those making a Commercial Use Request shall not be charged a fee unless the total cost of a Search in excess of two hours plus the cost of Duplication in excess of 100 pages totals more than $50.00.

(g) If the NCPC determines or estimates fees in excess of $50.00, the NCPC shall notify the Requester of the actual or estimated amount of total fees, unless in its initial Request the Requester has indicated a willingness to pay fees as high as those determined or estimated. If only a portion of the fee can be estimated, the NCPC shall advise the Requester that the estimated fee constitutes only a portion of the total fee. If the NCPC notifies a Requester that actual or estimated fees amount to more than $50.00, the Request shall not be considered received for purposes of calculating the time-frame for a Response, and no further work shall be undertaken on the Request until the Requester agrees to pay the anticipated total fee. Any such agreement shall be memorialized in writing. A notice under this paragraph shall offer the Requester an opportunity to work with the NCPC to reformulate the Request to meet the Requester's needs at a lower cost.

(h) Apart from other provisions of this section, if the Requester asks for, or the NCPC chooses as a matter of administrative discretion to provide a special service—such as certifying that Records are true copies or sending them by other than ordinary mail, the actual costs of special service shall be charged.

(i) The NCPC shall charge interest on any unpaid fee starting on the 31st day following the date of billing the Requester. Interest charges will be assessed at the rate provided in 31 U.S.C. 3717 (Interest and Penalty on Claims) and will accrue from the date of the billing until payment is received by the NCPC. The NCPC shall follow the provisions of the Debt Collection Act of 1982 (Pub. L. 97–365, 96 Stat. 1749), as amended, and its administrative procedures, including the use of consumer reporting agencies, collection agencies, and offset.

(j) Where the NCPC reasonably believes that one or more Requesters are acting in concert to subdivide a Request into a series of Requests to avoid fees, the NCPC may aggregate the Requests and charge accordingly. The NCPC shall presume that multiple Requests of this type made within a 30-day period have been made to avoid fees. Where Requests are separated by a time period in excess of 30 days, the NCPC shall aggregate the multiple Requests if a solid basis exists for determining aggregation is warranted under all circumstances involved.

(k) Advance payments shall be treated as follows:

(1) For Requests other than those described in paragraphs (k)(2) and (3) of this section, the NCPC shall not require an advance payment. An advance payment refers to a payment made before work on a Request is begun or continued after being stopped for any reason but does not extend to payment owed for work already completed but not sent to a Requester.

(2) If the NCPC determines or estimates a total fee under this section of more than $250.00, it shall require an advance payment of all or part of the anticipated fee before beginning to process a Request, unless the Requester provides satisfactory assurance of full payment or has a history of prompt payment.

(3) If a Requester previously failed to pay a properly charged FOIA fee to the NCPC within 30 days of the date of billing, the NCPC shall require the Requester to pay the full amount due, plus any applicable interest, and to make an advance payment of the full amount of any anticipated fee, before the NCPC begins to process a new Request or continues processing a pending Request from that Requester.

(4) If the NCPC requires advance payment or payment due under paragraphs (k)(2) or (3) of this section, the Request shall not be considered received and no further work will be undertaken on the Request until the required payment is received.

(1) Where Records responsive to Requests are maintained for distribution by Agencies operating statutorily based fee schedule programs, the NCPC shall inform Requesters of the steps for obtaining Records from those sources so that they may do so most economically.

(m) All fees shall be paid by personal check, money order or bank draft drawn on a bank of the United States, made payable to the order of the Treasurer of the United States.

§602.14 **Fee waiver requirements.**

(a) Records responsive to a Request shall be furnished without charge or at a reduced charge below that established under §602.13. If the Requester demonstrates to the NCPC, and the NCPC determines, based on all available information, that Disclosure of the Requested information is in the public interest because it is likely to contribute significantly to public understanding of the operations or activities of the government, and disclosure of the information is not primarily in the commercial interest of the Requester.

(b) To determine if disclosure of the Requested information is in the public interest because it is likely to contribute significantly to public understanding of the operations or activities of the government, the Requester shall demonstrate, and NCPC shall consider, the following factors:

(1) Whether the subject of the Requested Records concerns the operations or activities of the government. The subject of the Requested Records must concern identifiable operations or activities of the federal government, with a connection that is direct and clear, not remote or attenuated.

(2) Whether the disclosure is likely to contribute to an understanding of government operations or activities. The portions of the Requested Records eligible for disclosure must be meaningfully informative about government operations or activities. The disclosure of information that already is in the public domain, in either a duplicative or a substantially identical form, is not likely to contribute to an understanding of government operations and

activities because this information is already known.

(3) Whether disclosure of the Requested information will contribute to public understanding. The disclosure must contribute to the understanding of a reasonably broad audience of persons interested in the subject, as opposed to the individual understanding of the Requester. A Requester's expertise in the subject area and ability and intention to effectively convey information to the public shall be considered. It shall be presumed that a Representative of the News Media satisfies this consideration.

(4) Whether the disclosure is likely to contribute significantly to public understanding of government operations or activities. The public's understanding of the subject in question must be enhanced by the disclosure to a significant extent, as compared to the level of public understanding existing prior to the disclosure. The NCPC shall not make value judgments about whether information that would contribute significantly to public understanding of the operations or activities of the government is important enough to be made public.

(c) To determine whether disclosure of the information is not primarily in the commercial interest of the Requester, the Requester shall demonstrate, and NCPC shall consider, the following factors:

(1) Whether the Requester has a commercial interest that would be furthered by the Requested disclosure. The NCPC shall consider any commercial interest of the Requester (with reference to the definition of Commercial Use Request in § 602.3(f)), or of any person on whose behalf the Requester may be acting, that would be furthered by the Requested disclosure. Requesters shall be given an opportunity in the administrative process to provide explanatory information regarding this consideration.

(2) Whether any identified commercial interest of the Requester is sufficiently large in comparison with the public interest in disclosure that disclosure is primarily in the commercial interest of the Requester. A Fee Waiver is justified where the public interest standard of paragraph (b) of this section is satisfied and that public interest is greater in magnitude than that of any identified commercial interest in disclosure. The NCPC ordinarily shall presume that a Representative of the News Media satisfies the public interest standard, and the public interest will be the interest primarily served by disclosure to that Requester. Disclosure to data brokers or others who merely compile and market government information for direct economic return shall not be presumed to primarily serve the public interest.

(d) Where only some of the Records to be released satisfy the requirements for a Fee Waiver, a Fee Waiver shall be granted for those Records.

(e) Requests for a Fee Waiver should address the factors listed in paragraphs (a) through (c) of this section, insofar as they apply to each Request. The NCPC shall exercise its discretion to consider the cost-effectiveness of its investment of administrative resources in this decision-making process in deciding to grant Fee Waivers.

[82 FR 44037, Sept. 20, 2017; 82 FR 44879, Oct. 19, 2017]

§ 602.15 Preservation of FOIA records.

(a) The NCPC shall preserve all correspondence pertaining to FOIA Requests received and copies or Records provided until disposition or destruction is authorized by the NCPC's General Records schedule established in accordance with the National Archives and Records Administration (NARA) approved schedule.

(b) Materials that are responsive to a FOIA Request shall not be disposed of or destroyed while the Request or a related lawsuit is pending even if the Records would otherwise be authorized for disposition under the NCPC's General Records Schedule or NARA or other NARA-approved records schedule.

PART 603—PRIVACY ACT REGULATIONS

AUTHORITY: 5 U.S.C. 552a as amended and 44 U.S.C. ch. 36.

SOURCE: 82 FR 44046, Sept. 20, 2017, unless otherwise noted.

§ 603.1 Purpose and scope.

(a) This part contain the rules the National Capital Planning Commission (NCPC) shall follow to implement a privacy program as required by the Privacy Act of 1974, 5 U.S.C. 552a (Privacy Act or Act) and the privacy provisions of the E-Government Act of 2002 (44 U.S.C. ch. 36) (E-Government Act). These rules should be read together with the Privacy Act and the privacy related provisions of the E-Government Act, which provide additional information respectively about Records maintained on individuals and protections for the privacy of personal information as agencies implement citizen-centered electronic Government.

(b) Consistent with the requirements of the Privacy Act, the rules in this part apply to all Records maintained by NCPC in a System of Records; the responsibilities of theNCPC to safeguard this information; the procedures by which Individuals may request notification of the existence of a record, request access to Records about themselves, request an amendment to or correction of those Records, and request an accounting of disclosures of those Records by the NCPC; and the procedures by which an Individual may appeal an Adverse Determination.

(c) Consistent with the privacy related requirements of the E-Government Act, the rules in this part also address the conduct of a privacy impact assessment prior to developing or procuring information technology that collects, maintains, or disseminates information in an identifiable form, initiating a new electronic collection of information in identifiable form for 10 or more persons excluding agencies, instrumentalities or employees of the federal government, or changing an existing System that creates new privacy risks.

(d) In addition to the rules in this part, the NCPC shall process all Privacy Act Requests for Access to Records in accordance with the Freedom of Information Act (FOIA), 5 U.S.C. 552, and part 602 of this chapter.

§ 603.2 Definitions.

For purposes of this part, the following definitions shall apply:

Adverse Determination shall mean a decision to withhold any requested Record in whole or in part; a decision that the requested Record does not exist or cannot be located; a decision that the requested information is not a Record subject to the Privacy Act; a decision that a Record, or part thereof, does not require amendment or correction; a decision to refuse to disclose an accounting of disclosure; and a decision to deny a fee waiver. The term shall also encompass a challenge to NCPC's determination that Records have not been described adequately, that there are no responsive Records or that an adequate search has been conducted.

E-Government Act of 2002 shall mean Public Law 107-347, Dec. 17, 2002, 116 Stat. 2899, the privacy portions of which are set out as a note under section 3501 of title 44.

Individual shall mean a citizen of the United States or an alien lawfully admitted for permanent residence.

Information in Identifiable Form (IIF) shall mean information in an Information Technology system or an online collection that directly identifies an individual, *e.g.*, name, address, social security number or other identifying number or code, telephone number, email address and the like; or information by which the NCPC intends to identify specific individuals in conjunction with other data elements, *e.g.*, indirect identification that may include a combination of gender, race, birth date, geographic identifiers, and other descriptions.

Information Technology (IT) shall mean, as defined in the Clinger Cohen Act (40 U.S.C. 11101(6)), any equipment, software or interconnected system or subsystem that is used in the automatic acquisition, storage, manipulation, management, movement, control, display, switching, interchange, transmission or reception of data.

Maintain shall include maintain, collect, use or disseminate a Record.

Privacy Act Officer shall mean the individual within the NCPC charged with responsibility for coordinating and implementing NCPC's Privacy Act program.

Privacy Act or Act shall mean the Privacy Act of 1974, as amended and codified at 5 U.S.C. 552a.

Privacy Impact Assessment (PIA) shall mean an analysis of how information is handled to ensure handling conforms to applicable legal, regulatory, and policy requirements regarding privacy; to determine the risks and effects of collecting, maintaining and disseminating information in identifiable form in an electronic system; and to examine and evaluate protections and alternative processes for handling information to mitigate potential privacy risks.

Record shall mean any item, collection, or grouping of information about an Individual that is Maintained by the NCPC, including, but not limited to, an Individual's education, financial transactions, medical history, and criminal or employment history and that contains a name, or identifying number, symbol, or other identifying particular assigned to the Individual, such as a finger or voice print or photograph.

Requester shall mean an Individual who makes a Request for Access to a Record, a Request for Amendment or Correction of a Record, or a Request for Accounting of a Record under the Privacy Act.

Request for Access to a Record shall mean a request by an Individual made to the NCPC pursuant to subsection (d)(1) of the Privacy Act to gain access to his/her Records or to any information pertaining to him/her in the system and to permit him/her, or a person of his/her choosing, to review and copy all or any portion thereof.

Request for Amendment or Correction of a Record shall mean a request made by an Individual to the NCPC pursuant to subsection (d)(2) of the Privacy Act to amend or correct a Record pertaining to him/her.

Routine Use shall mean with respect to disclosure of a Record, the use of such Record for a purpose which is compatible with the purpose for which the Record is collected.

Senior Agency Official for Privacy (SAOP) shall mean the individual within NCPC responsible for establishing and overseeing the NCPC's Privacy Act program.

System of Records or System (SOR or Systems) shall mean a group of any Records under the control of the NCPC from which information is retrieved by the name of the individual or by some identifying number, symbol, or other identifying particular assigned to the individual.

System of Record Notice (SORN) shall mean a notice published in the FEDERAL REGISTER by the NCPC for each new or revised System of Records intended to solicit public comment on the System prior to implementation.

Workday shall mean a regular Federal workday excluding Saturday, Sunday and legal Federal holidays when the federal government is closed.

§ 603.3 Privacy Act program responsibilities.

(a) The NCPC shall designate a Senior Agency Official for Privacy (SAOP) to establish and oversee the NCPC's Privacy Act Program and ensure compliance with privacy laws, regulations and the NCPC's privacy policies. Specific responsibilities of the SAOP shall include:

(1) Reporting to the Office of Management and Budget (OMB) and Congress on the establishment of or revision to Privacy Act Systems;

(2) Reporting periodically to OMB on Privacy Act activities as required by law and OMB;

(3) Signing Privacy Act SORNS for publication in the FEDERAL REGISTER;

(4) Approving and signing PIAs; and

(5) Serving as head of the agency response team when responding to a large-scale information breach.

(b) The NCPC shall designate a Privacy Act Officer (PAO) to coordinate and implement the NCPC's Privacy Act program. Specific responsibilities of the PAO shall include:

(1) Developing, issuing and updating, as necessary, the NCPC's Privacy Act policies, standards, and procedures;

(2) Maintaining Privacy Act program Records and documentation;

(3) Responding to Privacy Act Requests for Records and coordinating appeals of Adverse Determinations for Requests for access to Records, Requests for Amendment orCorrection of Records, and Requests for accounting for disclosures;

(4) Informing Individuals of information disclosures;

(5) Working with the NCPC's Division Directors or designated staff to develop an appropriate form for collection of Privacy Act information and including in the form a Privacy Act statement explaining the purpose for collecting the information, how it will be used, the authority for such collection, its routine uses, and the effect upon the Individual of not providing the requested information;

(6) Assisting in the development of new or revised SORNs;

(7) Developing SORN reports for OMB and Congress;

(8) Submitting new or revised SORNS to the FEDERAL REGISTER for publication;

(9) Assisting in the development of computer matching systems;

(10) Preparing Privacy Act, Computer Matching, and other reports to OMB as required; and

(11) Evaluating PIA to ensure compliance with E-Government Act requirements.

(c) Other Privacy related responsibilities shall be shared by the NCPC Division Directors, the NCPC Chief Information Officer (CIO), the NCPC System Developers and Designers, the NCPC Configuration Control Board, the NCPC employees, and theChairman of the Commission.

(1) The NCPC Division Directors shall be responsible for coordinating with the PAO the implementation of the requirements set forth in this part for Systems of Records applicable to their area of management and the preparation of PIA prior to development or procurement of new systems that collect, maintain or disseminate IIF. Specific responsibilities include:

(i) Reviewing existing SOR for need, relevance, and purpose for existence, and proposing SOR changes to the PAO as necessary in response to altered circumstances;

(ii) Reviewing existing SOR to ensure information is accurate, complete and up to date;

(iii) Coordinating with the PAO the preparation of new or revised SORN;

(iv) Coordinating with the PAO the development of an appropriate form for collection of Privacy Act information and including in the form a Privacy Act statement explaining the purpose for collecting the information, how it will be used, the authority for such collection, its routine uses, and the effect upon the Individual of not providing the requested information;

(v) Collecting information directly from individuals whenever possible;

(vi) Assisting the PAO with providing access to Individuals who request information in accordance with the procedures established in §§ 603.12, 603.13, 603.14 and 603.15.

(vii) Amending Records if and when appropriate, and working with the PAO to inform recipients of former Records of such amendments;

(viii) Ensuring that System information is used only for its stated purpose;

(ix) Establishing and overseeing appropriate administrative, technical, and physical safeguards to ensure security and confidentiality of Records; and

(x) Working with the SAOP, the PAO and Configuration Control Board (CCB) on SORs, preparing a PIA, if needed, and obtaining SAOP approval for a PIA prior to its publication on the NCPC Web site.

(2) The CIO shall be responsible for implementing IT security management to include security for information protected by the Privacy Act and the E-Government Act of 2002.Specific responsibilities include:

(i) Overseeing security policy for privacy data; and

(ii) Reviewing PIAs prepared for information security considerations.

(3) The NCPC System Developers and Designers shall be responsible for ensuring that the IT system design and specifications conform to privacy standards and requirements and that technical controls are in place for safeguarding personal information from unauthorized access.

(4) The NCPC CCB shall, among other responsibilities, verify that a PIA has been prepared prior to approving a request to develop or procure information technology that collects, maintains, or disseminates Information in Identifiable Form.

(5) The NCPC employees shall ensure that any personal information they use in the conduct of their official responsibilities is protected in accordance with the rules set forth in this part.

(6) The Chairman of the Commission shall be responsible for acting on all appeals of Adverse Determinations.

[82 FR 44046, Sept. 20, 2017; 82 FR 44879, Sept. 27, 2017]

§ 603.4 Standards used to Maintain Records.

(a) Records Maintained by the NCPC shall contain only such information about an Individual as is relevant and necessary to accomplish a purpose NCPC must accomplish to comply with relevant statutes or Executive Orders of the President.

(b) Records Maintained by the NCPC and used to make a determination about an Individual shall be accurate, relevant, timely, and complete to assure a fair determination.

(c) Information used by the NCPC in making a determination about an Individual's rights, benefits, and privileges under federal programs shall be collected, to the greatest extent practicable, directly from the Individual. In deciding whether collection of information about an Individual, as opposed to a third party is practicable, the NCPC shall consider the following:

(1) Whether the information sought can only be obtained from a third party;

(2) Whether the cost to collect the information from an Individual is unreasonable compared to the cost of collecting the information from a third party;

(3) Whether there is a risk of collecting inaccurate information from a third party that could result in a determination adverse to the Individual concerned;

(4) Whether the information collected from an Individual requires verification by a third party; and

(5) Whether the Individual can verify information collected from third parties.

(d) The NCPC shall not Maintain Records describing how an Individual exercises rights guaranteed by the First Amendment to the Constitution unless the maintenance of the Record is expressly authorized by statute or by the Individual about whom the Record is Maintained or pertinent to and within the scope of an authorized law enforcement activity.

§ 603.5 Notice to Individuals supplying information.

(a) Each Individual asked to supply information about himself/herself to be added to a System of Records shall be informed by the NCPC of the basis for requesting the information, its potential use, and the consequences, if any, of not supplying the information. Notice to the Individual shall state at a minimum:

(1) The legal authority for NCPC's solicitation of the information and whether disclosure is mandatory or voluntary;

(2) The principal purpose(s) for which the NCPC intends to use the information;

(3) The potential routine uses of the information by the NCPC as published in a Systems of Records Notice; and

(4) The effects upon the individual, if any, of not providing all or any part of the requested Information to the NCPC.

(b) When NCPC collects information on a standard form, the notice to the Individual shall either be provided on the form, on a tear off sheet attached to the form, or on a separate form, whichever is deemed the most practical by the NCPC.

(c) NCPC may ask an Individual to acknowledge, in writing, receipt of the notice required by this section.

§603.6 System of Records Notice or SORN.

(a) The NCPC shall publish a notice in the FEDERAL REGISTER describing each System of Records 40-days prior to the establishment of a new or revision to an existing System of Records.

(b) The SORN shall include:

(1) The name and location of the System of Records. The name shall identify the general purpose, and the location shall include whether the system is located on the NCPC's main server or central files. The physical address of either shall also be included.

(2) The categories or types of Individuals on whom NCPC Maintains Records in the System of Records;

(3) The categories or types of Records in the System;

(4) The statutory or Executive Order authority for Maintenance of the System;

(5) The purpose(s) or explanation of why the NCPC collects the particular Records including identification of all internal and routine uses;

(6) The policies and practices of the NCPC regarding storage, retrieval, access controls, retention and disposal of Records;

(7) The title and business address of the agency official responsible for the identified System of Records;

(8) The NCPC procedures for notification to an Individual who requests if a System of Records contains a Record about the Individual; and

(9) The NCPC sources of Records in the System.

§603.7 Procedures to safeguard Records.

(a) The NCPC shall implement the procedures set forth in this section to insure sufficient administrative, technical and physical safeguards exist to protect the security and confidentiality of Records. The enumerated procedures shall also protect against any anticipated threats or hazards to the security of Records with the potential to cause substantial harm, embarrassment, inconvenience, or unfairness to any Individual on whom information is Maintained.

(b) Manual Records subject to the Privacy Act shall be maintained by the NCPC in a manner commensurate with the sensitivity of the information contained in the Records. The following minimum safeguards or safeguards affording comparable protection shall apply to manual Systems of Records:

(1) The NCPC shall post areas where Records are maintained or regularly used with an appropriate warning sign stating access to the Records shall be limited to authorized persons. The warning shall also advise that the Privacy Act prescribes criminal penalties for unauthorized disclosure of Records subject to the Act.

(2) During work hours, the NCPC shall protect areas in which Records are Maintained or regularly used by restricting occupancy of the area to authorized persons or storing the Records in a locked container and room.

(3) During non-working hours, access to Records shall be restricted by their storage in a locked storage container and room.

(4) Any lock used to secure a room where Records are stored shall not be capable of being disengaged with a master key that opens rooms other than those in which Records are stored.

(c) Computerized Records subject to the Privacy Act shall be maintained, at a minimum, subject to the safeguards recommended by the National Institute of Standards and Technology (NIST) Special Publications 800–53, Recommended Security Controls for Federal Information Systems and Organizations as revised from time to time or any superseding guidance offered by NIST or other federal agency charged with the responsibility for providing recommended safeguards for computerized Records subject to the Privacy Act.

(d) NCPC shall maintain a System of Records comprised of Office of Personnel Management (OPM) personnel Records in accordance with standards prescribed by OPM and published at 5 CFR 293.106–293.107.

§603.8 Employee conduct.

(a) Employees with duties requiring access to and handling of Records shall, at all times, take care to protect the integrity, security, and confidentiality of the Records.

(b) No employee of the NCPC shall disclose Records unless disclosure is permitted by § 603.10(b), by part 602 of this chapter, or disclosed to the Individual to whom the Record pertains.

(c) No employee of the NCPC shall alter or destroy a Record unless such Record or destruction is undertaken in the course of the employee's regular duties or such alteration or destruction is allowed pursuant to regulations published by the National Archives and Records Administration (NARA) or required by a court of competent jurisdiction. Records shall not be destroyed or disposed of while they are the subject of a pending request, appeal or lawsuit under the Privacy Act.

§ 603.9 Government contracts.

(a) When a contract provides for third party operation of a SOR on behalf of the NCPC to accomplish a NCPC function, the contract shall require that the requirements of the Privacy Act and the rules in this part be applied to such System.

(b) The Division Director responsible for the contract shall designate a NCPC employee to oversee and manage the SOR operated by the contractor.

§ 603.10 Conditions for disclosure.

(a) Except as set forth in paragraph (b) of this section, no Record contained in a SOR shall be disclosed by any means of communication to any person, or to another agency, unless prior written consent is obtained from the Individual to whom the Record pertains.

(b) The limitations on disclosure contained in paragraph (a) of this section shall not apply when disclosure of a Record is:

(1) To employees of the NCPC for use in the performance of their duties;

(2) Required by the Freedom of Information Act (FOIA), 5 U.S.C. 555;

(3) For a Routine Use as described in a SORN;

(4) To the Bureau of Census for statistical purposes, provided that the Record must be transferred in a form that precludes individual identification;

(5) To an Individual who provides NCPC adequate written assurance that the Record shall be used solely for statistical or research purposes, provided that the Record must be transferred in a form that precludes Individual identification;

(6) To the NARA because the Record warrants permanent retention because of historical or other national value as determined by NARA or to permit NARA to determine whether the Record has such value;

(7) To a law enforcement agency for a civil or criminal law enforcement activity, provided that the law enforcement agency must submit a written request to the NCPC specifying the Record(s) sought and the purpose for which they will be used;

(8) To any person upon demonstration of compelling information that an Individual's health or safety is at stake and provided that upon disclosure, notification is given to the Individual to whom the Record pertains at that Individual's last known address;

(9) To either House of Congress, and any committee or subcommittee thereof, to include joint committees of both houses and any subcommittees thereof, when a Record falls within their jurisdiction;

(10) To the Comptroller General, or any of his authorized representatives, to allow the Government Accountability Office to perform its duties;

(11) Pursuant to a court order by a court of competent jurisdiction; and

(12) To a consumer reporting agency trying to collect a claim of the government as authorized by 31 U.S.C. 3711(e).

§ 603.11 Accounting of disclosures.

(a) Except for disclosures made under §§ 603.10(b)(1)–(2), when a Record is disclosed to any person, or to another agency, NCPC shall prepare an accounting of the disclosure. The accounting shall Record the date, nature, and purpose of the disclosure and the name and address of the person or agency to whom the disclosure was made. The NCPC shall maintain all accountings for a minimum of five years or the life of the Record, whichever is greatest, after the disclosure is made.

(b) Except for disclosures under § 603.10(b)(7), accountings of all disclosures shall be made available to the Individual about whom the disclosed Records pertains at his/her request. Such request shall be made in accordance with the requirements of § 603.15.

(c) For any disclosure for which an accounting is made, if a subsequent amendment or correction or notation of dispute is made to a Record by the NCPC in accordance with the requirements of §603.14, the Individual and/or agency to whom the Record was originally disclosed shall be informed.

§603.12 Requests for notification of the existence of Records.

(a) An Individual seeking to determine whether a System of Records contains Records pertaining to him/her shall do so by appearing in person at NCPC's official place of business or by written correspondence to the NCPC PAO. In-person requests shall be by appointment only with the PAO on a Workday during regular office hours. Written requests sent via the U.S. mail shall be directed to the Privacy Act Officer at NCPC's official address listed at *www.ncpc.gov*. If sent via email or facsimile, the request shall be directed to the email address or facsimile number indicated on the NCPC Web site. To expedite internal handling of Privacy Act Requests, the words Privacy Act Request shall appear prominently on the envelop or the subject line of an email or facsimile cover sheet.

(b) The Request shall state that the Individual is seeking information concerning the existence of Records about himself/herself and shall supply information describing the System where such Records might be maintained as set forth in a System of Record Notice.

(c) The NCPC PAO shall notify the Requester in writing within 20 Workdays of the Request whether a System contains Records pertaining to him/her unless the Records were compiled in reasonable anticipation of a civil action or proceeding or the Records are NCPC employee Records under the jurisdiction of the OPM. In both of the later cases the Request shall be denied. If the Request is denied because the Record(s) is/are under the jurisdiction of the OPM, the response shall advise the Requester to contact OPM. If the PAO denies the Request, the response shall state the reason for the denial and advise the Requester of the right to appeal the decision within 60 days of the date of the letter denying the re-

quest in accordance with the requirements set forth in §603.16.

§603.13 Requests for access to Records.

(a) An Individual seeking access to Records about himself/herself shall do so by appearing in person at NCPC's official place of business or by written correspondence to the NCPC Privacy Act Officer. In-person requests shall be by appointment only with the Privacy Act Officer on a Workday during regular office hours. For written requests sent via the U.S. mail, the Request shall be directed to the Privacy Act Officer at NCPC's official address listed at *www.ncpc.gov*. If sent via email or facsimile, the request shall be directed to the email address or facsimile number indicated on the NCPC Web site. To expedite internal handling of Privacy Act Requests, the words Privacy Act Request shall appear prominently on the envelop or the subject line of an email or facsimile cover sheet.

(b) The Request shall:

(1) State the Request is made pursuant to the Privacy Act;

(2) Describe the requested Records in sufficient detail to enable their location including, without limitation, the dates the Records were compiled and the name or identifying number of each System of Record in which they are kept as identified in the list of NCPC's SORNs published on its Web site; and

(3) State pursuant to the fee schedule in set forth in §603.17 a willingness to pay all fees associated with the Privacy Act Request or the maximum fee the Requester is willing to pay.

(c) The NCPC shall require identification as follows before releasing Records to an Individual:

(1) An Individual Requesting Privacy Act Records in person shall present a valid, photographic form of identification such as a driver's license, employee identification card, or passport that renders it possible for the PAO to verify that the Individual is the same Individual as contained in the requested Records.

(2) An Individual Requesting Privacy Act Records by mail shall state their full name, address and date of birth in their correspondence. The Request must be signed and the signature must

either be notarized or submitted with a statement signed and dated as follows: I declare under penalty of perjury that the foregoing facts establishing my identification are true and correct.

(d) The PAO shall determine within 20 Workdays whether to grant or deny an Individual's Request for Access to the requested Record(s) and notify the Individual in writing accordingly. The PAO's response shall state his/her determination and the reasons therefor. If the Request is denied because the Record(s) is/are under the jurisdiction of the OPM, the response shall advise the Requester to contact OPM. In the case of an Adverse Determination, the written notification shall advise the Individual of his/her right to appeal the Adverse Determination in accordance with the requirements of § 603.16.

§ 603.14 Requests for Amendment or Correction of Records.

(a) An Individual seeking to amend or correct a Record pertaining to him/her that he/she believes to be inaccurate, irrelevant, untimely or incomplete shall submit a written request to the PAO at the address listed on NCPC's official Web site *www.ncpc.gov.* If sent via email or facsimile, the Request shall be directed to the email address or facsimile number indicated on the NCPC Web site. To expedite internal handling, the words Privacy Act Request shall appear prominently on the envelop or the subject line of an email or facsimile cover sheet.

(b) The Request shall:

(1) State the Request is made pursuant to the Privacy Act;

(2) Describe the requested Record in sufficient detail to enable its location including, without limitation, the dates the Records was compiled and the name or identifying number of the System of Record in which the Record is kept as identified in the list of NCPC's SORNs published on its Web site;

(3) State in detail the reasons why the Record, or objectionable portion(s) thereof, is/are not accurate, relevant, timely or complete.

(4) Include copies of documents or evidence relied upon in support of the Request for Amendment or Correction; and

(5) State specifically, and in detail, the changes sought to the Record, and if the changes include rewriting the Record, or portions thereof, or adding new language, the Individual shall propose specific language to implement the requested changes.

(c) A request to Amend or Correct a Record shall be submitted only if the Requester has previously requested and been granted access to the Record and has inspected or been given a copy of the Record.

(d) The PAO shall render a decision within 20 Workdays. If the Request for an Amendment or Correction fails to meet the requirements of paragraphs (b)(1)–(5) of this section, the PAO shall advise the Individual of the deficiency and advise what additional information is required to act upon the Request. The timeframe for a decision on the Request shall be tolled (stopped) during the pendency of a request for additional information and shall resume when the additional information is received. If the Requester fails to submit the requested additional information within a reasonable time, the PAO shall reject the Request.

(e) The PAO's decision on a Request for Amendment or Correction shall be in writing and state the basis for the decision. If the Request is denied because the Record(s) is/are under the jurisdiction of the OPM, the response shall advise the Requester to contact OPM. In the event of an Adverse Determination, the written notification shall advise the Individual of his/her right to appeal the Adverse Determination in accordance with the requirements of § 603.16.

(f) If the PAO approves the Request for Amendment or Correction, the PAO shall ensure that subject Record is amended or corrected, in whole or in part. If the PAO denies the Request for Amendment or Correction, a notation of dispute shall be noted on the Record. If an accounting of disclosure has been made pursuant to § 603.11, the PAO shall advise all previous recipients of the Record that an amendment or correction or notation of dispute has been made and, if applicable, the substance of the change.

§ 603.15 Requests for Accounting of Record disclosures.

(a) An Individual seeking information regarding an accounting of disclosure of a Record pertaining to him/her made in accordance with § 603.11 shall submit a written request to the PAO at the address listed on NCPC's official Web site *www.ncpc.gov.* If sent via email or facsimile, the Request shall be directed to the email address or facsimile number indicated on the NCPC Web site. To expedite internal handling, the words Privacy Act Request shall appear prominently on the envelop or the subject line of an email or facsimile cover sheet.

(b) The Request shall:

(1) State the Request is made pursuant to the Privacy Act; and

(2) Describe the requested Record in sufficient detail to determine whether it is or is not contained in an accounting of disclosure.

(c) The NCPC PAO shall notify the Requester in writing within 20 Workdays of the Request and advise if the Record was included in an accounting of disclosure. In the event of a disclosure, the response shall include the date, nature, and purpose of the disclosure and the name and address of the person or agency to whom the disclosure was made. If the Request is denied because the Record(s) is/are under the jurisdiction of the OPM, the response shall advise the Requester to contact OPM. In the event of an Adverse Determination, the written notification shall advise the Individual of his/her right to appeal the Adverse Determination in accordance with the requirements of § 603.16.

§ 603.16 Appeals of Adverse Determinations.

(a) Except for appeals pursuant to paragraph (d) of this section, an appeal of an Adverse Determination shall be made in writing addressed to the Chairman (Chairman) of the National Capital Planning Commission at the address listed on NCPC's official Web site *www.ncpc.gov.* If sent via email or facsimile, the Request shall be directed to the email address or facsimile number indicated on the NCPC Web site. To expedite internal handling, the words Privacy Act Request shall appear

prominently on the envelop or the subject line of an email or facsimile cover sheet. An appeal of an Adverse Determination shall be made within 30 Workdays of the date of the decision.

(b) An appeal of an Adverse Determination shall include a statement of the legal, factual or other basis for the Requester's objection to an Adverse Determination; a daytime phone number or email where the Requester can be reached if the Chairman requires additional information or clarification regarding the appeal; copies of the initial request and the PAO's written response; and for an Adverse Determination regarding a fee waiver, a demonstration of compliance with part 602 of this chapter.

(c) The Chairman shall respond to an appeal of an Adverse Determination in writing within 20 Workdays of receipt of the appeal. If the Chairman grants the appeal, the Chairman shall notify the Requester, and the NCPC shall take prompt action to respond affirmatively to the original Request upon receipt of any fees that may be required. If the Chairman denies the appeal, the letter shall state the reason(s) for the denial, a statement that the decision is final, and advise the Requester of the right to seek judicial review of the denial in the District Court of the United States in either the district in which the Requester resides, the district in which the Requester has his/her principal place of business or the District of Columbia.

(d) The appeal of an Adverse Determination based on OPM jurisdiction of the Records shall be made to OPM pursuant to 5 CFR 297.306.

(e) The NCPC shall not act on an appeal of an Adverse Determination if the underlying Request becomes the subject of litigation.

(f) A party seeking court review of an Adverse Determination must first appeal the Adverse Determination under this section.

§ 603.17 Fees.

(a) The NCPC shall charge for the duplication of Records under this subpart in accordance with the schedule of fees set forth in part 602 of this chapter. The NCPC shall not charge duplication fees when the Requester asks to inspect the Records personally but is provided copies at the discretion of the agency.

(b) The NCPC shall not charge any fees for the search for or review of Records requested by an Individual.

§ 603.18   Privacy Impact Assessments.

(a) Consistent with the requirements of the E-Government Act and OMB Memorandum M-03-22, the NCPC shall conduct a PIA before:

(1) Developing or procuring IT systems or projects that collect, maintain, or disseminate IIF; or

(2) Installing a new collection of information that will be collected, maintained, or disseminated using IT and includes IIF for 10 or more persons (excluding agencies, instrumentalities or employees of the federal government).

(b) The PIA shall be prepared through the coordinated effort of the NCPC's privacy Officers (SAOP, PAO), Division Directors, CIO, and IT staff.

(c) As a general rule, the level of detail and content of a PIA shall be commensurate with the nature of the information to be collected and the size and complexity of the IT system involved. Specifically, a PIA shall analyze and describe:

(1) The information to be collected;

(2) The reason the information is being collected;

(3) The intended use for the information;

(4) The identity of those with whom the information will be shared;

(5) The opportunities Individuals have to decline to provide the information or to consent to particular uses and how to consent;

(6) The manner in which the information will be secured; and

(7) The extent to which the system of records is being created under the Privacy Act.

(d) In addition to the information specified in paragraphs (b)(1)-(7) of this section, the PIA must also identify the choices NCPC made regarding an IT system or collection of information as result of preparing the PIA.

(e) The CCB shall verify that a PIA has been prepared prior to approving a request to develop or procure information technology that collects, maintains, or disseminates Information in Identifiable Form.

(f) The SAOP shall approve and sign the NCPC's PIA. If the SAOP is the Contracting Officer for the IT system that necessitated preparation of the PIA, the Executive Director shall approve and sign the PIA.

(g) Following approval of the PIA, the NCPC shall post the PIA document on the NCPC Web site located at *www.ncpc.gov.*

FINDING AIDS

A list of CFR titles, subtitles, chapters, subchapters and parts and an alphabetical list of agencies publishing in the CFR are included in the CFR Index and Finding Aids volume to the Code of Federal Regulations which is published separately and revised annually.

Table of CFR Titles and Chapters

(Revised as of January 1, 2019)

Title 1—General Provisions

Title 2—Grants and Agreements

Title 2—Grants and Agreements—Continued

Title 3—The President

Title 4—Accounts

Title 5—Administrative Personnel

Title 5—Administrative Personnel—Continued

Title 6—Domestic Security

Title 7—Agriculture

Title 7—Agriculture—Continued

Title 8—Aliens and Nationality

Title 9—Animals and Animal Products

Title 10—Energy

Title 11—Federal Elections

Title 12—Banks and Banking

144

146

Title 25—Indians

Title 26—Internal Revenue

Title 27—Alcohol, Tobacco Products and Firearms

Title 28—Judicial Administration

Title 29—Labor

148

Title 32—National Defense

Title 33—Navigation and Navigable Waters

Title 34—Education

Title 34—Education—Continued

Title 35 [Reserved]

Title 36—Parks, Forests, and Public Property

Title 37—Patents, Trademarks, and Copyrights

Title 38—Pensions, Bonuses, and Veterans' Relief

Title 39—Postal Service

Title 40—Protection of Environment

Title 41—Public Contracts and Property Management

Title 45—Public Welfare—Continued

Title 46—Shipping

Title 47—Telecommunication

153

Title 48—Federal Acquisition Regulations System

Title 49—Transportation

Title 50—Wildlife and Fisheries

Alphabetical List of Agencies Appearing in the CFR

(Revised as of January 1, 2019)

Agency	CFR Title, Subtitle or Chapter
Administrative Conference of the United States	1, III
Advisory Council on Historic Preservation	36, VIII
Advocacy and Outreach, Office of	7, XXV
Afghanistan Reconstruction, Special Inspector General for	5, LXXXIII
African Development Foundation	22, XV
Federal Acquisition Regulation	48, 57
Agency for International Development	2, VII; 22, II
Federal Acquisition Regulation	48, 7
Agricultural Marketing Service	7, I, IX, X, XI
Agricultural Research Service	7, V
Agriculture, Department of	2, IV; 5, LXXIII
Advocacy and Outreach, Office of	7, XXV
Agricultural Marketing Service	7, I, IX, X, XI
Agricultural Research Service	7, V
Animal and Plant Health Inspection Service	7, III; 9, I
Chief Financial Officer, Office of	7, XXX
Commodity Credit Corporation	7, XIV
Economic Research Service	7, XXXVII
Energy Policy and New Uses, Office of	2, IX; 7, XXIX
Environmental Quality, Office of	7, XXXI
Farm Service Agency	7, VII, XVIII
Federal Acquisition Regulation	48, 4
Federal Crop Insurance Corporation	7, IV
Food and Nutrition Service	7, II
Food Safety and Inspection Service	9, III
Foreign Agricultural Service	7, XV
Forest Service	36, II
Grain Inspection, Packers and Stockyards Administration	7, VIII; 9, II
Information Resources Management, Office of	7, XXVII
Inspector General, Office of	7, XXVI
National Agricultural Library	7, XLI
National Agricultural Statistics Service	7, XXXVI
National Institute of Food and Agriculture	7, XXXIV
Natural Resources Conservation Service	7, VI
Operations, Office of	7, XXVIII
Procurement and Property Management, Office of	7, XXXII
Rural Business-Cooperative Service	7, XVIII, XLII
Rural Development Administration	7, XLII
Rural Housing Service	7, XVIII, XXXV
Rural Telephone Bank	7, XVI
Rural Utilities Service	7, XVII, XVIII, XLII
Secretary of Agriculture, Office of	7, Subtitle A
Transportation, Office of	7, XXXIII
World Agricultural Outlook Board	7, XXXVIII
Air Force, Department of	32, VII
Federal Acquisition Regulation Supplement	48, 53
Air Transportation Stabilization Board	14, VI
Alcohol and Tobacco Tax and Trade Bureau	27, I
Alcohol, Tobacco, Firearms, and Explosives, Bureau of	27, II
AMTRAK	49, VII
American Battle Monuments Commission	36, IV
American Indians, Office of the Special Trustee	25, VII
Animal and Plant Health Inspection Service	7, III; 9, I

Agency	CFR Title, Subtitle or Chapter
Appalachian Regional Commission	5, IX
Architectural and Transportation Barriers Compliance Board	36, XI
Arctic Research Commission	45, XXIII
Armed Forces Retirement Home	5, XI
Army, Department of	32, V
Engineers, Corps of	33, II; 36, III
Federal Acquisition Regulation	48, 51
Bilingual Education and Minority Languages Affairs, Office of	34, V
Blind or Severely Disabled, Committee for Purchase from People Who Are	41, 51
Broadcasting Board of Governors	22, V
Federal Acquisition Regulation	48, 19
Career, Technical, and Adult Education, Office of	34, IV
Census Bureau	15, I
Centers for Medicare & Medicaid Services	42, IV
Central Intelligence Agency	32, XIX
Chemical Safety and Hazardous Investigation Board	40, VI
Chief Financial Officer, Office of	7, XXX
Child Support Enforcement, Office of	45, III
Children and Families, Administration for	45, II, III, IV, X, XIII
Civil Rights, Commission on	5, LXVIII; 45, VII
Civil Rights, Office for	34, I
Council of the Inspectors General on Integrity and Efficiency	5, XCVIII
Court Services and Offender Supervision Agency for the District of Columbia	5, LXX
Coast Guard	33, I; 46, I; 49, IV
Coast Guard (Great Lakes Pilotage)	46, III
Commerce, Department of	2, XIII; 44, IV; 50, VI
Census Bureau	15, I
Economic Analysis, Bureau of	15, VIII
Economic Development Administration	13, III
Emergency Management and Assistance	44, IV
Federal Acquisition Regulation	48, 13
Foreign-Trade Zones Board	15, IV
Industry and Security, Bureau of	15, VII
International Trade Administration	15, III; 19, III
National Institute of Standards and Technology	15, II; 37, IV
National Marine Fisheries Service	50, II, IV
National Oceanic and Atmospheric Administration	15, IX; 50, II, III, IV, VI
National Technical Information Service	15, XI
National Telecommunications and Information Administration	15, XXIII; 47, III, IV
National Weather Service	15, IX
Patent and Trademark Office, United States	37, I
Secretary of Commerce, Office of	15, Subtitle A
Commercial Space Transportation	14, III
Commodity Credit Corporation	7, XIV
Commodity Futures Trading Commission	5, XLI; 17, I
Community Planning and Development, Office of Assistant Secretary for	24, V, VI
Community Services, Office of	45, X
Comptroller of the Currency	12, I
Construction Industry Collective Bargaining Commission	29, IX
Consumer Financial Protection Bureau	5, LXXXIV; 12, X
Consumer Product Safety Commission	5, LXXI; 16, II
Copyright Royalty Board	37, III
Corporation for National and Community Service	2, XXII; 45, XII, XXV
Cost Accounting Standards Board	48, 99
Council on Environmental Quality	40, V
Court Services and Offender Supervision Agency for the District of Columbia	5, LXX; 28, VIII
Customs and Border Protection	19, I
Defense Contract Audit Agency	32, I
Defense, Department of	2, XI; 5, XXVI; 32, Subtitle A; 40, VII
Advanced Research Projects Agency	32, I
Air Force Department	32, VII

158

Agency	CFR Title, Subtitle or Chapter
Contract Appeals, Board of	48, 61
Federal Acquisition Regulation	48, 5
Federal Management Regulation	41, 102
Federal Property Management Regulations	41, 101
Federal Travel Regulation System	41, Subtitle F
General	41, 300
Payment From a Non-Federal Source for Travel Expenses	41, 304
Payment of Expenses Connected With the Death of Certain Employees	41, 303
Relocation Allowances	41, 302
Temporary Duty (TDY) Travel Allowances	41, 301
Geological Survey	30, IV
Government Accountability Office	4, I
Government Ethics, Office of	5, XVI
Government National Mortgage Association	24, III
Grain Inspection, Packers and Stockyards Administration	7, VIII; 9, II
Gulf Coast Ecosystem Restoration Council	2, LIX; 40, VIII
Harry S. Truman Scholarship Foundation	45, XVIII
Health and Human Services, Department of	2, III; 5, XLV; 45, Subtitle A
Centers for Medicare & Medicaid Services	42, IV
Child Support Enforcement, Office of	45, III
Children and Families, Administration for	45, II, III, IV, X, XIII
Community Services, Office of	45, X
Family Assistance, Office of	45, II
Federal Acquisition Regulation	48, 3
Food and Drug Administration	21, I
Indian Health Service	25, V
Inspector General (Health Care), Office of	42, V
Public Health Service	42, I
Refugee Resettlement, Office of	45, IV
Homeland Security, Department of	2, XXX; 5, XXXVI; 6, I; 8, I
Coast Guard	33, I; 46, I; 49, IV
Coast Guard (Great Lakes Pilotage)	46, III
Customs and Border Protection	19, I
Federal Emergency Management Agency	44, I
Human Resources Management and Labor Relations Systems	5, XCVII
Immigration and Customs Enforcement Bureau	19, IV
Transportation Security Administration	49, XII
HOPE for Homeowners Program, Board of Directors of	24, XXIV
Housing and Urban Development, Department of	2, XXIV; 5, LXV; 24, Subtitle B
Community Planning and Development, Office of Assistant Secretary for	24, V, VI
Equal Opportunity, Office of Assistant Secretary for	24, I
Federal Acquisition Regulation	48, 24
Federal Housing Enterprise Oversight, Office of	12, XVII
Government National Mortgage Association	24, III
Housing—Federal Housing Commissioner, Office of Assistant Secretary for	24, II, VIII, X, XX
Housing, Office of, and Multifamily Housing Assistance Restructuring, Office of	24, IV
Inspector General, Office of	24, XII
Public and Indian Housing, Office of Assistant Secretary for	24, IX
Secretary, Office of	24, Subtitle A, VII
Housing—Federal Housing Commissioner, Office of Assistant Secretary for	24, II, VIII, X, XX
Housing, Office of, and Multifamily Housing Assistance Restructuring, Office of	24, IV
Immigration and Customs Enforcement Bureau	19, IV
Immigration Review, Executive Office for	8, V
Independent Counsel, Office of	28, VII
Independent Counsel, Offices of	28, VI
Indian Affairs, Bureau of	25, I, V
Indian Affairs, Office of the Assistant Secretary	25, VI

161

162

Agency	CFR Title, Subtitle or Chapter
Selective Service System	32, XVI
Small Business Administration	2, XXVII; 13, I
Smithsonian Institution	36, V
Social Security Administration	2, XXIII; 20, III; 48, 23
Soldiers' and Airmen's Home, United States	5, XI
Special Counsel, Office of	5, VIII
Special Education and Rehabilitative Services, Office of	34, III
State, Department of	2, VI; 22, I; 28, XI
Federal Acquisition Regulation	48, 6
Surface Mining Reclamation and Enforcement, Office of	30, VII
Surface Transportation Board	49, X
Susquehanna River Basin Commission	18, VIII
Tennessee Valley Authority	5, LXIX; 18, XIII
Trade Representative, United States, Office of	15, XX
Transportation, Department of	2, XII; 5, L
Commercial Space Transportation	14, III
Emergency Management and Assistance	44, IV
Federal Acquisition Regulation	48, 12
Federal Aviation Administration	14, I
Federal Highway Administration	23, I, II
Federal Motor Carrier Safety Administration	49, III
Federal Railroad Administration	49, II
Federal Transit Administration	49, VI
Maritime Administration	46, II
National Highway Traffic Safety Administration	23, II, III; 47, IV; 49, V
Pipeline and Hazardous Materials Safety Administration	49, I
Saint Lawrence Seaway Development Corporation	33, IV
Secretary of Transportation, Office of	14, II; 49, Subtitle A
Transportation Statistics Bureau	49, XI
Transportation, Office of	7, XXXIII
Transportation Security Administration	49, XII
Transportation Statistics Bureau	49, XI
Travel Allowances, Temporary Duty (TDY)	41, 301
Treasury, Department of the	2, X;5, XXI; 12, XV; 17, IV; 31, IX
Alcohol and Tobacco Tax and Trade Bureau	27, I
Community Development Financial Institutions Fund	12, XVIII
Comptroller of the Currency	12, I
Customs and Border Protection	19, I
Engraving and Printing, Bureau of	31, VI
Federal Acquisition Regulation	48, 10
Federal Claims Collection Standards	31, IX
Federal Law Enforcement Training Center	31, VII
Financial Crimes Enforcement Network	31, X
Fiscal Service	31, II
Foreign Assets Control, Office of	31, V
Internal Revenue Service	26, I
Investment Security, Office of	31, VIII
Monetary Offices	31, I
Secret Service	31, IV
Secretary of the Treasury, Office of	31, Subtitle A
Truman, Harry S. Scholarship Foundation	45, XVIII
United States and Canada, International Joint Commission	22, IV
United States and Mexico, International Boundary and Water Commission, United States Section	22, XI
U.S. Copyright Office	37, II
Utah Reclamation Mitigation and Conservation Commission	43, III
Veterans Affairs, Department of	2, VIII; 38, I
Federal Acquisition Regulation	48, 8
Veterans' Employment and Training Service, Office of the Assistant Secretary for	41, 61; 20, IX
Vice President of the United States, Office of	32, XXVIII
Wage and Hour Division	29, V
Water Resources Council	18, VI
Workers' Compensation Programs, Office of	20, I, VII
World Agricultural Outlook Board	7, XXXVIII

List of CFR Sections Affected

All changes in this volume of the Code of Federal Regulations (CFR) that were made by documents published in the FEDERAL REGISTER since January 1, 2014 are enumerated in the following list. Entries indicate the nature of the changes effected. Page numbers refer to FEDERAL REGISTER pages. The user should consult the entries for chapters, parts and subparts as well as sections for revisions.

For changes to this volume of the CFR prior to this listing, consult the annual edition of the monthly List of CFR Sections Affected (LSA). The LSA is available at *www.govinfo.gov*. For changes to this volume of the CFR prior to 2001, see the "List of CFR Sections Affected, 1949–1963, 1964–1972, 1973–1985, and 1986–2000" published in 11 separate volumes. The "List of CFR Sections Affected 1986–2000" is available at *www.govinfo.gov*.